Evoking Genocide

Also by Adam Jones

Gender Inclusive: Essays on Violence, Men, and Feminist International Relations. Routledge, 2009.

(ed. with Nicholas Robins) *Genocides by the Oppressed: Subaltern Genocide in Theory and Practice.* Indiana University Press, 2009.

(ed.) *Genocide* (4 vols.). Sage Publications, 2008.
    v. 1: *Genocide in Theory and Law*
    v. 2: *Genocide in History*
    v. 3: *Perpetrators, Victims, Bystanders, Rescuers*
    v. 4: *Prevention, Intervention, and Restitution*

Crimes Against Humanity: A Beginner's Guide. Oneworld Publications, 2008.

Genocide: A Comprehensive Introduction. Routledge, 2006.

(ed.) *Men of the Global South: A Reader.* Zed Books, 2006.

(ed.) *Política Mundial: Cambio y Conflicto: Ensayos Escogidos de Kal Holsti* [World Politics: Change and Conflict: Selected Essays of Kal Holsti], trans. Atenea Acevedo. CIDE, 2005.

(ed.) *Genocide, War Crimes & the West: History and Complicity.* Zed Books, 2004.

(ed.) *Gendercide and Genocide.* Vanderbilt University Press, 2004.

Beyond the Barricades: Nicaragua and the Struggle for the Sandinista Press, 1979–1998. Ohio University Press, 2002.

The Press in Transition: A Comparative Study of Nicaragua, South Africa, Jordan, and Russia. German Overseas Institute, 2002.

Travel Photography
Latin American Portraits. The Key Publishing House Inc., 2008.

Evoking Genocide

Scholars and Activists Describe the Works That Shaped Their Lives

Edited by
Adam Jones

The Key Publishing House Inc.

The editor and publisher gratefully acknowledge the permission granted to reproduce the copyright material in this book. Every effort has been made to trace copyright holders and to obtain their permission for the use of copyright material. Please notify the publisher at info@thekeypublish.com of any copyright issue that should be addressed.

First Edition 2009
The Key Publishing House Inc.
Toronto, Canada
Website: www.thekeypublish.com
E-mail: info@thekeypublish.com

ISBN 978–0–9782526–9–4 paperback

Cover design, layout design and typesetting Olga Lagounova
Indexer Jennifer South

Printed and bound in USA. This book is printed on paper suitable for recycling and made from fully sustained forest sources.

Library and Archives Canada Cataloguing in Publication

Evoking genocide : scholars and activists describe the works that shaped their lives/editor, Adam Jones.— 1st ed.
Back cover photo by Griselda Ramírez

Includes bibliographical references and index.
ISBN 978-0-9782526-9-4

1. Genocide. 2. Genocide—Psychological aspects. 3. Genocide in literature.
4. Genocide in art. 5. Scholars—Biography. 6. Social reformers—Biography.
7. Political activists—Biography.
I. Jones, Adam, 1963–

HV6322.7.E96 2009   364.15'1   C2009–900699–5

Published in association and with a grant from The Key Research Centre (www.thekeyresearch. org). The Key Publishing promotes mutual understanding, respect and peaceful coexistence among the people of the world. We represent unique and unconventional voices whose objective is to bring tolerance, peace, harmony, and happiness to human society.

The Key Publishing House Inc.
www.thekeypublish.com

Table of Contents

Preface

"I remember when I first read . . . saw . . . heard . . . visited . . ."

For years, genocide scholars and activists have made these comments in my hearing, or in correspondence. They usually presaged an off-the-cuff tribute to a work of art or communication—a book, film, song, painting, photograph, document, monument, reportage, personal testimony—that had a formative impact on the individual's evolution in the field.

I felt it would be enlightening to compile a series of short essays paying homage to such works. The response to my call for submissions was livelier than I had expected, and *Evoking Genocide* is the gratifying result. Contributors were invited to explore intersections of history, cultural criticism, and autobiography: to engage both with the works themselves, and with their influence on the author's own evolution. I was also curious to know whether contributors had used the work in their teaching or activism. If so, how, and with what reaction from students or other audiences?

Along these general lines, different authors weighted their pieces differently. I saw my editorial role as respecting and preserving their voices, not imposing a uniform tone. Their contributions range from the angry to the elegiac, sometimes within the space of a single essay.

Not all books are a joy to edit, but this one has been a labor of love. A number of contributors also emphasized how much they had enjoyed writing their pieces—a welcome relief, they said, from the more detached and "objective" style that scholars are often confined by. I hope the freshness and vitality of the engagement with their chosen subjects comes through. I also hope that the diverse materials presented here will inspire readers, as they have inspired me, to seek out a personal engagement with works they may not have encountered—or even heard of. A section of further reading and links is provided for this purpose at the end of the volume.

I have chosen to organize the essays in broadly chronological order, according to the historical events that each addresses. *Evoking Genocide* begins with the European conquest of the Americas, and moves through the Armenian genocide, Aboriginal "residential schools," and the Jewish Holocaust, to key post-World War Two events like the birth of the Genocide Convention and the Eichmann trial in Jerusalem. It then alights on Cambodia, Vietnam, Argentina, Guatemala, the anti-nuclear movement of the 1980s, events surrounding East Timor's struggle for independence, the Rwandan apocalypse of 1994, and finally the Darfur genocide. There are occasional minor shadings on this chronological scheme throughout the text, for improved "flow" as I perceive it. I hope the overall effect is to convey something of the scope and scale of genocide in history, while also highlighting the human beings who intervened in it, bore witness to it, struggled against it, and strove to memorialize it.

Inevitably, there is a heavy—some might say disproportionate—emphasis in this book on works that deal with the Jewish Holocaust and the Nazis' other genocidal crimes. My own writing on genocide sets these seminal events in comparative perspective, rejecting any notion that they are "uniquely unique."[1] But the predominance of a Holocaust theme here is predictable, and I think defensible. Most contributors grew up when the Holocaust was the paradigmatic genocide, the *ne plus ultra*. For many people, it still is, and it has given rise to a far vaster body of artistic representations and scholarly investigations than all other genocides combined. The Rwandan and Darfur genocides may be beginning to play something of a similar anchoring role for a new generation of scholars and activists, and a sense of this is conveyed by the closing essays in the volume.

Readers who are well-grounded in genocide studies should delight in the vistas that this book opens to them. But I also hope that *Evoking Genocide* will serve as an accessible introduction to genocide for those who are new to this field of study. Sometimes, the sheer accumulation of grim historical and empirical detail can make the initial engagement with the subject of mass crimes a daunting one. And it is true that there is no shortage of "hearts of darkness" and "grey zones" ahead of you in the volume. But there may also be a catharsis in witnessing works of art and communication forged from the raw trauma of genocide, and the pleasure of sharing contributors' sense of discovery as they explore these works with you. I hope you will emerge sobered and informed—but also captivated, and energized to make your own contribution.

www.evokinggenocide.org

Accompanying this edited volume is a website, www.evokinggenocide.org, which serves both to publicize the book and as a forum for readers and others to offer their thoughts on works that have influenced them personally.

Readers are invited to visit the website and consider contributing their own essay, which may be incorporated in any future editions of the book. All correspondence regarding the website may be addressed to the editor at adam.jones@ubc.ca, or to the individual authors whose email addresses appear in the biographical notes.

Acknowledgments

Evoking Genocide was substantially compiled and edited during my time as an Associate Research Fellow in the Genocide Studies Program at Yale University. I am deeply grateful to the program's director, Ben Kiernan, and to Frederick J. Iseman of Caxton-Iseman Capital, Inc., who personally funded much of the fellowship that brought me to Yale. Thanks also to Ian Shapiro, Richard Kane, and Nancy Ruther of the Whitney and Betty MacMillan Center for International and Area Studies at Yale. Work on the book concluded after I moved to my new post at the University of British Columbia Okanagan. My UBCO colleagues, like my family and friends, have been stalwart in their support.

Working at long distance with the book's terrific designer, Olga Lagounova, was a constant (indeed, for a stretch, almost daily) pleasure. Special thanks to Olga for incorporating a deluge of minor alterations and adjustments along the way, and doing so with good humor and professionalism.

Dedication

By common agreement, the editor and contributors to this volume dedicate it to the memory of two leading genocide scholars, for many of us dear friends.

Eric Markusen died after a long illness in January 2007. He was one of the first genocide scholars I ever met, and I took to him instantly, as everyone did. Eric was a gracious, loving man who made a seminal contribution to genocide studies on subjects like the bombing of German and Japanese cities during World War Two, the "genocidal mentality," and genocide denial.

Stephen C. Feinstein, who passed with shocking suddenness in March 2008, contributes a searching essay to this book (see p. 148) that stands as one of his final testimonials. Examining Zbigniew Libera's Lego crematorium, it displays something of Stephen's eclecticism and cultural astuteness, as well as his readiness to tackle offbeat and controversial subjects. From the warm welcome he extended to me on visits to Minneapolis, I know how gregarious and generous he was personally.[2]

Both of these men left us unfairly soon; both will inspire and inform the work in our field for decades.

Adam Jones
Kelowna, BC, Canada
September 2009

Notes

[1] See the discussion in Adam Jones, *Genocide: A Comprehensive Introduction* (London: Routledge, 2006), pp. 162–63.

[2] See Ben Cohen's tribute, "Eric Markusen Studied Roots of Genocide," *Minneapolis Star-Tribune*, 31 January 2007, http://www.startribune.com/obituaries/11604066. html; and Kathryn Nelson's warm tribute to Stephen Feinstein, "Historian's Death Called Loss to Study of the Nazi Holocaust," *Minneapolis Star-Tribune*, 5 March 2008, http://www.startribune.com/local/16319736.html.

"All My Inner Self Protested"

Raphael Lemkin

Genocide scholars and activists, it seems, have always drawn inspiration from creative and communicative works — beginning with the first such scholar, Raphael Lemkin (1900–59), who coined the term "genocide" in 1944. In this excerpt from his unpublished autobiography, edited by Samuel Totten and Steven L. Jacobs for publication in their volume Pioneers of Genocide Studies *(Transaction Publishers, 2002), Lemkin describes the impact on his emerging world-view of stories and songs he heard, books he read, and news reports that reached him as a child growing up in Poland.*

I was born and lived my first ten years on a farm called "Ozerisko," fourteen miles from the city of Wolkowysk. Through this city marched the Swedish and Napoleonic armies, and innumerable tussles in this area took place between the Russians and the Poles, Lithuanians and Ukrainians, and earlier, among the Mongols and the Tartars.

The farm of "Ozerisko" lay in a large clearing between huge forests. It was a joint tenancy of two families, my father's and that of my uncle. The children, who were mostly of the same age, spent their days together in one happy gang. The forest was the heart of the farm.

The ground of the forest was covered with dried leaves and pine needles, which was a ready-made bed for tired heads of children explorers, hungry for dreams. This was my world that I learned to love and that gave me the first lessons in aloneness. From my early years I took a special delight in being alone, so that I could think and feel without outer disturbances. At that time I did not understand the meaning and purpose of this feeling, but I fully enjoyed the delight of contemplation. Lost from my companions, I spent hours in the forest listening through my third ear how the story of life was sung by the sparrows, robins, crows, and blackbirds, innumerable mosquitoes, and insects. Though they were playing on discordant instruments, they still were producing harmonious melodies . . .

The evenings were a delight. My mother gathered us near the warm stove. She taught us to sing songs and taught us poetry through the songs by Nadson.[1] As I [try] to reconstruct the content of these sonnet-songs, the following picture of the world appears from them. There is much evil on earth and there is much injustice. The innocent and the poor suffer. They are often murdered in cold blood. People bow to false gods, which are the gods of greed and power. The poor and the innocent must be helped. Those who suffer must be loved and raised from their destitution. The songs offered hope for a betterment of the world, for the cessation of evil, for the protection of the weak.

The appeal for the protection of the innocent from destruction set a chain reaction in my mind. It followed me all my life. When I learned to read, I started to devour books on the subject of persecution of religious, racial, or other minority groups. I was startled by the destruction of the Christians by Nero. They were thrown to the lions while the Emperor sat laughing in the Roman arena. A book on the subject by the Polish writer Henryk Sienkiewicz, under the title *Quo Vadis*, made a strong impression on me and I re-read and discussed [it] many times. I was indignant at the French king, who watched the hanging of the Huguenots from his balcony. The king ordered [that] more light [be thrown] on the scene so that he might better see the tormented faces of the dying. All my inner self protested when I read that the Huguenots in Lyon were compelled to sit with naked bodies on heated irons and [be] roasted alive. The Moors, in the fifteenth century, were deported on boats, and, while on the decks, they were stripped of their clothes and exposed to the sun, which finally killed them. Why should the sun, which brought life to our farm and reddened the cherries on our trees, be turned into an agent of murder?

News of a pogrom in the city of Bialystok, fifty miles away, came to our farm. The mobs opened the stomachs of their victims and stuffed them with the feathers from the pillows and feather comforters.

A line of blood led from the Roman arena through the gallows of France to the pogrom of Bialystok. I could not define history with my childish mind, but I saw it vividly and strongly with my eyes, as a huge torture place of the innocent. And, in my childish way, I joined with Nadson in protesting the grotesque mockery that men have perpetrated on [other] men.

Our mother [also] read to us [Aesop's] fables. Equity, justice, and fairness are basic elements of reason. The unjust is made a fool because he destroys the reasonable bases of life. To us, the lesson from these fables was plain: the unjust are basically fools. I grew up with a strong sense of feeling that persecution must cease and that justice and love will finally prevail. I did not differentiate at that time between human beings, animals, and birds.

When winter came, we moved to Bella's house where the [Hebrew] teacher lived. More boys from the village joined us in common classes. Because our parents taught us well to read Hebrew we were able to join higher classes in studying the Bible. The chanting voice of the teacher would set the tone. The brevity of the Hebrew language consisting of words loaded with meaning made a lasting impression on my style in writing and speaking in other languages.

I felt deep compassion for the prophets who had to suffer for what they believed. The lives and deeds of poor men, who challenged kings and priests to obey the religion of my heart, kindled fire in the heart of a small village boy studying the Bible.

Notes

[1] Siemlon Nadson (1882–1887) was a Russian nationalistic poet whose works were translated into Polish by Zaruskie in 1887, thirteen years before Lemkin's birth.

Diego Rivera, "La Gran Tenochtitlán" (1945)

Lost Worlds

John M. Cox

> Dumbfounded by the beauty of it, the conquistadors ride down the causeway. Tenochtitlán seems to have been torn from the pages of Amadís, *things never heard of, never seen, nor even dreamed . . .* The Sun rises behind the volcanoes, enters the lake, and breaks the floating mist into shreds. The city—streets, canals, high-towered temples—glitters before them. A multitude comes out to greet the invaders, silent and unhurried, while innumerable canoes open furrows in the cobalt waters.
>
> —Eduardo Galeano[1]

Lost in the library one day in my undergraduate years—and desperately seeking an excuse to avoid completing a term paper that was already overdue—I stumbled upon a book of reproductions of Diego Rivera's murals. I was awestruck by the force of Rivera's images of the depredations of the Spanish conquistadors in such works as "De la Conquista a 1930" ("From Conquest to 1930") and "Desembarco de Españoles en Veracruz" ("Disembarkation of the Spanish in Veracruz").

But one work in particular captured my imagination: the artist's recreation of the great Aztec capital, Tenochtitlán, on the eve of its destruction.[2] Rivera's homage to pre-Conquest Mexico—"La Gran Tenochtitlán" ("The Great City of Tenochtitlán")—is among an enormous series of frescoes that adorns the stairwells and walls of the third floor of the Palacio Nacional in Mexico City.

Most of the action in Rivera's "Tenochtitlán" occurs in the foreground, behind which looms the magnificent city, replete with temples, streets, marketplaces, and plazas, surrounded by towering mountains. Characteristically, Rivera notes the distinctions between rich and poor, rulers and subjects; but the most lasting impression is one of a centuries-old culture of elaborate symbolism and rituals. Rivera's fresco is not only a celebration of a vanquished people who had given much to his own, modern Mexico, but also an indictment of the Conquest—for we know, unlike the Indians painted by Rivera, that this way of life would shortly be destroyed, along with the city itself, by Cortés and his successors.[3]

At the time I encountered this work, I was a young student fascinated with the history of Nazi Germany, an era that raises many troubling and profound questions. My introduction to the Holocaust had led me to look deeper into the long and grim history of genocide—learning, for example, about the mass murder of indigenous peoples in the Americas. But in viewing Rivera's fresco, even in the book's pale reproduction, it dawned on me that history could have taken other paths. I was compelled to discover those civilizations that had been erased from the earth, and often from historical memory, because of genocide.

Our work as historians of geno-cide tends to dwell upon the crimes of the perpetrators and the suffering of the victims. Much is known today about the suffering of the Armenian people during World War I, the horrors under the Khmer Rouge in Cambodia, the genocide that eradicated three-fourths of Rwanda's Tutsi population. But

"La Gran Tenochtitlán" (1945).
Diego Rivera.
See Color Plate I

much less is known of the lives these people led before the tragedies that befell them, and of the cultures that were dispersed or destroyed. Some, like the East Timorese, have managed to persevere and keep alive their cultural identity. Others were less fortunate.

"La Gran Tenochtitlán" would serve as a lingering inspiration for my own research, some years later, into German-Jewish life before the Holocaust, and specifically the underground anti-Nazi resistance that originated in left-wing Jewish youth subcultures. It is tempting to view all of pre–1933 German-Jewish history as a prelude to the Holocaust. In fact, by the time of its unification, Germany was actually seen by European Jews as a haven from the much harsher antisemitism of neighboring lands.

Jews lived in Germany for many centuries, and gave Europe some of its greatest talents, from Moses Mendelssohn and Heinrich Heine to Alfred Einstein, Kurt Weill, and Walter Benjamin—products not purely of Jewish life, but of cultural syntheses. German-Jewish intellectual traditions and youth subcultures would later foment a determined and creative resistance to Nazism—resistance that took many forms, and was much larger than is commonly believed. While in Germany a Jewish community has reemerged in recent years, it is in many ways cut off from the vibrant pre–1933 traditions of German Jewry, which can never be rebuilt or resurrected. Not only did the Jewish people suffer an irreparable tragedy in the Holocaust: Europe and the world lost something irreplaceable as well.

It was only recently that I finally had the privilege of viewing Rivera's murals at various sites around Mexico City — the teeming metropolis that rests, layer upon layer, above the ruins of Tenochtitlán. Groups of school-children milled about the frescoes of the Palacio Nacional, reminding me that Rivera's work continues to resonate, and that the pre-Spanish civilization he depicted is seen by Mexicans as part of their heritage. Yet the frescoes remain as poignant reminders that what is lost can never be regained.

Notes

[1]   Eduardo Galeano, *Memory of Fire: Genesis* (New York: W.W. Norton, 1998), p. 67.

[2]   "Aztec" is a popular term that is not entirely accurate, but I use it for clarity. The Aztecs referred to themselves as Culhua-Mexica, and many scholars today prefer "Mexica."

[3]   The revolutionary artist and *bon vivant* ran afoul of his comrades in the Communist Party for his portrayal of pre-Conquest Mexico, which expressed too unambiguously his admiration of Indian culture and veered too far from the deadening "socialist realism" then in vogue.

Roland Joffé (dir.), *The Mission* (1986)

The Wound at the Heart of the World

Christopher Powell

When I first watched *The Mission* almost twenty years ago, I was sixteen and a Christian. I am neither of those things now, but when I watched it again last night, I realized that the film had sunk into me like a stone into a stream, disappearing from sight and changing me forever.

What I remember of my first impressions, or imagine I remember, concerns the Christian themes — martyrdom, redemption, guilt. Mendoza's harrowing penance, the forgiveness he wins, and how he finds redemption despite his own intentions. Father Gabriel's courage: facing his own murderers with love. The hands that pick up his cross when he falls, his evanescent vindication. A diplomat's rationalization: "We must work in the world, and the world is thus," and Altamirano's remorse: "No . . . thus have we *made* the world. Thus have I made it."

Even as I write these words, the images shift, and I have to concentrate to tell you what I saw then, without adding to it what I see now, which is this: that the Guaraní who die in battle win as

In *The Mission*, **Rodrigo Mendoza** is a mercenary and slave hunter who operates in Guaraní territory. After he kills his brother in a fit of rage, his remorse drives him to an unusual and dangerous penance: carrying his own armor and weaponry up the cliffs of Iguazú Falls, where he is forgiven by the very people he has been persecuting. He abandons the sword and becomes a Jesuit, serving the mission founded by Father Gabriel. When the mission is attacked, Mendoza takes up his sword again, and leads its military defence. But as soldiers storm the village, he pauses to rescue a child at the river's edge rather than fire his cannon, and this act of compassion unexpectedly becomes his final deed.

Gabriel is a Jesuit Father who risks martyrdom to found a mission among the Guaraní Indians. Gabriel's Christianity is that of 1 Corinthians 13, a Christianity whose highest virtue is love. He rebels against the orders of Altamirano, choosing to stay with the Guaraní after their abandonment, even though it means his certain death. As soldiers storm the mission and massacre its inhabitants, Gabriel holds a mass, and then calmly walks into the gunfire with a cross in his hands, followed by his congregation.

Jeremy Irons, as Father Gabriel, leads a procession of Guaraní Indians at the climax of *The Mission* (courtesy Warner Bros. Entertainment Inc.).

much or as little redemption as the Christian converts who walk into gunfire. That Gabriel is brave but also cowardly: "If might is right, then love has no place in the world. It may be so . . . But I don't have the strength to live in a world like that." He is unwilling to violate his sense of self in order to survive. But he is also indomitable, daring to refuse the patriarchal authority that says: learn to be violent to others, as I am violent unto you. What Bourdieu might have called "disinvesting in the field." The genius of martyrdom, which institutionalized Christianity both valorizes and co-opts. Lines of flight and apparatuses of capture. In the midst of which — out of which — we make our lives.

(Nothing can exist without form, and all forms are limiting and mortal.)

Disinvest in the field of power, and you die. Invest, and you buy life, but at the price of submission. Or so it was for the priest and the mercenary. Sooner or later, each had to lose his self, either by submitting or by refusing to submit. So too with the Guaraní, facing the choice that has confronted indigenous peoples in the Americas for half a millennium: assimilate or be exterminated. What a colossal mistake those Guaraní made, coming out of the forest! Listening to Gabriel with his talk of God's love. Letting themselves become something recognizable to the colonizer: an Other whom I must exterminate because it is like my self, and I know my self to be violent, annihilatory.

Altamirano is the papal emissary sent to decide whether the Jesuit missions south and east of the Rio Uruguay should be ceded to Portugal, in keeping with the 1750 Treaty of Madrid, or remain under papal protection. At stake is the very survival of these missions, since Portugal practices slavery against indigenous peoples in its colonial territories. Altamirano stalls by conducting a tour of the missions, but his conclusion is foregone: the Catholic Church is under political pressure in Europe, and he believes the missions must be sacrificed to save the Jesuit order from extinction.

Pierre Bourdieu used the term "**field**" to refer to a network of strategic relationships that constitute and are constituted by practical social action. Our need or desire for the goods each field provides (economic, cultural, political) draws us to invest our selves, through our practices, in the relations of domination and subordination that each field produces.

The conceptual terminology proposed by Gilles Deleuze and Félix Guattari in *1,000 Plateaus* is notoriously obscure and elliptical. But we could say that a **line of flight** occurs when the logic of a system generates a course of action that tends to violate the system and escape beyond it. An **apparatus of capture** traps the energies of divergent, open-ended, liberatory impulses in a relatively closed and stable structure: as market forces commodify and co-opt the revolutionary aspirations of the counterculture, for example.

Sociology understands the **self** as constructed or produced through social action: as we do, so we are. Being intersubjective or relational, the self cannot be reduced either to the body or to the mind, and so can at least partly survive the death of both; conversely, the self can be destroyed even when the body and mind survive.

Why did they trust that priest, who lured them meekly with his oboe and then taught that the Devil lives in the forest? Probably to disinvest in some local field. That's tragedy: seeking freedom, only to find our selves in a larger, crueler trap — not by accident, but through our very means of escape. Civilization and heroin have that in common.

Why do you keep calling atrocity "tragedy"? That usage itself is atrocious. In tragedy, annihilation is fated, or flows from the hero's tragic flaw; the violence of tragedy is that of the order of the world restoring itself. It is meaningful. Genocide annihilates not just meaning, but the very condition of its arising. Altamirano's remorse counts for *nothing* against the nothing that the Guaraní he betrayed have now become: the nothing that was made of their world, with his permission.

A world is a fragile thing, after all: a skein of meaning and practice, a juggling act, complementarity in motion. Elias's dance, which only ever seems to *be*. The best of all worlds are those in which we don't have to defend ourselves, can be defenseless, can love. That was the dream of the carpenter's son, and every time we call genocide *tragic* we spit on that dream.

To commit or condone or enable atrocity is always a choice. The Pope's agent saw that in the end. The world is thus, thus have we made the world: structure and agency, making history under conditions not of our choosing. Labor. The atrocity is that these other worlds, the defenseless ones, *could* exist. What is the function of sovereignty, except to defend us from sovereigns? The meaning of "contradiction": laboring to obtain our freedom, we produce the very forces that dominate us. Denial of contradiction: the fantasy that might serves right, that power is moral. The romance of heroism. But Odysseus was a pirate who sacked defenseless towns for booty. Nothing romantic about that—nor incongruous. Power, like capital, has its inhuman and so amoral logic, which includes dissemination of the fantasy that obscures it.

Phenomenological sociology treats existence in terms of experience, and observes that socially constructed relationships and meanings are inseparable from the supposed intransigence of objects. So we can say that a **world** is a matrix of actual or possible experiences. In this sense, human beings inhabit as many different worlds as there are irreducibly different cultures.

Norbert Elias used the metaphor of a **dance** to illustrate how cultures or societies can be understood purely as processes, always in motion, which only seem to be static objects.

Marx spoke of **contradiction** not only in the realm of logic or ideas, but in that of practice. How does this make sense? In this way, I think: workers seeking to produce their own wealth obtain greater wealth for the owners of capital than for themselves, and so make themselves relatively poorer. In all class societies, creative human effort is turned against itself; our efforts to realize ourselves in the world produce the forces that negate us.

The puncturing of that fantasy is left to those who die violently practicing nonviolence, who love even their oppressors. Gabriel's revenge: to give to Altamirano, with his dying breath, that sensation which precedes guilt, and of which guilt is a misdirection, the sense of intolerable contradiction, of the self-contradictions of the field of practice knitted into our very souls. The sensation is produced in this way: I act as you would act, in perfect fulfillment of your rules; I act out your ideals; I am your idealized self; yet I act against you, against the actual you. I force the actual you to act against me, the ideal you; I die, you see yourself die, at your hands, your self turns against itself. I sacrifice my self to wound your self so that you will feel the pain of the wounded world and doubt the deadly fantasies of power.

To accomplish this, Gabriel and the Guaraní who celebrated mass with him had to die, sacrifice their selves—which they had to give up in any case, whether by submitting or resisting. By their death, they increased the symbolic

The laws that defined **Jewishness** under the Third Reich differed substantially from how Jews were defined either in their own religious tradition or in their everyday lives. The Nazis manufactured and imposed on people a social identity that had not previously existed.

Raphael Lemkin was the Polish jurist who coined the term "genocide," and campaigned for its criminalization, in response to the annihilation campaigns against Armenians in the Ottoman Empire during the First World War and against multiple ethnic groups, including Jews, in the Axis-occupied countries during the Second World War.

Bartolomé de las Casas was a Spanish priest who documented and campaigned against the mass enslavement, torture, and slaughter of indigenous peoples by colonizers in the Americas in the early 16th century.

costs of genocide, just as those who took up arms increased its material costs, demanding more soldiers, guns, powder, uniforms, transport, provisions. Under more favorable circumstances, it might have worked: either strategy, or both in combination. But in that moment, it couldn't. That is the horrifying thing about genocide: the extremity of its unfairness. There is no right thing to do to escape being victimized. Just as Jews under the Third Reich could not escape a Jewishness that was thrust upon them, a kind of Jewishness of which they had previously been unaware and which, in fact, had not previously existed, so too the Guaraní under European colonialism could not escape an aboriginality, nonwhiteness, animalism, disposability, that was alien to them, brought over the ocean in the same ships that carried muskets and shot and powder.

Genocide destroys not just a people, but a world: a universe of meaning and of possible experiences. The diminution of humanity, one world at a time: it's this that Lemkin intuited when he wrote about the contribution that all nations make to humankind, though he was narrow and ethnocentric to speak only of "nations." The holocausts of the Armenians and the Jews traumatized Europe in a way that centuries of holocaust in the Americas had not, a system with nowhere left to expand, forced to turn in on itself, an involution so devastating as to trouble the colonizers' sense of themselves and their superiority. What would the word 'genocide' mean to us, if Bartolomé de las Casas and not Raphael Lemkin had been its prophet? But such ifs are in vain. As their blithe misnomer confirms, what and who the so-called Indians were to *themselves* mattered far less in the racist imaginary than was true even for Jews.

Impunity, identity, interest. The colonizers knew who they were or, more to the point, they knew how to separate inside from outside. They knew what their interests were, and how to protect them. Two sides of the same coin. An astonishing thing, those Guaraní/Jesuit reductions, another of history's appalling losses: a chance for the Guaraní to enter the modern world on their own terms. If only people meant what they said about civilizing missions, about loving their neighbours. But to cite Marx again, you know a person by what they do, rather than by what they say about themselves. Let's distinguish cake from icing. Altamirano's argument: the very existence of the Jesuit Order is imperiled. Gabriel's response: "Is that to stand in our way?" Everything dies; some deaths have meaning. Altamirano is pained by the beauty of the limb he came to

Although missionary activity in the Americas has often been itself a vehicle for genocide, the **Guaraní/Jesuit reductions** (called "missions" in *The Mission*) seem to have been anomalous, in that they allowed indigenous people to benefit from the fruits of European civilization while maintaining the distinctiveness and cohesiveness of their culture. Fields and workshops were owned and operated collectively. Community members were provided with advanced social services and education. The working day was less than half the European norm. Advanced handicrafts included sculpture, woodcarving, the making of clocks and violins. Operating over a large area of contemporary Paraguay, Argentina, and Brazil, and at their peak including over one hundred thousand Christian Guaraní, the reductions operated independently of, and competed economically with, the neighboring settler societies. Begun in 1609, their independence was broken after the military defeat of the Guaraní in the 1750s and the expulsion of the Jesuit order from the Spanish and Portuguese empires in 1767.

The notion of a world-system, as developed by Immanuel Wallerstein, recognizes that a single social system may be constituted by a network of production relations, without being politically or culturally unified. In the modern **world-system**, the system of (formally) sovereign and independent states is coextensive with the capitalist mode of production. Where previous world-systems, such as the Roman or Chinese empires, achieved only regional dominance, the modern world-system is unique in being the first world-system to achieve global hegemony.

sever to save the body; Gabriel knows that Christ sacrificed himself to save others, not the other way around. But Altamirano's inability to paper over the slippage between doctrine and practice barely impeded that practice.

For over five hundred years, the modern world-system has exploded across the Earth, and with it a single interconnected (but not unified) ensemble of social relations, fields, meanings, and possible experiences. The myriad worlds in which human beings lived have been smashed, torn apart, swallowed and digested, to an extent limited only by the ability of the colonized to resist. The many are becoming one: a single world-system has brought with it a single phenomenological world, expanding like a nova, a cancer, an event horizon. Or not exactly; human beings can live in the New World, after all. The settlers do. It's the expanding, devouring boundary *between* the worlds that is so lethal. A holocaustic passage, this forced migration of the spirit. And yet, almost miraculously, there are survivors: not only individuals, but collectivities, the Guaraní among them. Conquered and wounded, the Guaraní have managed to transport pieces of their old world across the boundary—enough to preserve self and community, to be a part of the modern New World even without being accepted by it, even though it goes on trying to reject them as uselessly and stupidly as a host body rejects a transplanted organ. Enough to be a part of the field, to make demands, to fight.

The many indigenous peoples of the Americas refuse to disappear. In their struggles for life and for renaissance, they give to their colonizers, their oppressors, their génocidaires, an astonishing gift, painful and precious: that of a world that has failed to erase the memory of its atrocities; a world that cannot deny its contradictions completely. A world that might still be redeemed.

Buffy Sainte-Marie, "My Country 'Tis of Thy People You're Dying" (1966)

"A Bargain Indeed"

Ward Churchill

Hear how the bargain was made for the West:
With her shivering children in zero degrees,
Blankets for your land — so the treaties attest,
Oh well, blankets for land, that's a bargain indeed.
And the blankets were those Uncle Sam had collected
From smallpox diseased soldiers that day.
And the tribes were wiped out and the history books censored,
A hundred years of your statesmen have felt it's better that way.
— Buffy Sainte-Marie,
"My Country 'Tis of Thy People You're Dying"

I honestly can't remember when I first encountered this verse, penned by Cree singer-songwriter Buffy Sainte-Marie in 1965 and released on her album *Little Wheel Spin and Spin* a year later. It's vaguely possible that I came across it before I was drafted in November 1966. More likely, it was during my two-year stint in the army, either while I was marking time for the better part of a year at Custer's old post of Fort Riley, Kansas, or during the eleven months I then spent in Vietnam's Central Highlands. The passage of time, the sheer intensity of that period, and probably the amphetamines on which I then routinely relied, have conspired to defeat precise recollection. I'm quite sure, however, that I was familiar with the song well before I made the transition, in mid-summer 1969, from serving as a downstate organizer for Black Panther Fred Hampton's Chicago-based Rainbow Coalition to what were then called "Weather" politics.

I also know that, irrespective of the exact moment of my initial exposure to it, the impact of Buffy's potent depiction of the microbiological genocide inflicted by the United States upon American Indians was for me profoundly confirming, rather than revelatory. This was because stories of soldiers distributing smallpox-infested blankets, integral to traditional *Indian*

Buffy Sainte-Marie (Photo courtesy www.creative-native.com).

understandings of "American" history, had been told, retold, and sometimes read to me by my mother since childhood. The knowledge that smallpox had been employed as a means of committing genocide against native peoples, not least the Cherokees from whom I am descended, was part of the bedrock in which my apprehension of meaning in the world was anchored by the time I was ten or twelve. So it has remained, because, as with much else imparted by my elders over the years, I've never found reason to question the validity of what was explained to me early on. Quite the contrary: while I've not approached the matter systematically until recently, I have regularly stumbled on information in the course of other research which has tended to corroborate what Mom had told me all along.

Among Cherokees, it has never been doubted that the devastating smallpox epidemic of 1738 resulted from the English deliberately including infected blankets in a batch of trade goods. Other items I've come across include Squanto's 1620 warning to the few surviving Wampanoags near Plymouth Plantation that the English had not only deliberately infected them with the pox two years earlier, but retained the means to do so again; evidence that the exterminatory Pequot War of 1637 resulted from the Indians' belief that they had been deliberately infected by the Plymouth colonists; and the conviction of the Wampanoags and Narragansetts that the very same English colonists had once again deliberately infected several of their villages, a matter precipitating "King Philip's War" in 1675–76. Apart from the well-documented instance involving English nobleman Jeffery Amherst in 1763, there is evidence that the English used infected blankets to spark an epidemic of smallpox among the peoples of the Ohio River Valley in 1752; they appear also to have engaged in biowarfare against insurgents during the U.S. War for Independence which, though unsuccessful in eliminating its intended target, unleashed a pandemic among American Indians that swept into the western regions of the continent as far north as central Canada and south into Mexico.

That's to speak only of the English (the French and Spanish have their own grisly histories); only of smallpox (measles and chickenpox were also rife); and of both in an undoubtedly incomplete manner (as I said, I've started to examine the matter systematically only recently). There is no shortage of similar examples pertaining to England's offshoot, the United States. These include not only the pandemic engineered by the War Department among the peoples of the upper Missouri River in 1837, claiming upwards of 100,000 lives, but the report of U.S. official Isaac McCoy that the Pawnees and other peoples to the south had been deliberately infected a year earlier. Sam Houston, the first president of Texas, almost certainly used blankets to infect the Wichitas with smallpox in 1843. This sort of thing was actually reported in newspapers from time to time, as when, on March 6, 1853, the *Daily Alta California* announced that smallpox had been used to rid the northern portion of the state of its last remaining Indians.

Buffy's verse was written with the 1837 pandemic specifically in mind, but she could as easily have been singing about any number of comparable "incidents," many of them already known to me. I thus received her harsh yet elegant lyrics with a sense of relief — not dissimilar to the feeling I've sometimes had when, adrift in a city of strangers, I spotted the face of an acquaintance. What *we* know to be true — the truth of which *they*, the primary beneficiaries of what was done, seek most desperately to deny — had finally been said to a relatively large audience, the words spoken with the utmost eloquence, but without a trace of sugar-coating or equivocation, delivered through a medium that compelled even the reluctant to listen. In that, I found great comfort at the time — and do so now, perhaps more profoundly still.

In retrospect, I find it probable that in the moment, whenever it was, I simply slipped into the song as if it were an old and intimately familiar shirt: appreciating the perfect feel of it, but unable to recall when or where I'd acquired it; wearing it as if, somehow, it had always been with me. I complemented it whenever I could with items exhibiting a similar texture and fit: Vine Deloria, Jr.'s observation in *Custer Died for Your Sins* about how in "the old days" the army gave "blankets infected with smallpox . . . to the tribes" as a means of exterminating them; Ann Ramenofsky's statement in *Vectors of Death* that "in the nineteenth century, the U.S. Army sent contaminated blankets to Native Americans [to] control the Indian problem"; Jared Diamond's assertion in *Guns, Germs, and Steel* that "U.S. whites bent on wiping out 'belligerent' Native Americans sent them gifts of blankets previously used by smallpox patients."[1] Over the years, I've catalogued scores of such passages, each reinforcing the knowledge bestowed in my youth, as well as that shared later by the elders of other peoples.

Long since, the sum of these parts has congealed into a core confidence that the extermination of American Indians by disease is a historical fact, no less self-evident than that the Japanese navy attacked its U.S. counterpart at Pearl Harbor, and that the U.S. employed nuclear weapons against Japanese civilians at Hiroshima and Nagasaki. This foundation, concretized by the words of a "folk song" of the mid–1960s, has stood me in good stead these past couple of years, as my passing references to the causes of the 1616 and 1837 smallpox outbreaks became the focal point of attack for deniers of the American holocaust, ranging from Guenter Lewy, to University of Colorado "distinguished historian" Marjorie McIntosh, to such self-anointed enforcers of "scholarly integrity" as David Horowitz and Bill O'Reilly. Standing on the strong base provided by those who came before has allowed me to remain unflinching in the face of this literal onslaught of denial.

It is this refusal to "cut my conscience to the fashion of the day" — if I may borrow from Lillian Hellman — to never compromise what I know to be true in the interest of expediency, convenience, or even personal safety, that I hope to pass along as an example to coming generations. For my ability to do so, however limited, I owe a great debt to those who passed along examples to which I, in my own way, now aspire. Prominent among them is Buffy Sainte-Marie. To her, I must seize this opportunity to say what I should have said long ago: "Thank you, sister. May what I've spent my life struggling to achieve have been worthy of your gift."

Postscript

In April 2009, a jury in Denver, Colorado found that Ward Churchill had been wrongfully dismissed in 2005 from his position at the University of Colorado.

Notes

[1] Vine Deloria, Jr., *Custer Died for Your Sins: An Indian Manifesto* (New York: Macmillan, 1969), p. 54; Ann F. Ramenofsky, *Vectors of Death: The Archaeology of European Contact* (Albuquerque, NM: University of New Mexico Press, 1987), p. 148; Jared Diamond, *Guns, Germs, and Steel: The Fates of Human Societies* (New York: W.W. Norton, 1997), p. 199.

The Westering Holocaust

Benjamin Whitmer

The first time I read *Blood Meridian*, I was tempted to make the mistake made by so many of the novel's proponents. Published in 1985, Cormac McCarthy's Indian-hating epic was acclaimed as a realistic corrective to the latest wave of romantic depictions of American Indians.[1] True, the scalp-hunting Glanton gang is presented as a band of genocidal thugs, murdering Indians for profit; but the Comanche they war with are depicted in little better light: as sodomites, cannibals, and "stoneage savages."[2] Reviewers tied their tongues in knots working to find new ways to praise McCarthy's historical accuracy.

There were two things that kept me from joining in the acclaim. The first was that the realistic/romantic dichotomy is one of the oldest tropes of American Indian-hating. Since the days of Thomas Morton, any text daring to affirm the humanity of even a single Indian has been met with a virulently racist corrective flying the flag of hard-headed realism. The archetypal example is James Fenimore Cooper's *Last of the Mohicans*. Granted, Cooper's novel was only romantic enough to posit that there were two good Indians on the continent—and those only because they were vastly superior to the rest of their race. But even this was too much for contemporary critics. Hence, Robert Montgomery Bird penned *Nick of the Woods*, a grisly extermination fantasy shot through with an orgiastic display of racial epithets that would have made Julius Streicher stutter. Nor has the tradition lost any steam. After being appalled by Kevin Costner's 1990 film *Dances with Wolves*, film critics across the nation could barely contain themselves upon viewing *Black Robe*—a dismal flick which, among other absurdities, represented the entire panoply of indigenous spirituality in the form of a malevolent dwarf.[3]

But, as I said, there were two things that kept me from joining the hype about *Blood Meridian*'s realism. The first was a rejection of the entire premise, but the second was the character of Judge Holden.

Though there was a historical Judge Holden, McCarthy's creation is all his own. A massive bald albino, he dances through *Blood Meridian* spouting a racialist pseudo-philosophy that reads like Nietzsche as interpreted by Charles Manson, butchering Indians indiscriminately. As Melville showed us in the *Confidence Man* (and Melville is McCarthy's favorite novelist), the frontier narrative is a confidence game, and the game is extermination. Judge Holden is that story writ large: a hypercivilized emissary of Manifest Destiny, advancing across the continent as a "westering holocaust."[4]

Like the so-called realistic texts that McCarthy is riffing on, Holden contains his own parody. He's a pedophile, of course — how could any monster created in our time not be? — and as such, in one of the novel's funnier moments, we find him trying to lure children into his clutches with candy. He's a caricature of evil, and that's the point. Near the end, when we find him stalking members of the gang across a desert, naked save for a parasol and leading a gibbering moron on a leash, it's nearly impossible not to see him as an exercise in kitsch. As with the dwarf in *Black Robe* or the schizophrenic Quaker in *Nick of the Woods*, it's a testament to the power of the Indian-hating tradition that anyone takes him seriously. But literary critics did, touting the philosophical soundness of Judge Holden's historical model.

That this model is so instantly recognizable speaks to its power. As Holden gives it to us in a long soliloquy on the disappearance of the Anasazi, it's a narrative of continual racial warfare, of the universality of wars of extermination. It's the hard-headed realism of Francis Parkman, Theodore Roosevelt, and T.R. Fehrenbach, the historical counterparts to novelists like Robert Montgomery Bird. Like Melville before him, McCarthy locates the contemporary metanarrative of Indian-hating upon which all lesser narratives hinge: that the exterminations enacted here in the United States were inevitable and natural, a result of the natural propulsion of history, of an ever-expanding frontier — never the result of deliberate decisions made by genocidal agents.

There are no boundaries to this narrative. Holden's story informs the scientific and the legal as thoroughly as the historical. As such, Holden is what every Indian-hater before him has been: an interdisciplinary huckster. It may be helpful here to think of Theodore Roosevelt, whose impressively interdisciplinary approach to Indian-hating included historical philosophy, natural science, and of course a U.S. foreign policy predicated on the extermination of savages. So, as an anthropologist, Holden discourses at length on the origin of the American Indian, from the lost tribes of Israel to the currently fashionable Bering Strait land-bridge theory. As a natural scientist, he lectures the gang on his ability to read universal law in the bones of the world. And, then, as a confidence man, he mocks his acolytes as fools for believing him.

His work is to do to the American Indian what white experts have done for four hundred years: to define them out of existence. Indians, like the natural world that Holden conflates them with, are only suffered to exist within his own framework. It's a point he drives home when, during one of his Socratic sessions with the gang, a member questions him as to exactly what it is that they're doing. The judge answers:

> War. War is your trade. Is it not?
> And it ain't yours?
> Mine too. Very much so.
> What about all them notebooks and bones and stuff?
> All other trades are contained in that of war.[5]

This is reified when we get a glimpse into Holden's method, as he comes across a series of petroglyphs and traces them into his sketchbook. Then, for no apparent reason, "he rose and with a piece of broken chert he scrappled away one of the designs, leaving no trace of it only a raw place on the stone where it had been."[6] As anthropologist and scientific researcher, what Holden encodes into his book, he eradicates, never allowing the original to exist in its original context. He contains all things, and will allow nothing outside himself. This is the key to one of McCarthy's most memorable puzzles, which comes in a discussion of Judge Holden's weight, given to us as twenty-four stone. One stone equals roughly fourteen pounds. Multiplying this hairless albino judge's twenty-four stone by fourteen gives us 336, or the exact number of *Blood Meridian*'s pages, excluding the prologue. It's a page count that has been a constant through several editions, and it means that the book's characterization of the Comanche has nothing to do with realism — rather, it has to do with the impossibility of escaping the narrative that Holden embodies.

Judge Holden's lesson is that there's no way of extricating the genocidal practice of clearing the continent from what's been constructed on those corpses, and there's no kinder, gentler version of our national identity. We live buried under the mass graves at Mystic and Wounded Knee, and the contortions we undergo to wriggle out from under them only serve to reenact them in newly tortured forms. Our Indian Wars not only haven't ceased, they haven't even significantly evolved, and neither have we. It's a horrifying understanding, and it's at the heart of what it has always meant to me to be a radical.

Utah Phillips once said that he saw liberals as the kind of folks who'd rearrange deck chairs on the Titanic. I've often thought of the radicals as down below in the hold, hacking holes in the hull with any tool at hand. As many critics have noted, *Blood Meridian* is heavily imbued with the psychological residue of another Indian war: Vietnam. In fact, like the Judge himself, the novel seems to contain all our Indian wars. The Pequot child roasting alive at Mystic is a progenitor of the Vietnamese child roasted alive in napalm. As we find ourselves embroiled in yet another Indian war, with Iraqi children shredded by our cluster bombs and a civilian death-count beginning to rival Pol Pot's, I find myself rereading *Blood Meridian*. And as I do so, I find myself thinking it's high time I headed down to the hold, and started looking for a hatchet.

Notes

[1]   Cormac McCarthy, *Blood Meridian*, or The Evening Redness in the West (New York: Random House, 1985).

[2]   McCarthy, *Blood Meridian*, p. 228.

[3]   Even positive reviews of *Dances with Wolves* were generally delivered with the caveat that the movie's depiction of American Indians was hopelessly romantic. *Black Robe*, on the other hand, was almost universally lauded for its historically authenticity. For instance, Victor Canby's November 9, 1990 *New York Times* review of *Dances with Wolves* decried the movie's Lakota camp as "on the brink of earnest silliness" and "a theme-park evocation, without rude odors to offend the sensitive nostril," while his October 31, 1991 review of *Black Robe* stated unequivocally that, "[*Black Robe*] is historically authentic not only in its locations but also in the picture it gives of the conditions in which these people lived. Unlike the scenery, these conditions are not pretty." One has to wonder what exactly Victor Canby's credentials are when it comes to assessing the historical authenticity of early 17th century Iroquois life.

[4]   See Benjamin Whitmer, review of Cormac McCarthy, *The Road*, in *The Modern World*, 23 October 2006. http://www.themodernword.com/reviews/mccarthy_road.html.

[5]   McCarthy, *Blood Meridian*, p. 249.

[6]   McCarthy, *Blood Meridian*, p. 173.

My Grandfather's Testimony

Sara Cohan

My engagement with human rights, and specifically with the issue of genocide, began in an intensely personal way at a young age. My father is Jewish and my mother Armenian: enough said. My family's history on both sides is marred, slashed, pulverized by the genocides of the twentieth century. I joke with friends that I should marry a Cambodian, Rwandan, or maybe a Ukrainian, to ensure that my child, like me, will be raised with a morbid subtext of genocide permeating an otherwise healthy and privileged childhood.

My father's family history with regard to the Holocaust was vague to me at best. A branch of our family tree was lost forever in the Shoah. But the specific experiences of those who died were subsumed by the intense desire of my paternal grandparents to assimilate in the United States. They died many years ago, and took all the clues to the fate of my great-aunts and great-uncles with them.

My mother's side was a little different. My maternal grandfather, Garo Aivazian, was a survivor of the Armenian Genocide. I spent a great deal of time with him until his death in 2005. It was not his intention to make me an activist by sharing his testimony about genocide with me. In fact, he very much wanted me to be an "American," and not to be bothered with past events. He was a psychiatrist, and was always trying to broach sensitive subjects with me in a way he felt would help me to lead a happy and well-adjusted life.

I do live as my grandfather wanted me to, but at the same time, I cannot quite be an "all-American girl" as he desired. As a child, I learned that much of the maternal side of my family had been killed in the Armenian Genocide; my grandfather had survived against the odds. What I did not know were the details of his life in the Ottoman Empire: the names of the villages our family had resided in for hundreds of years; the personal anecdotes about those who had not escaped—people we would have known as aunties and uncles, held reunions with, celebrated marriages and births with, mourned deaths with.

The bare bones of my family history in tow, I seized every opportunity to write school papers and create projects on the Armenian genocide. I regularly asked my grandfather about his own experiences, and received

Garabed Aivazian (courtesy Sara Cohan).

the same succinct answers I had become accustomed to over the years. I pep-
pered my research papers with odd facts about famous Armenian-Americans,
but my understanding of the genocide was basic at best. I remember excitedly
coming across Peter Balakian's poetry at the local library. Sitting in the book

stacks, I read again and again Balakian's poem "History of Armenia," which juxtaposed life in East Orange, New Jersey, with the intimate experiences of his grandmother's experience during the Armenian genocide. I tried to connect with his well-crafted words, but I could not. The history felt distant and foreign. I lacked the strong grasp of my own family's experiences that would allow me truly to connect with Balakian's verses.

About ten years ago, my grandfather sat me down and told me he had five years to live. He cited the results of a test he had taken in a health magazine to prove his point. He knew I would not take his passing well, and felt it was in my best interest to prepare me for it. Shortly after his declaration, I attended a seminar for educators sponsored by the National Endowment for the Humanities on Islam in Europe, and held at New York University. The lead professor at the month-long seminar openly denied the Armenian Genocide. During the last week of the seminar, she lectured on aspects of Ottoman history. Suddenly, she raised her head and voice, and announced that "so-called survivors" of the Armenian genocide were liars. I challenged her, but she did not back down.

A rage consumed me. It was the year 2000. I had learned of Rwanda's genocide; I knew the fate of the Bosnians, and had read about the crimes against humanity committed by Pol Pot and the Khmer Rouge in Cambodia. I had studied the Holocaust, taught it in my classes, and knew it was a part of my own story. On a personal level, my maternal grandfather had suffered more than anyone should have to in a thousand lifetimes. To have someone use his or her power as a professor to deny my family's tragedy, and the fate of 1.5 million martyrs, was the single most humiliating and hurtful moment of my life.

Soon after I returned from New York, I bought a cassette recorder and four blank tapes. Then I traveled to visit my grandfather in Memphis, Tennessee, where he had lived since the 1950s. I asked him to provide me with his testimony—a detailed testimony this time. He agreed, and set about filling the tapes with his memories of a childhood perverted by genocide. I expected to receive the tapes, transcribe them, and finally have his complete life history. But when I sat down to listen, I realized he was not parting with many of the details that I needed to know. We began a dialogue about his experiences that lasted until his death. Through the tapes and our long chats, the blank spaces began to disappear.

I listened to my grandfather's voice as he recounted his father's murder, his extended family's demise, and his struggle for survival in an empire that hated him for being Armenian. He was very young in 1915—just four years old. He and one of his sisters found themselves moved from orphanage to orphanage over the next four years. In one orphanage run by Turks, he was renamed "Mehmet," a traditional Turkish name. But his mother had written his Armenian name in his shirt before she was deported, to remind him who he was, wherever he might be sent. He described being so hungry at the same orphanage that he buried a "little red tomato" in the fields he was forced to work in, and snuck out in the evening to retrieve it. He was caught, and the tomato was confiscated. He was then six years old.

When I visited my grandfather in Memphis, he would cook for me. Our first course was always a simple salad with little red tomatoes. I never asked him if his orphanage experience had spurred him to eat cherry tomatoes with his meals. I *couldn't* ask him: it just seemed too sad, too personal. But every time I ate his salads, I couldn't help but think how hungry he must have been for that tiny tomato to hold such a powerful place in his memory. Now Balakian's poem was beginning to sink in. I realized that when one is a survivor of genocide, or a descendant of a survivor, the genocide experience is everywhere. It is on the dinner table in Memphis, Tennessee; or, as in the poem, on a parkway in East Orange, New Jersey.

Genocide is a plague that infects everything, and even when denied, seeps into each new generation. I decided I would not allow my grandfather's suffering to be denied any longer; I never wanted another child to suffer as he had. A professor with a fine Ivy League degree should not announce from her podium—with confidence, authority, and government funding—that genocide survivors were liars. I had to do something.

The classroom was the only tool available in my small community to assert my newfound activism. I developed lessons on human rights issues and genocide. As a history teacher, I needed to make sure my students knew the historical facts surrounding human rights atrocities. Next, they had to be equipped with an understanding of how to address such violations today. Later, I left the classroom environment for the Southern Poverty Law Center, where I wrote an article about the Armenian genocide for educators. From there, I moved to Washington D.C. and worked for Armenian organizations, assisting in historical research and educational outreach. I also used my time in Washington to volunteer at the United States Holocaust Memorial Museum and with the "Save Darfur Coalition." Currently, I teach world history, and serve as Education Director of the Genocide Education Project. The mission of the organization is also my own: to ensure that the history of genocide is remembered, analyzed, and discussed, and to use that history to find ways to thwart future genocides. Through education, I am contributing to the fight against genocide, and paying homage to my family's history at the same time.

A few years ago, I read the poem "After the Survivors are Gone," by Peter Balakian. It explores how we remember survivors—or rather why, once we hear their words, we cannot forget their pain. The last stanza of the poem reads:

> *We shall not forget the earth,*
> *the artifact, the particular song,*
> *the dirt of an idiom —*
> *things that stick in the ear.*

My grandfather knew his testimony was not just his own, but was mine as well. He felt a moral responsibility to leave his words with us after he was gone. For my part, I have a duty to ensure that his story is not forgotten—for the sake of the particular history he endured, and for those suffering from genocide today. Maybe, if I yell loud enough and long enough, his words will stick in others' ears as well.

Werfel, *Musa Dagh* and the Armenian Genocide

William Schabas

Franz Werfel's *The Forty Days of Musa Dagh* was probably the book that first provoked my interest in genocide. My father had an old copy that I suppose he had bought in the 1930s, when it first came out. He urged me to read it. It was one of those books that you couldn't put down. Full of heroism and personal tragedy, and of course beautifully written. It tells a true story, but through fiction, describing the defense of Musa Dagh's Damlayik, where Armenians had gathered in a last-ditch struggle for survival. Eventually, they were rescued by a French warship.

I'd love to know the whole story about why it was never made into a Hollywood film, because it would make a great one. Apparently, during the 1930s, MGM Studies was considering the project. Turkey intervened with the United States Department of State, which in turn put pressure on the filmmakers to abandon the project. *Plus ça change* . . . Sometime in the early 1980s, a low-budget film version was released, but has never been widely distributed. Early in 2007, it was rumored that Sylvester Stallone was planning his own version.[1]

Perhaps the most important aspect of the book was its unintended message that there were other victims of genocide than the Jews. Obviously, the book was written before the Holocaust. It appeared in 1933, when Werfel could hardly have imagined what awaited his fellow European Jews. He was of Czech origin, but lived in Vienna, and fled after the *Anschluss*. Eventually he made it to the United States.

In April 2005, I had the privilege of speaking at the conference organized in Armenia in commemoration of the 1915 genocide. My remarks began with a reminiscence about learning of the Armenian genocide from Franz Werfel. I will long remember the knowing and appreciative looks of those in the audience, almost all of whom were descendants of survivors. There may have been a few survivors in the audience as well, I am not sure. Later in

Crowds at the genocide memorial in Yerevan, Armenia
(courtesy Otto de Voogd, www.7is7.com/otto).

the day, I went to the very stirring memorial on the outskirts of Yerevan. One looks out over the city, in one direction, and in the other to the twin peaks of Mount Ararat. Of course, it is not possible to visit Ararat, because it lies just across the border in Turkey. The border remains closed because Turkey insists that Armenia acknowledge the genocide did not take place.

A year later, I gave the same lecture in Ankara, at the invitation of the Ankara Bar Association. Orhan Pamuk was facing charges at the time for his alleged insults to "Turkishness," and I wasn't at all sure what would happen to me when I spoke of the Armenian genocide. There was some grumbling in the hall, and a few rather feeble attempts at hostile questions. Then, to my great surprise and satisfaction, when the talk was over and we were milling around in the lobby of the hotel, some Turkish colleagues came over and thanked me for my remarks. It wasn't as warm a welcome as I had received in Yerevan; but I sensed that there are cracks in the Turkish position.

All of this started for me when I was about twelve, and read *The Forty Days of Musa Dagh*. My father still has his battered copy. Recently, my mother told me she was reading it for the first time! Some years ago, I decided I needed a copy of my own, and found a more recent edition through an online book vendor. It now sits in my library, surrounded by books on the law and history of genocide.

Notes

[1] For more information, see David Welky, "Global Hollywood versus National Pride: The Battle to Film *The Forty Days of Musa Dagh*," *Film Quarterly*, 59: 3 (Spring 2006), pp. 35–43.

Armin T. Wegner, photographs and letters

"The Desire to Communicate Something of My Torment"

Nina Krieger

Armin T. Wegner confronted two of the twentieth century's nadirs with words and images. An expressionist writer who photographed Armenian deportation camps while serving with the German Army in World War I, and who later protested against Nazi Germany's anti-Semitic policies, his actions hint at issues central to my abiding interest in genocide studies. As a museum educator who facilitates interaction with traces of the past, I am drawn to remnants that prompt a consideration of what is at stake when we attempt to document, represent, and learn from atrocities. Wegner left records of events he witnessed, and articulated responses to them, that offer compelling entry-points to such discussions.

I first learned of Wegner's remarkable story when I began research for a school program to coincide with an exhibition of his photographs.[1] In April 1915, following the military alliance of Germany and Turkey, Wegner left his post as a medic on the Eastern Front to join the German Sanitary Corps in the Middle East. His writings reveal a youthful optimism: "Now I hold the helm of my life in my own hands. I shall see Baghdad, the Tigris, Mossul, Babylon. I am fully aware of the choice I have made . . . I have become a soldier . . . I have put my life at stake for my soul's sake."[2] Perhaps it was this same wanderlust and yearning for self-discovery that prompted Wegner to use his leave between July and August to investigate rumors about the massacre of Armenians. Travelling along the Baghdad Railway, he observed the Ottoman army leading the empire's Armenian population on forced marches through the Syrian desert, and encountered scenes of starvation, disease, and murder.

Disobeying orders intended to prevent the spread of information about the atrocities, Wegner collected notes, documents, letters, and took photographs in the Armenian deportation camps. In a diary entry, Wegner describes the risk associated with his documentary enterprise:

Armin Wegner smuggled out this photograph of Armenian refugee children during the genocide. (Courtesy Friends of Armenian Cultural Treasures, Inc. [FACT] and Armin T. Wegner Society of USA. © Wallstein Verlag, Germany.)

> *I have taken numerous photographs . . . on penalty of death. I do not doubt for a moment that I am committing a treasonable act. And yet I am inspired by the knowledge that I have helped these poor people in some small way. . . . Hunger, death, disease, despair shout at me from all sides. Wretched me, for I carried neither bandages nor medications . . . I was overcome by dizziness, as if the earth were collapsing on both sides of me into an abyss . . .*[3]

At the request of the Turkish Command, Wegner was arrested and recalled to Germany. While many of his photographs were confiscated and destroyed, he succeeded in smuggling images to Germany and the United States through clandestine mail. In looking at Wegner's photographs, which have defied the odds to reach museum audiences, the students I work with consider the danger sometimes associated with image making, and encounter a context and moral universe very different from their own.

Wegner's belief that documentation could *in some small way help* the victims is a historically specific one. Noting the challenge to language represented by the Great War, American novelist and critic Henry James suggested in 1915 that "one finds it in the midst of all this as hard to apply one's words as endure one's thoughts. The war has used up words; they have weakened, they have deteriorated . . ."[4] Alongside this erosion of linguistic power, photography emerged as a medium capable of conveying the grim realities of conflict, and of stimulating moral outrage. In *Regarding the Pain of Others*, Susan Sontag traces the changing relationship between war photography and affect in viewers.[5]

Wegner's images, which cannot be viewed by audiences today without subsequent war images—many of them strikingly similar—coming to mind, provide an opportunity to consider the shifting meaning of still images. According to Sontag, "photographs echo photographs."[6] These echoes can supply fertile entry-points for self-reflective viewing. In a school program, I might ask students to consider Wegner's photograph of young orphans in an Armenian deportation camp, a haunting image that invariably activates students' mental storehouse of images—perhaps of Jewish children in camp liberation photographs from 1945, or crowded refugee camps in Sudan. The point is not to compare the experiences of these victims, but to stimulate discussion about what these images tell us about such events, and how photographs function to construct our apprehension of human suffering. Wegner's images leave us with a springboard for thinking about the motivations and implications of the witness's gaze, and the power (and limitations) of a photograph as evidence and catalyst for action.

Sontag provocatively suggests that "harrowing photographs . . . are not much help if the task is to understand. Narratives can make us understand."[7] Wegner fortuitously provides us with both image and narrative. His writings, both private and published, reveal an individual struggling with how to respond to what he had witnessed. In March 1916 Wegner wrote to his mother from Baghdad: "Can I still live? Do I still have the right to breathe, to make plans for a future which seems so insubstantial, when all about me lies an abyss filled with the eyes of the dead?"[8] Wegner's choice of words is of course worth noting. Drawing on the expressionist style and often creating turgid and sentimental passages, Wegner mined language for its power to stir emotions and promote the idea of a common humanity.[9] Working through the representational challenge described by Henry James and later by post-Holocaust philosophers,[10] Wegner demonstrates the capacity of language to wrestle with conveying horrific experiences and, he would hope, to stimulate understanding, perhaps even intervention.

In a 1919 collection of letters from his time in the Middle East, Wegner wrote: ". . . with memories of the massacres still alive and set against the pale horizon of the scorched steppe, there arose in me, quite involuntarily, the desire to communicate something of my torment, not only to personal friends, but to a wider, invisible community."[11] This notion of sharing what he had witnessed with an undefined audience (humanity, perhaps?) suggests narration as a possible counterpoint to paralysis and despair. Wegner's impulse, regardless of its arguably naïve motivations and failed outcomes, is a powerful one that left remarkable traces.

In 1919 Wegner directed his words toward a very precise target: United States President Woodrow Wilson, then attending the Paris Peace Conference. In an open letter, he wrote:

> As one of the few Europeans who have been eyewitnesses of the dreadful destruction of the Armenian people from the beginning in the flourishing towns and fruitful fields of Anatolia to the wiping out of their miserable remains on the banks of the Euphrates the desolate, stony Mesopotamian desert, I dare claim the right of bringing to your attention this picture of misery and terror which passed before my eyes for nearly two years, and which will never be obliterated from my mind. The Armenian Question is a question for Christendom, for the whole human race. . . . The voice of conscience and humanity will never be silenced in me, and therefore I address these words to you. This document is a request. In it the tongues of thousands dead speak.[12]

Wegner again assumed the role of spokesperson for justice in a 1933 letter to Adolf Hitler. Written on April 11th—immediately following the Nazi state's first coordinated anti-Jewish policy, a boycott of Jewish businesses and the offices of Jewish doctors and lawyers—the letter is worth quoting at length:

> Righteousness was always the jewel in the crown of the nations, and Herr Reichskanzler, it is not just a matter of the fate of our Jewish brethren, the fate of Germany is also at stake! As a German born and bred, I appeal to you to put a stop to all this. I have both the right and the duty to appeal to you, for my heart is seething with indignation, and I was not endowed with the gift of speech merely to make myself an accomplice by remaining silent. The Jews have survived captivity

in Babylon, slavery in Egypt, the Inquisition in Spain, the oppression of the crusades and sixteen hundred pogroms in Russia. The resilience that has enabled this people to survive to the present day will also enable them to overcome this threat. But the opprobrium and ignominy which now adhere to Germany as a result of this will not be forgotten for a long time!

> *I dispute the foolish notion that the Jews should be blamed for the world's misfortunes. I repudiate this charge, based on the judgment, testimony and voice of the centuries. And if I turn to you now in the form of a letter, it is because I see no other way for being given a hearing. I appeal to you not as a friend of the Jews but . . . out of love for my people. Though all prefer today to stand mute, I for one can no longer.*

> *What would Germany be without Truth, Beauty and Justice? If one day our cities were to lie in ruins, generation upon generation had bled to death and words of tolerance had died away forever, the mountains of our homeland, covered by their everlasting rustling forests, would of course still stand out defiantly against the sky—but they would no longer breathe the air of freedom and justice of our ancestors. They would, with shame and contempt, tell of the generations which had recklessly gambled with the good of our country and disgraced its memory for all time. In demanding justice we want dignity. I implore you! Preserve magnanimity, conscience and a sense of pride, without which we cannot live. Preserve the dignity of the German people!*[13]

Each time I read Wegner's urgent words, I am struck by their resonance. The 1919 letter was written as an eyewitness testimony and petition for victims' rights following genocide; the 1933 letter is written at genocide's dawn, in an attempt to alter the course of events. Both dimensions of witnessing and responding to injustice are significant, even though (or perhaps because) neither of Wegner's protests produced their desired effects.[14]

Uttered before the Nuremberg Laws, before *Kristallnacht*, before Auschwitz, before the Nuremberg Tribunals, Wegner's predictions about the consequences of Nazi anti-Semitism are eerily accurate. Wegner speaks to early warning signs—restriction of civil liberties; removal from professions;

fear, hate and scapegoating—integral to the systematic targeting of a particular group. He speaks of the consequences of inhumanity for not only the victims, but also the perpetrators. Yet the letter's power lies as much in its temporality as in its prophecy. Wegner speaks to *us*, *here* and *now* because his words are painfully oblivious to the cataclysmic events that would follow.

Articulations inevitably circumscribed by time, Wegner's letters seem to speak presciently to future audiences. This "invisible community"—an audience that includes readers of books, visitors to museums, students in classrooms—is also implied by the harrowing observations written during the Holocaust by Jews in ghettoes, grappling with rapidly changing circumstances and a growing realization that they would likely not survive the Nazi roundups. The chronicles of the Warsaw ghetto—Chaim Kaplan's *Scroll of Agony*, or the collected diaries and last wills and testaments of the *Oyneg Shabbes*, for instance—are some of the most powerful teaching texts I have encountered.[15] Such writings seem almost unbearably *human* because they offer access to specific and, with hindsight, inevitably limited perspectives. In many of these instances, texts survived when their authors did not.

In his excellent co-edited volume exploring the "gray zones" introduced by Primo Levi, John K. Roth discusses the "double bind" navigated by those who search for meaning in such historical events. Roth suggests that a "sense of ethical responsibility, real though it is, remains hopelessly optimistic and naïve unless it grapples with the despair that encounters with the Holocaust and other genocides are bound to produce."[16] Between despair and hope, between the inability to articulate the crime of genocide and the necessity to do so—as educators, students, and citizens we occupy the in-between.

The traces left by Armin Wegner hint at the potential of this space. Wegner's legacy reveals the fragmentary character of our understanding of genocide and the value of response, even if limited or failed. In reading his letters we imagine *what might have been* and confront the non-inevitability of history. Just as photographs echo photographs (often revealing painful repetitions), so documents echo historic moments, sounding the distance between past events and our own time. Words, Wegner reminds us, have special potential. At times they can be life-saving: names typed on a list of "essential workers," for instance. At times they can be soul-saving: a way to make sense of unimaginable suffering. And at times words can reach through time to shake us, to affirm the possibility—the necessity, even—of testimony and protest.

Notes

[1] *Armin T. Wegner & the Armenians in Anatolia*, 1915–1916, a travelling photographic exhibition produced by Friends of Armenian Cultural Treasures, Inc. and the Armin T. Wegner Society USA, was presented at the Vancouver Holocaust Education Centre in partnership with the Armenian National Committee of Canada, February-May 2009. Although the promotion of genocide awareness is part of the VHEC's mandate, the exhibition of Wegner's 1915–16 photographs was the first project and school program to have a genocide other that the Holocaust as its primary focus.

[2] Armin T. Wegner, *Der Weg ohne Heimkehr: Ein Martyrium in Briefen* (Berlin: Egon Fleischel & Co., 1919), p. 13, quoted in the exhibition catalogue, *Armin T. Wegner and the Armenians of Anatolia, 1915: Images and Testimonies* (Milan: Guerini E Associati, 1996).

[3] Wegner diary entry quoted on the PBS website, *The Great War and the Shaping of the 20th Century*: http://www.pbs.org/greatwar/chapters/ch2_voices2.html.

[4] Henry James, *The New York Times* (March 21, 1915).

[5] Susan Sontag, *Regarding the Pain of Others* (New York: Picador, 2003), particularly pp. 79–80.

[6] *Ibid.*, p. 84.

[7] *Ibid.*, p. 89.

[8] Wegner, *The Way of No Return: A Martyrdom in Letters*, original title: *Der Weg ohne Heimkehr: Ein Martyrium in Briefen* (Berlin: E. Fleischel & Co., 1919), p. 64, quoted in the Wegner exhibition catalogue.

[9] For a perspective on the relationship between Wegner and the internationalism of American poet Walt Whitman, see Betsy Erkkila and Jay Grossman, *Breaking Bounds: Whitman and American Cultural Studies* (New York: Oxford University Press, 1996), pp. 242–3.

[10] For perspectives on this issue, see Saul Friedlander, ed., *Probing the Limits of Representation: Nazism and the "Final Solution"* (Boston: Harvard University Press, 1992).

[11] Wegner, *The Way of No Return*, quoted in the exhibition catalogue.

[12] Quoted in the Wegner exhibition catalogue.

[13] Wolfgang Gerlach, trans., "Document: Armin T. Wegner's Letter to German Chancellor Adolf Hilter, Berlin, Easter Monday, April 11, 1933," *Holocaust and Genocide Studies*, 8: 3 (1994), pp. 395–409.

[14] Wegner's calls for an independent Armenian Republic and reparations to victims in the 1919 letter came to naught. When no newspaper would print his 1933 letter, Wegner delivered it directly to NSDAP party headquarters in Munich with a request

that it be forwarded directly to Hitler. Wegner was promptly arrested, tortured and interned in three concentration camps: Oranienberg, Borgermoor and Licthenberg. Incarceration in seven different prisons was followed by years of exile in England, Poland, and Italy. Wegner's actions, however, were later acknowledged. He was awarded the Highest Order of Merit by the Federal German Government (1956), the Eduard von der Heydt Prize by his birthplace, Wuppertal (1962), the designation of Righteous Among the Nations by Yad Vashem (1967), and the Order of Saint Gregory the Illuminator by the Catholicos of all Armenians (1968). Wegner died in Rome in 1978. See Gerlach, trans.

[15]   See *Scroll of Agony: The Warsaw Diary of Chaim A. Kaplan* (London: Hamish Hamilton, 1966); *Scream the Truth at the World: Emanuel Ringelbum and the Hidden Archive of the Warsaw Ghetto* (Warsaw: Zydowski Instytut Historyczy, 2001).

[16]   John K. Roth, "Gray-Zoned Ethics: Morality's Double Binds During and After the Holocaust" in Jonathan Petropoulous and John K. Roth, eds., *Gray Zones: Ambiguity and Compromise in the Holocaust and its Aftermath* (New York: Berghahn Books, 2005), p. 375.

Warning: Here There Be Experts

Benjamin Lieberman

Among all the many works that seek to explain or represent genocide, I find firsthand accounts most powerful: books by survivors such as Primo Levi, or documents left by victims such as Dawid Sierakowiak, the teenage boy who wrote a remarkable diary detailing the pain of life in the Lodz Ghetto before he died in August 1943. These works, and others by authors such as Mihail Sebastian, who survived the Second World War in Romania only to die when he was hit by a truck, are the kind of books that I most often tell people about. However, the works that most powerfully evoked genocide for me did so almost unintentionally. These books, written after the invention and then broad dissemination of the concept, do not mention genocide at all—or rather, they do not use the term to refer to the Armenian genocide.

I first became aware of the controversy over the Armenian genocide around the time that I started teaching college courses in the early 1990s. Knowing little about the subject, I did what I had learned to do in graduate school: I consulted the work of experts with the goal of learning the basics, so that I could say a few words to my class about the fate of the Armenians. This turned out to be a major error. One of the experts whose work I consulted was Bernard Lewis, and my brief survey of him and other authorities persuaded me that one could not speak of an Armenian genocide. Certainly, there had been appalling loss of life—Lewis did *not* minimize the death toll, and even wrote in the second

The missing volume of
Ottoman history.
Poster by Yervant Herian.
See Color Plate II

edition of *The Emergence of Modern Turkey* of a "terrible Holocaust" and of the death of as many as 1.5 million Armenians. But the overall impression I gained was of a terrible war in the east between Turks and Armenians, rather than of a genocide comparable in intent, organization, and planning to the Jewish Holocaust. Lewis described Armenians as posing a very real threat to Turkey, and he cast the killing in 1915 as the result of a "struggle between two nations for the possession of a single homeland . . ."[1] Prepared with this information, and trusting in the authority of well-known historians, I distinctly remember telling something of this sort to my class—that the killing of Armenians was mainly the result of a war between rival nations. I gave my students the impression that this was something different than genocide, and I can only hope that particular class was not paying close attention at that time.

I doubt these arguments would have made such a strong impression on me if I had not subsequently rejected them. A few years later, I read *Ambassador Morgenthau's Story*, by the then-US ambassador in Constantinople; and from there I turned to the German documents collected by Johannes Lepsius, who publicized the plight of Armenians, while obscuring some of the more embarrassing evidence of official German passivity. These and other sources shocked me, but the gap between their accounts of an extermination of Armenians and Bernard Lewis's portrait of a conflict between nations proved a far more powerful influence than any particular anecdote or detail of the suffering. I simply could not reconcile the reality I was now reading with the interpretations in the books I had pulled from the library shelves to provide a sketchy background for a few minutes of lectures. The clash between expert interpretation and very personal glimpses of extermination came to drive my own interest in detailing and comprehending genocide.

I still read and benefit from the work of historians, but the clash between my initial and subsequent encounters with the Armenian genocide also transformed my approach to history. While I benefit from learning about diverse interpretations and models, I now believe that no professorship at a famous university, no long list of awards, no impressive sequence of blurbs, and no amount of praise from fellow historians guarantees the authority of any argument or interpretation. Evidence cannot speak for itself, but evidence must always come before expertise if it presents a picture that is fundamentally at odds with expert opinion.

Notes

[1] Bernard Lewis, *The Emergence of Modern Turkey*, 2nd ed. (London: Oxford University Press, 1968).

J. Michael Hagopian (prod.), *Voices from the Lake* (2003)

Conspiracy of Silence

Ani Kalayjian

My father was a survivor of the Ottoman Turkish genocide against Armenians and other minorities, and my mother is a child of survivors. But they told us very little about the horrific events of 1915, in order to "protect" us from the negative emotions generated by those events. Years later, when I conducted research with forty survivors of this same genocide, the majority of respondents (75 percent) likewise stated that they avoided discussing their traumatic experiences, for the same reason. "The ones who witnessed [the genocide] know about it; the others don't want to know." Some survivors explained that during the genocide and immediately afterward, they were unable to talk about their experiences and feelings out of fear. "We were scared to talk to anyone. The Turks wouldn't even let us talk in Armenian with one another; so do you think we were going to talk about what they [Turks] did? They would have definitely finished us."[1]

As a young girl growing up in an Armenian neighborhood in Aleppo, Syria, this silence was extremely confusing to me. I would see my mother with neighbors gathered around and crying when I came home from school. I never knew what had happened, and always wondered about the cause of this visible pain.

In 1988, I organized a group of mental health professionals to establish a charitable organization dedicated to the research and recovery of survivors of genocide, as well as those suffering from other mass traumas. Under the auspices of this organization (the Armenian-American Society for Studies on Stress and Genocide), we have not only conducted scholarly studies, but arranged for dialogues between groups of Armenians and Turks, to allow subsequent generations to process their peoples' pasts. Representatives of the Turkish side frequently spoke of feelings of humiliation, while the most frequently expressed emotions from the Armenians were anger and sadness. Our desire to arrive at truth and reconciliation is challenged in these group settings. Turkish citizens state that the genocide is not a priority for them—although, in my analysis, they are unconsciously avoiding the need to address their dark history.

Armenians, meanwhile, are left to process their own trauma, not only without the active participation of the Turks, but in the face of the denialist and revisionist Turkish policies.

In 1999, I went to Istanbul to present one of our research papers at an international conference on "Psychotraumatology and Human Rights." All my friends and colleagues were against my going to Turkey to present our findings on the Armenian genocide. I decided to proceed, but being fully cognizant of Turkish denialism, I revised our research paper to avoid the word "genocide," titling it instead: "Mass Human Rights Violations: Resilience vs. Resignation." My paper was accepted with a few revisions.

Upon arriving at the conference, I noticed how the keynote speakers talked freely about Turkish human rights violations perpetrated against the Kurds. Encouraged by these candid remarks, I decided to distribute my original abstract on the Armenian genocide. At that point, the travails began.

First, my life was threatened by two men who claimed to represent the MIT (the Turkish equivalent of the CIA). I responded skeptically, saying that I doubted anyone would dare kill me in front of the 650 scholars from some 48 countries who were present at the conference. The next day, I was threatened with torture if I talked about the genocide. On the third day, the abstracts were snatched from my hands; and on the final day of the conference, when my actual lecture was scheduled, I was called by the Turkish organizers and the British head of the European Society for Traumatic Stress Studies for a private meeting in the basement of the hotel. There, I was presented with an ultimatum: either sign a letter, or leave without delivering our research paper. The letter stated that I would refrain from talking about the Ottoman Turkish genocide of the Armenians. It was handed to me only twenty minutes before my lecture, which was scheduled to take place at the very end of the conference. I tried to remind my interlocutors that this was a human rights conference, and told them they were actually violating my human rights by dictating what I could and could not talk about. But it was to no avail. They reiterated that because of the political situation, they had to "protect the Turkish organizers." To avoid losing the opportunity to address the conference, I decided to sign the letter.

The audio-visual department helped me to revise my accompanying transparencies, covering up identifying words such as "Genocide," "Armenian," and "Ottoman Turkish" with a special black-transparency marker. When I began delivering my lecture and the first transparency was projected, I apologized for the black lines, without glancing at the screen. But I noticed that many of my European and American colleagues had smirks on their faces. When I turned to look, I saw that the identifying words were showing through the black censoring marks. I instantly quipped: "Whoops, it is coming through. I guess we could not hide it any longer."

There was a hubbub in the audience. The Turkish attendees were extremely tense, while other participants were laughing at the irony in my statement. I asked the audiovisual person to stop displaying the transparencies, and focused on the theme of forgiveness as a therapeutic intervention. I felt apprehensive as I did so, trying to decipher what I should say and what I should avoid saying. Eventually, I felt I managed to communicate the importance of spiritual forgiveness as a means of transcending resentment and moving toward healthy dialogue.

When I returned safely to New York, I felt drained both emotionally and physically. It was then that I was handed a video called *Voices from the Lake*. It is an Armenian documentary, produced by J. Michael Hagopian, about the Ottoman Turkish genocide. What makes the film unique is that it consists of the voices of *American* missionaries who were working in Anatolia in 1915, when the genocide erupted. The validation I received from this film was extraordinary: I did not realize until that point how the Turkish government's revisionist agenda had impacted on me. When I heard recitations of the diary entries of these missionaries, who were themselves terrorized and traumatized by their experiences, it felt like a profound validation. Here was a group of non-Turkish, non-Armenian witnesses describing the atrocities, recording the exact colors of the clouds on a particular day in 1915, and reporting that although the chirping of birds could be heard, the noise of the guns that the Turkish gendarmes were using to kill Armenian civilians overpowered all else. They described the rape of young Armenian girls, and how gendarmes forced family members and neighbors to watch these crimes against humanity.

What perplexes me is that these American missionaries wrote to their parishes, their church leaders, the American Embassy, the President of United States—all to no avail. The genocide was written about in the *New York Times* and other widely-read newspapers—again, to no avail. This reinforced my sense of a pervasive "conspiracy of silence," one that still continues, long after the genocide ended. There has been no validation of the Armenian experience, no reparations, and no formal acknowledgment, even from the American government. As an American, this saddens me.

When I was being harassed in Istanbul, a good friend, Hrant Dink—an Armenian journalist born and living in Turkey—acted as my protector.

In January 2007, my dear friend was assassinated by a Turkish extremist for his views on freedom of speech. In fact, Turkey has regressed since my 1999 visit. It has adopted Resolution 301, stating that anyone who issues criticisms of Turkey or mentions the Armenian genocide will be imprisoned for insulting "Turkishness." When a Turk, Orhan Pamuk, was awarded the Nobel Prize in 2006, in part for his novel *Snow* which touches on the genocide, he was subjected to threats and legal harassment.

Despite these setbacks, I celebrate those American missionaries who tried to assist victims of the Ottoman Turkish genocide against Armenians, Greeks, Assyrians, and other minorities. I come alive in my work as a human rights advocate, and I use *Voices from the Lake* along with other works to convey the importance of witnessing, advocating, and collaborating for the good of humanity. As the popular proverb has it: When one helps another, both are stronger.

Notes

[1]   Ani Kalayjian et al., *Coping with Genocide: An Exploration of the Experiences of Armenian Survivors* (1996).

Letter from Ambassador R. Henry Norweb to President Franklin Delano Roosevelt (1937)

Discovering the Haitian Massacre

Edward Paulino

The first time I read them, I could not foresee that two sentences would transform my sense of history, memory, cultural identity, and genocide.

In 1989, I was an undergraduate at the College of New Paltz in upstate New York. My mentor, the historian Dr. Laurence Hauptman, invited me to visit the Franklin D. Roosevelt Presidential Library in Hyde Park, across the river in Poughkeepsie, New York, to conduct research for my undergraduate senior thesis. My thesis focused on the 1937 Haitian Massacre in the Dominican Republic — a genocidal killing spree ordered by the Dominican dictator Rafael Trujillo, in which between 12,000 and 20,000 ethnic Haitians were murdered [1] — and Dr. Hauptman thought I might find some interesting and relevant diplomatic documents. It was the first time I had visited an archive, and it would prove pivotal not only to my research, but to a process of reassessment of my ancestral home.

At the FDR Library, I reviewed several documents and photographs, including a black-and-white image from 1934 that showed Eleanor Roosevelt, holding a big bouquet of roses, standing next to Trujillo and his second wife in the port city of San Pedro de Macorís. (FDR himself never set foot on the island of Hispaniola.)

My main objective, though, was to discover the extent of the American government's knowledge of the 1937 massacre. At the time of the killings, the official narrative emanating from the Dominican Republic had depicted the massacre as a "skirmish" between farmers. The Trujillo dictatorship had censored all news of the killings, which began in September of 1937 and continued until November. In his correspondence with the Roosevelt administration, Trujillo lied about the massacre, reassuring the US president that allegations of the mass killing of Haitians was a fabrication by political exiles seeking his overthrow.

At the FDR Library, I uncovered diplomatic correspondence that showed a widespread government-sponsored killing spree had indeed taken place, and that Roosevelt knew Trujillo was lying about his regime's orchestration of it.

Ciudad Trujillo, Santo Domingo, D. R.,

October 11, 1937.

No. 16

Subject: Slaughter of Haitians on Northwest Frontier.

The Honorable

The Secretary of State,

Washington, D. C.

Sir:

I have the honor to confirm my telegram No. 30 of October 11 - 9 a.m., reporting that approximately one thousand Haitian residents on the northwest frontier of the Dominican Republic had been killed by the Dominican National Police and Army.

As was indicated in my telegram No. 29 of October 9 - 9 a.m. and my despatch No. 13 of the same date, Major Norris, the Auditor of the Receivership General of Dominican Customs, in the course of an inspection trip to Monte Cristi and Dajabón last Saturday and Sunday was able thoroughly to investigate the extent of

the

First page of the Norweb Communiqué
(courtesy Franklin D. Roosevelt Presidential Library and Museum, Hyde Park, NY).

Particularly startling was a diplomatic communiqué from R. Henry Norweb, then the US Ambassador to the Dominican Republic. "Apparently with the approval of President Trujillo," Norweb wrote,

> . . . a systematic campaign of extermination was directed against all Haitian residents . . . the drive was conducted with ruthless efficiency by the National Police and Army. The technique used is of special importance in that it was designed to give the Dominican Government an opportunity to disclaim all responsibility for the killings. Following a house to house canvass of Haitians resident in the area between Dajabón and the sea, all who had not previously fled across the border were rounded up and cited for deportation proceedings. Their *cedulas* [identity cards] and passports were examined and they were passed through the immigration control offices at Dajabón and Monte Cristi which in turn reported to the Fiscal of the district at Monte Cristi that the persons so indicated had been deported to Haiti. The Haitians were then quietly murdered by the Dominican troops. On three successive nights groups of Haitian men, women, and children were herded to the end of the customs wharf at Monte Cristi and there dispatched by the soldiers. They were clubbed over the head and thrown into the sea where the sharks completed the task by destroying the evidence. This slaughter on the dock was corroborated by the eye-witness reports of a watchman in the service of the Receivership who personally related to [U.S. Army] Major Norris what he had seen. Other bands of Haitian "deportees" were taken under guard down to the sea, ostensibly to embark on ships for Haiti. However, as Major Norris trenchantly remarked, "There were no ships." These persons were knocked on the head and run through by bayonets and knives. Other groups of Haitian victims were seen being conducted under armed guard to the fortress at Monte Cristi. They did not emerge . . . As a result of this campaign, the entire northwest of the frontier on the Dajabón side is absolutely devoid of Haitians. Those not slain either fled across the frontier or are still in hiding in the bush.[2]

Prior to this, I hadn't connected this relatively unknown Caribbean massacre with the larger history of genocide. As a young Dominican kid growing up in the Lower East Side in New York City, I first learned about genocide through Milton Metzer's book *The Holocaust*. I was fifteen years old, and was shocked to learn that places like Auschwitz had existed and were created specifically to destroy other human beings based on racist ideologies. Over the next few years, I would read more books and watch documentaries on genocides ranging from Cambodia to Rwanda to Darfur. Though always compelling, they were distant to my culture and identity: I was related to neither the victims nor the perpetrators. But the Norweb communiqué was different. It forced me to ponder my own relationship to this legacy of mass murder, and my identity as an ethnic Dominican bearing witness to the crime.

For someone born and raised in New York City, the Dominican Republic had seemed an idyllic place. During Christmas holidays and summer vacations, Santo Domingo served as a peaceful refuge, where I could bask under a limoncillo (Spanish lime) fruit tree on my family's cocoa farm in the town of San Francisco de Macorís and watch the guaraguaos (hawks) soaring high above in a royal-blue sky. It was my paradise. There, I felt at home, one of the majority—something denied me in the United States. During my adolescence in the 1980s, when my neighborhood, like others in New York and the United States, succumbed to the ravages of the crack epidemic, I yearned to leave the United States and return to my parents' country. I often argued fruitlessly with my mother to let me move to the Dominican Republic. In my college years, the joy and pride I felt toward the Dominican Republic and in being Dominican, and my need to understand why my parents had left their country in the late 1960s, drove me to read obsessively about Dominican history and culture. And, as an aspiring historian, I even memorized the root Library of Congress code for the section of our library stacks in the Sojourner Truth Library that held Dominican books: F1938.

It was thus disconcerting, indeed a jolting surprise, when I came across Norweb's document in the FDR Library. The communiqué alerting FDR to the 1937 Haitian massacre forced me to see the Dominican Republic and its history in a different light. How could "my people" participate in genocidal massacres? How could a culture, which spoke to me in ways that American culture did not, especially as a politically radicalized Latino undergraduate in a predominantly white college, also be the site of a mass murder not unlike the other genocides I had read about? At the time, I'd had an insatiable desire to condemn the European conquest of the Americas, the decimation of hundreds of indigenous nations, and the enslavement of Africans, thereby reaffirming my Dominican identity by romanticizing "the folk." Yet I was unprepared to expand my anti-colonial perspective to a critique of my own heritage of violence and racialism.

Since that first encounter, I have come to rely on the Norweb communiqué, and to use it consistently in my writings. Why? Because the document validates the historical reality of the massacre, when Trujillo himself never accepted responsibility for his leadership role in perpetrating it. It offers powerful documentary evidence that an intentional campaign to "exterminate" Haitians took place. Moreover, the document is part of a diplomatic skein running from US Ambassador Morgenthau's dispatches to his superiors in Washington about the Armenian Genocide in 1915, to the communications relayed to the US government during the mass killings of Tutsis by Hutus in Rwanda in 1994. It is also part of the trend that Samantha Power has identified in twentieth-century genocides: of US indifference and failure to intervene in global atrocities. Indeed, the Roosevelt administration's response was deeply cautious. War loomed with Germany, and Washington was keen to project to the world a united hemispheric front. It was not until Haiti invoked the Gondra Treaty of 1923 and the Conciliation Convention — treaties created to resolve hemispheric disputes — that the United States, along with Mexico and Cuba, officially entered the public process of a peace settlement between the two nations. Thereby, President Roosevelt achieved his objective of maintaining the hemispheric peace he espoused under the Good Neighbor Policy.[3] Four years later, the United States entered World War II, and all was forgotten. Trujillo was never punished for this crime against humanity. Indeed, he ingratiated himself even more with Washington by accepting several hundred Jewish refugees to settle on the northern side of the island (today the town of Sosúa), at a time when most countries, including the United States, refused European Jews entry into their ports.

For me, the relevance of the Norweb document is also deeply personal. As a Dominican-American, I realize that my legacy is not just that of the victim, but also of the perpetrator. Before, the *génocidaires* were Nazis, Hutus, Khmer Rouge, Serbs, Turks, Japanese, Europeans in the Americas and Africa — always the Other. Surely not *me*, a Dominican-American, a Latino, a New Yorker, an American. Through the Norweb communiqué, I stumbled on a heritage that forced me to reevaluate my youthful romanticism about a country in which, today, a poor, dark-skinned Haitian lacks a racial, ethnic, and class privilege that I, as a light-skinned American of Dominican descent with a precious blue passport, possess but do not deserve.[4]

Notes

[1]   The 1937 Haitian Massacre was one of the most egregious examples of twentieth-century collective violence in the Americas. In a period of several weeks army soldiers and conscripted civilians were mobilized to arrest, deport, and kill Haitian men, women, and children throughout the three hundred mile Dominican side of the Dominican-Haitian border. The killings were not limited to the border and occurred as far away as the northeastern coastal town of Puerto Plata—a distance of over eight days' travel by foot, according to several of the Haitian survivors I interviewed. Since many of the soldiers were unfamiliar with the border region, they relied on Dominican civilians to guide them to Haitian rural hamlets. Several Dominican Haitian interviewees mentioned soldiers burning corpses to destroy the evidence of a state-sponsored killing spree. In late 1937, the massacre was an international *cause célèbre*, and the outcry forced Trujillo to forgo running in the 1938 presidential elections. For articles on the 1937 massacre, see Richard Turit's excellent "A World Destroyed, A Nation Imposed: The 1937 Haitian Massacre in the Dominican Republic," *Hispanic American Historical Review*, 82:3 (2002), pp. 589–635; and my article "Forgotten Atrocities: The 1937 Genocidal Haitian Massacre in the Dominican Republic," in Roger W. Smith, ed., *Genocide: Essays Towards Understanding, Early-Warning, and Prevention* (Williamsburg, VA: The College of William and Mary, 1999), pp. 79–99. For the diplomatic dimension, see Eric Paul Roorda's archival gem, "Genocide Next Door: The Haitian Massacre of 1937 and the Sosúa Jewish Refugee Settlement," in his book *The Dictator Next Door: The Good Neighbor Policy and the Trujillo Regime in the Dominican Republic, 1933–1945* (Durham, NC: Duke University Press, 1998). A literary treatment is Edwidge Danticat, *The Farming of Bones* (New York: Penguin, 1998).

[2]   Letter from Ambassador R. Henry Norweb to President Franklin Delano Roosevelt, FDR Library, Hyde Park, NY, Box 70 State, 1937, pp. 2–3.

[3]   By December 20, the invocation of the hemispheric treaties had averted a diplomatic crisis, and President Roosevelt was congratulating Trujillo for accepting the terms of the treaty and supporting an American foreign policy of collaboration in Latin America. "Permit me further to express my gratification by reason of Your Excellency's statement that the Government of the Dominican Republic will not give the slightest ground for disturbance of the peace of America, in the preservation of which all peoples of the New World have so great and legitimate an interest. I extend to your Excellency my most sincere wishes that the controversy which regrettably exists between the two sister republics may obtain rapid, just, and pacific solution through the utilization of the Inter-American peace instruments to which they have now announced their determination to have recourse. I am your sincere friend." Diplomatic Letter from President Franklin D. Roosevelt to President Rafael Trujillo, December 20, 1937, OF 138 D.R. 1933-1937 FDR Presidential Library. The letter is also reprinted in the *Department of State Papers Relating to the Foreign Relations of the United States Diplomatic Papers* 1937 Vol. V The American Republics (Washington, DC: Government Printing Office, 1954), p. 141.

[4]   See Edward Paulino, "Anti-Haitianism, Historical Memory, and the Potential for Genocidal Violence in the Dominican Republic," *Genocide Studies and Prevention*, 1: 3 (Winter 2006), pp. 265–88.

Where It All Began

Paul R. Bartrop

Like many others, I came to the study of genocide from a background in the study of the Holocaust. However, despite the fact that my hometown of Melbourne has the largest *per capita* proportion of Holocaust survivors and their children of any Jewish community in the diaspora, I was not drawn to study the Holocaust by family connections or personal experience. (My family has roots in Australia extending back to the convict period in the early nineteenth century, and has seen a mixture of Jews and non-Jews throughout.)

When I attended La Trobe University as an undergraduate in the early 1970s, I entered into Holocaust studies through the side door, so to speak. Having completed a fourth-year Honors thesis in history on Sir Nevile Henderson, the British ambassador to Berlin from 1937 to 1939, I was seeking another Third Reich-related topic for a Master's thesis. When interviewed about my potential candidature by the then-head of the History department at La Trobe, the late Roger Joyce, I was asked what I was currently reading. As it turned out, I had just finished Stefan Lorant's memoir of his time in Nazi prisons during 1933: *I Was Hitler's Prisoner*. "Good," said Professor Joyce. "We'll put you down for a topic that we'll call 'Nazi Racial Theories and Imprisonment,' or something like that. Applications close tomorrow, and we have to have something for you. We can change it later if we need to."

That was that. My academic course was set for life.

Stefan Lorant's book is not, strictly speaking, a book about the Holocaust. A journalist, Lorant was born in Hungary in 1901, though he spent the most important part of his early career in Austria and Germany. In 1933, when the Nazis came to power, he was editor of the *Münchner Illustrierte Presse*, a nonpolitical illustrated newspaper with the largest circulation in southern Germany. On March 12, 1933, he was arrested by the Nazi authorities, and for six-and-a-half months was held in "protective custody" — *Schutzhaft* — as a political offender. In his book, he claimed that "To this day I do not know the real reason [why I was arrested]. I was never informed of it. My case never came up for hearing. No legal proceedings were ever instigated against me."[1]

The book took the form of a diary, which Lorant kept during his imprisonment. He noted down everything, so far as he could, on odd scraps of paper, pocket handkerchiefs, the backs of letters, envelopes, even toilet paper. These he managed to smuggle out of the prison; the published work appeared in English about eighteen months after his release, in April 1935, under the imprint of the left-wing British publisher Victor Gollancz.

What was it about this diary that had an impact on me so great that it would ultimately lead me to the academic study of the Holocaust, and, from there, to comparative genocide? A number of issues spring to mind.

In the first place, the very humanity of the subject-matter was immensely attractive to a young man in his early twenties. I had already examined one facet of the Third Reich, through the career of a British diplomat who had to confront it head on. I had seen something of the uncompromising nature of the dictatorship with which Sir Nevile Henderson had to deal on an official level. Here, in Lorant's diary, was an account of a different type of uncompromising intimidation: from Nazi guards, Nazi officials, and Nazi police. While Lorant's experience was nowhere near as brutal as what would come later in the Third Reich—and certainly bore little resemblance to the horrors of the Holocaust—it was, nonetheless, the shock of his transformation from life in a democratic society to one under Nazi dictatorship that moved me as I read the diary.

Second, having read and digested what Lorant had to say about his own experience, I was moved to learn more about the experience of others who found themselves similarly incarcerated. This led inevitably to accounts by other former prisoners: first from the 1930s, and then, by extension, from the camps of the Second World War period. I grew interested in how prisoners found ways to live in situations designed to minimize their opportunities to live—or, in the case of the extermination camps, that denied such opportunities utterly. This research produced a successful Master's thesis, and, much later, a published book, *Surviving the Camps*.[2]

Finally, reading Lorant's diary showed me that the comfortable world of middle-class, university-educated Melbourne was not everywhere the norm. Indeed, it seemed to me as I read Lorant's work that his experience was about as far removed from my own reality as could be. Only later, in direct confrontations with the 1970s and '80s variants of Holocaust denial, did I see that there was a nasty underbelly of bigotry, racism, and—it should be said—anti-Semitism that I had overlooked in earlier times. As I became more of a Holocaust scholar, I grew more sensitized to what was going on "out there," in the "real world." The line from there is fairly straightforward: from Nazi prisons came Nazi concentration camps; then the study of the Holocaust; then study of what were then contemporary events — in Bosnia and Rwanda. By 1996, I was teaching a course titled Comparative Genocide Studies at the University of South Australia. The rest, as the cliché has it (and with no pun intended), is history.

Stefan Lorant's diary is not a work of art, or a movie, or a television show. It was never made into a play or a miniseries. While you'll find his name and many references to him on Google, there are few analytical treatments of the diary. Yet it had a profound impact on me, and it is a shame that it has not been republished for new generations. Here was one of Hitler's first victims — arrested literally as Dachau, nearby, was being constructed. Stefan Lorant was in the belly of the beast from the outset of the Third Reich. Across the decades, his ordeal spoke to me at the beginning of my academic career. He will never know it, but the trial he underwent was not in vain.[3] It led one young man, who might otherwise have followed very different scholarly pursuits, to dedicate himself to alerting others about the type of regime that treated Lorant so cruelly — and where that regime ultimately led. Through Lorant's diary, I discovered my *menschlichkeit*: my sense of humanity. That is not a bad legacy by which to be remembered.

Notes

[1]   Stefan Lorant, *I Was Hitler's Prisoner: A Diary* (London: Victor Gollancz, 1935), p. v.

[2]   Paul Bartrop, *Surviving the Camps: Unity in Adversity during the Holocaust* (Lanham, MD: University Press of America, 2000).

[3]   Lorant's career after his release from the Nazi prisons — and subsequent departure from Germany — was one of pioneering excellence. In 1937, he started his own magazine, *Lilliput*. In 1938, he sold the magazine to British publisher Edward Hulton. It was then transformed into the iconic weekly magazine, *Picture Post*, which served as a model for other photographic periodicals like *Time* and *Life*. *Picture Post* was an immediate success, and even in Britain's austere wartime environment, it sold well over one million copies per week. Lorant emigrated from Britain to the United States in 1940, where he resided until his death, at the great age of 96, in 1997.

Karl Schwesig, *Schlegelkeller* (1983)

Documenting Torture in the Early Nazi Camps

Joseph Robert White

Contemplating the millions persecuted, enslaved, and murdered, Auschwitz survivor Jean Améry regarded torture as the "essential" characteristic of the Nazi regime.[1] Having read anti-Nazi exile publications, such as the *Neue Weltbühne* (Prague), in pre-Anschluss Vienna, Améry harbored few illusions about the Gestapo when he was arrested for resistance activities in Belgium in 1943. Recounting his ordeal at Fort Breendonk prison and at Auschwitz, he concluded that anyone who has undergone torture never fully recovers: they lose "trust in the world," the expectation that society will help when they are threatened.[2]

As Améry discovered in the exile press, the torture of political opponents began in the Nazi regime's first days. Among the fifty to one hundred thousand regime opponents taken into "protective custody" (*Schutzhaft*) in 1933–34 and victimized by Nazi brutality was the noted Düsseldorf artist Karl Schwesig. In a cycle of charcoal drawings, *Schlegelkeller*, Schwesig brought to light his ordeal and that of fellow sufferers of torture and incarceration.[3]

My encounter with *Schlegelkeller* began when I was invited to contribute some sixty entries about the early Nazi camps (1933–1937), including the camp at Düsseldorf (Ulmenstrasse), for the Center for Advanced Holocaust Studies' forthcoming seven-volume encyclopedia on camps and ghettos. My previous research prepared me to read about the SS's systematic torture of camp victims, such as "sport," a euphemism for penal exercises designed to demoralize and kill, and the *Prügelbock*, a pillory to which prisoners were fastened before SS officers (and later camp *Kapos*) administered up to two dozen cane blows on their buttocks. But early camp violence was more intimate and arbitrary. During the Nazi *Kampfzeit* (struggle for power), stormtroopers (SA) and SS men often kidnapped and abused "racial" or political enemies in the back rooms of their favorite pubs—a practice that continued after the Nazi takeover. Instead of thousands of prisoners being worked to death (*Vernichtung durch Arbeit*), a lone victim faced days of physical and psychological abuse. *Schlegelkeller* vividly brought home to me the descriptions of violence I found in early camp testimonies.[4]

At state (*Land*) and local behest, the Nazi regime established just over one hundred camps in 1933: around seventy concentration camps (*Konzentrationslager*) and over thirty "protective custody" camps (*Schutzhaftlager*). Intended for the temporary confinement of regime opponents, most had closed by year's end, and only a handful remained open in July 1934, when the SS reorganized them under the Inspectorate of Concentration Camps. The early camps were mostly ad hoc detention centers—disused factories, castles, workhouses, prisons, and penitentiaries. Apart from these facilities, the new police "auxiliaries," the SA and SS, established torture sites (*Folterstätten* or *Folterkeller*), approximately 150 in Berlin alone.[5] In a brazen display of schadenfreude, these "auxiliaries" sometimes situated torture chambers inside properties seized from the German Social Democratic and Communist Parties (SPD and KPD), including the national KPD headquarters in Berlin.[6] At Hamburg's Stadthaus, the police and auxiliaries decorated torture rooms with banners, flags, and posters seized from local KPD and SPD headquarters. The victim underwent "interrogation" (*Verhör*) with portraits of Lenin, Marx, or Bebel hanging above them. Not only did these early camps establish templates for Nazi persecution, but Adolf Hitler's dismissal of criminal cases against their staff created a legal vacuum in which the racist avant-garde—the Nazi SS—could operate, thus paving the way for more radical measures.[7]

During this deadly assault on the German Left, Karl Schwesig was arrested in July 1933. He was already known for lampooning the Nazis before their seizure of power, especially with his conceptual *Maskenball*, which depicts the Reichsbank president, Nazi supporter Hjalmar Schacht, and boxer Max Schmeling standing beside a woman wearing a gas mask. Upon his arrest, Schwesig was repeatedly "interrogated" for four days at the Schlegelkeller (the basement of the Schlegel Brewery).[8] In charcoal sketches drawn after his immigration to Belgium in 1935, he blended political satire with the graphic imagery of beatings and ritual humiliation. Before World War II, the *Schlegelkeller* was exhibited in Antwerp, Amsterdam, and Moscow. Schwesig gave Jewish émigré Aaron Bezdesky a photographic copy to take to New York City, which saved the cycle from destruction by the Nazis. Despite repeated attempts at publication, and a foreword to the manuscript by Heinrich Mann, *Schlegelkeller* only appeared in 1983, nearly thirty years after Schwesig's death in 1955.[9]

Two images from Karl Schwesig's cycle, *Schlegelkeller*
(courtesy Gallerie Remmert und Barth, Düsseldorf).

Called "Ulmer Höh" by the prisoners, Ulmenstrasse was a typical
pretrial detention center until the promulgation of the "Reichstag Fire
Decree" on February 28, 1933, when a portion of it became a *Schutzhaftlager*
for political detainees. Ulmenstrasse's best-known prisoner was the theater
impresario Wolfgang Langhoff, whose testimony, published in 1935, described
a diminutive prisoner, "Karlchen" (Little Karl), taken to Ulmer Höh shortly
before Langhoff's transport to Börgermoor. Karlchen was in terrible shape:
battered and begging his overseers not to beat him again; the brutality of his
treatment included a swastika carved into his scalp. Langhoff learned later
that Karlchen was Karl Schwesig.[10]

After reading Langhoff, I quickly located Schwesig's *Schlegelkeller*
and other collections of his work, including the unpublished *Rosenmontag*, a
blend of the satirical and the banal. One sketch of a water pitcher from his
Ulmer Höh cell in *Rosenmontag* represents the monotony of his detention.[11]
In Ulmer Höh, Schwesig awaited trial on the spurious charge of treason,
for opening his studio to leftist associates. Sentenced to sixteen months'

imprisonment, he was confined at Wuppertal-Bendahl prison from February to November 1934.

Opening with caricatures of Hitler, Himmler, and a Nazi, *Schlegelkeller* narrates in captioned images Schwesig's four days in the torture chamber and his subsequent incarceration. The captions do not name names, but his drawings clearly distinguish between SA and SS torturers. Entering the Folterstätte, Schwesig sees a woman crying over another woman's lifeless body, while the stormtroopers sneer. Inside his makeshift community cell, he encounters expressionless detainees seated at table, on which a stormtrooper has scrawled "HEIL HITLER"—likely a reference to political "re-education," the regime's official rationale for the early camps.[12]

The first evening's interrogation opens with a stormtrooper pointing a gun at Schwesig's temple, while an official presses a pen in his face. In the office, an SS member prepares to type Schwesig's confession, while an SA thug again aims a pistol at his head while clutching his throat. A first-aid kit and bullwhips hang on the walls. Later that evening, the second *Verhör* begins. A policeman looks on as Schwesig, straddled on a chair, is repeatedly beaten by three stormtroopers, a water pail visible in the foreground.[13]

The second evening opens with two SA and a policeman watching, while another stormtrooper shaves Schwesig's scalp and carves the swastika into his head. Later, the torturers take him to view another, shirtless victim, into whose back, according to the caption, a swastika has been carved. The stormtroopers taunt Schwesig, joking that someday the scene might inspire him to paint a "beautiful fairy tale of atrocity." (Since March 1933, the regime had dismissed as "atrocity stories" public references to murder or torture in the early camps, and cast the anti-Jewish boycott of April 1 as "retaliation" for the Jews' dissemination of such stories.) Next, Schwesig contrasts his status as a "worker of the head" (*Kopfarbeiter*, or intellectual), with the picture of three SA striking him on the head. Falling to his knees, he is revived with a pail of cold water. To remove the blood, the SA douse him under a faucet.[14]

Schwesig depicts himself as aged beyond his thirty-five years. He projects his body from the viewer's vantage-point, as if disembodied, thereby distancing himself from the trauma, except where the captions indicate his personal ordeal. This perspective not only facilitates the narration, but conveys how his torturers objectified him—much as Améry, years later, observed that the first thing torture accomplishes is to reduce its victim to flesh and blood.[15]

Other drawings portray Schwesig's fellow sufferers. One shows a Jewish torture victim in the police hospital in the Düsseldorf Polizeigefängnis, shortly before he expired of his injuries. Others are based on secondhand information, including one showing a woman whose torture may have taken place within earshot, but whose suffering Schwesig could only have imagined.[16] By incorporating others' experiences with his own, Schwesig follows a practice adopted in the early camp accounts (and later in many

Holocaust testimonies). After their release, former prisoners felt obligated to share their comrades' stories, though with the regime's continued existence, they had to take the precaution of changing the names.

In researching the early Nazi camps, the *Schlegelkeller* is never far from my mind. As I read early camp testimonies reporting torture in its innumerable forms, the images of Karlchen, alone and defenseless, facing repeated thrashings by the SA and SS, flash before me. *Schlegelkeller* lends a powerful visual dimension to Nazi persecution: before the Holocaust; before Raphael Lemkin's neologism "genocide"; and before the United Nations' conventions against genocide and, much later, against torture.

Notes

[1] Jean Améry, *At the Mind's Limits: Contemplations by a Survivor on Auschwitz and Its Realities*, trans. Sidney and Stella P. Rosenfeld (New York: Schocken Books, 1986), p. 24. The World Medical Association defines torture as "the deliberate, systematic, or wanton infliction of physical and mental suffering by one or more persons acting alone or on the orders of any authority, to force another person to yield information, to make a confession, or for any other reason." See World Medical Association, *Declaration of Tokyo* (1975). Adopted by the World Medical Association, Tokyo, Japan, October 1975, available at http://www.cirp.org/library/ethics/tokyo. This essay could not have been written without the support of a fellowship at the Center for Advanced Holocaust Studies (CAHS) at the United States Holocaust Memorial Museum (USHMM). I would like to thank the CAHS staff, in particular Jürgen Matthäus, Geoffrey P. Megargee, Center director Paul A. Shapiro, and Evelyn Zegenhagen. I also thank Philip W. Blood, Gerald H. Davis, Lee Hulteng, Judy Treible, and Laurie Anne Whitcomb-Norden.

[2] Améry, *At the Mind's Limits*, pp. 22, 24–25, 28 (quotation).

[3] Karl Schwesig, *Schlegelkeller* (Berlin: Frölich & Kaufmann, 1983). Pages 10–101 of this volume are unpaginated, but follow the numbers Schwesig assigned to the cycle's captions. Since Schwesig evidently never completed the cycle, as certain caption numbers lack a corresponding drawing, the unpaginated section is cited by caption (*Zeichnung*) number. The arrest estimate is from Jane Caplan, "Political Detention and the Origin of the Concentration Camps in Nazi Germany, 1933–1935/6," in Neil Gregor, ed., *Nazism, War and Genocide: Essays in Honour of Jeremy Noakes* (Exeter: University of Exeter Press, 2005), p. 23. Clouding the estimate of early camp detainees were the multiple arrests of the same person in 1933, and the SA's and SS's unauthorized seizure of detainees.

[4] Joseph Robert White, "Düsseldorf (Ulmenstrasse) [Ulmer Höh]," s.v. Geoffrey P. Megargee, ed., *United States Holocaust Memorial Museum Encyclopedia of Camps and Ghettos, Vol. 1: Early Camps, Youth Camps, and Concentration Camps and Subcamps under the SS-Business Administration Main Office (SS-WVHA)*, foreword by Elie Wiesel (Bloomington: Indiana University Press in association with USHMM, 2009).; White, "IG Auschwitz: The Primacy of Racial Politics" (unpublished dissertation, University of Nebraska-Lincoln, 2000).

[5]   For the camps typology, see the list in Klaus Drobisch and Günther Wieland, *System der NS-Konzentrationslager 1933–1939* (Berlin: Akademie Verlag, 1993), pp. 73–75; for the estimate of torture sites in Berlin, Helmut Bräutigam and Oliver C. Gleich, "Nationalsozialistische Zwangslager im Berlin I: Die 'wilden' Konzentrationslager und Folterkellern 1933/34," *Berlin-Forschung* II (1987), pp. 141–178.

[6]   Felix Bürger (comp.), "Kantor" (pseudonym), "10 Monate in Görings Ge-fängnissen und Konzentrationslagern," in Felix Bürger (comp.), *Aus Hitlers Konzentrationslagern* (Moscow: Verlagsgenossenschaft ausländischer Arbeiter in der UdSSR, 1934), p. 16.

[7]   Albert Peldszus testimony in Gewerkschaft Öffentliche Dienste, Transport und Verkehr (ÖTV), Bezirksverwaltung Hamburg, ed., *Dokumentation Stadthaus in Hamburg: Gestapo-Hauptquartier von 1933 bis 1943* (Hamburg: ÖTV, 1981), p. 15; for the same site, see also the novel by Willi Bredel, *Die Prüfung: Roman aus einem Konzentrationslager* (1935; repr. Berlin: Aufbau-Verlag, 1946), pp. 5, 42–62.

[8]   *Maskenball* appeared in the Nazi *Volksparole* (Düsseldorf), 25 July 1933, where it is called a "typical product of the painter of the Marxist Inflation" (*typische Produkte des Malers der marxistischen Inflation*). For reproductions, see Schwesig, *Schlegelkeller*, p. 144.

[9]   For biographies of Schwesig, see Schwesig, *Schlegelkeller*, pp. 137–151; and Annette Baumeister, "Verfolgung und Widerstand, 1933–1935," in Herbert Remmert and Peter Barth, eds., *Karl Schwesig: Leben und Werk* (Berlin: Frölich & Kaufmann, 1984), pp. 57–80. The reproductions of watercolors Schwesig painted during his Belgian, French, and German internment are available at *Learning about the Holocaust through Art*, http://art.holocaust-education.net. Schwesig donated these watercolors to the Leo Baeck Institute in New York City, which is today part of the Center for Jewish History. Although Schwesig was interned sporadically from 1940 to 1945, he was not sent to a wartime Nazi concentration camp.

[10]   Wolfgang Langhoff, *Die Moorsoldaten: 13 Monate Konzentrationslager* (Zurich: Schweizer Spiegel, 1935), p. 101.

[11]   "Zellenkrug Nr. 12 (Ulmer Höh)," in *Rosenmontag*, 1938, USHMM Art and Artifacts collection, Washington, DC.

[12]   Schwesig, *Schlegelkeller*, Captions 1–5; Schwesig does not comment on the nature of the relationship between the two women.

[13]   *Ibid.*, captions 6–8.

[14]   *Ibid.*, captions 9-14. The original quotation from Caption 10 reads, ". . . *damit du später ein schönes Greuelmärchen malen kannst.*"

[15]   Améry, *At the Mind's Limits*, pp. 33–34.

[16]   Schwesig, *Schlegelkeller*, Captions 15–18, 21, 29.

Sexuality and Genocide

Jack Nusan Porter

The two words in my title are rarely found together. Certainly, this was true in the time of Raphael Lemkin, who coined the term "genocide" in 1944. Not until the 1970s or 1980s, in the wake of the black, gay, and women's liberation movements, did we see such concepts combined: with terms like "the gay genocide," or, inelegantly, "homocide"; and in writings about rape and war.

But my own interest in issues of sexuality was not sparked by human rights issues, or the Holocaust, or war. Rather, it derived from my early training as a graduate student in the sociology department at Northwestern University, in Evanston, a suburb of Chicago, in the late 1960s. It was a radical time, both politically and methodologically. I was influenced by iconoclasts like Erving Goffman (especially his book *Stigma*) and Laud Humphreys (who wrote *Tearoom Trade: Impersonal Sex in Public Places*), and by Howard S. Becker, author of *Outsiders* and one of the founders of "labeling theory."[1]

In short, it was the work on what was called "social deviance" that ignited my interest in subcultures, especially "deviant" subcultures—especially the idea of studying them by ethnographic participant observation. I write out of an interest in history and sociology, with a fascination for the arcane, the oppressed, and the stigmatized.[2] While I am not gay, I am an advocate of gay rights. I am not a woman, but I passionately support women's rights. And I am not black, but I strongly defend civil rights.

The intellectual figure who had the greatest intellectual and emotional impact on me died over seventy years ago—Dr. Magnus Hirschfeld. Hirschfeld was one of the most "deviant" characters I had ever come across. He was a Jew, a sexologist, a pacifist, a radical reformer, a physician, a transvestite, and a homosexual activist. He was as famous in his day as Freud, yet few know of him today. Why?

There are several reasons. First, he was an open homosexual, and therefore his ideas were sometimes seen as special pleading. Second, some of his conclusions were erroneous. He felt, for example, that homosexuals were an "intermediate sex," a *zwischenstufen* in German—neither male nor female. This may describe certain cross-dressers, transgendered persons, and perhaps some bisexuals, but not homosexuals. Third, and most relevant, he fell into disfavor with Freud's disciples, and was marginalized by them, especially in the United States.

This treatment resembled that of the psychologist Wilhelm Reich, and in fact both Reich and Hirschfeld suffered similar academic and intellectual fates. Both had unusual theories that were rejected by orthodox Freudians and society in general; both were political activists who were shunned by "objective" social scientists; and both suffered from translations that were poorly done, not done at all, or poorly distributed. Furthermore, Hirschfeld lived and died in the era before mass-market paperbacks became popular. His books were usually sold in ponderous and expensive hardcover editions, strictly limiting their potential audience.

Nonetheless, in the early 1930s, Hirschfeld did make a triumphant tour of the world, including the United States. He was arguably the most famous German psychologist of his time. Sadly, though, his ideas were not adopted by prominent intellectuals, and he fell into oblivion until the 1960s, when radical activists like myself discovered him.

Hirschfeld would be pleasantly surprised to see himself cited as the "guru of the gay genocide," when all three of these terms were unknown in the 1920s and '30s. Yet he should be seen as a pioneer, not only in sexology and psychology, but in the study of genocide—or what Mary Anne Warren and Adam Jones have called "gendercide."[3]

Recently, a Russian-Jewish playwright and director Dale Gutzman of Milwaukee, Wisconsin, produced a play about Hirschfeld's life.[4] He has also been the focus of several documentaries. These film treatments should come as no surprise. Hirschfeld appeared in a famous movie titled *Anders als die Andern* (*Different from the Others*), produced in 1919–20 during the Weimar period in Germany, which was one of the first films openly to discuss the gay predicament. Several other films were inspired by Hirschfeld's work and life, including Fritz Lang's masterpiece, *M* (1931). His prominence and sexual dissidence, however, made him an irresistible target for the Nazis after they took power in 1933. One of their early acts of censorship and repression was the destruction of his Institute of Sexology and Foundation for Sexual Research. Hirschfeld fled into exile in Nice, France, where he died on May 14, 1935.

The key book of Hirschfeld's that influenced me was one of the few translated into English: *Sexual Anomalies: The Origins, Nature, and Treatment of Sexual Disorders* (1956). Edited by his students after his death, it basically

Above: Slide of Dr. Magnus Hirschfeld, from a Nazi propaganda lecture titled "Jewry, Its Blood-based Essence in Past and Future."
Below: Hirschfeld's Institute for Sexual Research in Berlin is plundered by students and Nazi SA troops, May 1933 (courtesy US Holocaust Memorial Museum).

served as a summary of Hirschfeld's work, a "humble memorial by his pupils" (as the title page noted), and a textbook for the "medical and legal professions, ministers, educators, psychologists, biologists, sociologists, and social workers, criminologists, and students in these fields."[5]

Along with *Sexual Anomalies*, I responded powerfully to the film *Different from the Others*, a successful *Aufklärungsfilm* (sexual enlightenment film), produced when censorship was briefly suspended by the Weimar government. This was the first work of cinema in which homosexuality occupied a central, unambiguous, and positive position. Directed by Richard Oswald, it was co-written by, and featured, Hirschfeld himself. It presented homosexuality as a natural phenomenon rather than an illness, and worked to counter hostile social attitudes engendered by the infamous Paragraph 175 of the German penal code, which punished "unnatural sexual acts" between persons of the male sex with up to five years' imprisonment.[6]

The film focuses on a violin virtuoso, Paul Korner (Conrad Veidt), and his romance with a pupil named Kurt (Fritz Schultz). Their liaison is cut short by Franz, a blackmailer (Reinhold Schunzel), who ensnares homosexuals with threats of exposure under Paragraph 175. Franz ultimately denounces Paul, leading to his imprisonment, loss of employment, and ultimately suicide. This was a common theme in Hirschfeld's work: that blackmail often results in suicide. Several of Hirschfeld's patients did indeed kill themselves in these circumstances.

The film is not only about homosexuality, but about all manner of "queer sexualities," including transvestism, cross-dressing by both men and women, and various kinds of "sexual intermediacy" ("*Sexuelle Zwischenstufen*"). Weimar's openness would soon be slammed shut by the Nazis, and Paragraph 175 would be sternly enforced, pushing thousands of gays and lesbians into an underground existence and dispatching thousands of male homosexuals to concentration camps.

Hirschfeld's books and films continue to mystify and intrigue. In studying the shift from the Wilhelminian to the Weimar to the Nazi periods of German history, we can trace the tortuous route of homosexual movements and public attitudes towards them. Hirschfeld, having lived through all three of these periods, played a central role in each. The full history of homosexual "genocide," and the destruction of "queer sexualities" in general, has yet to be written. When it is, Hirschfeld will merit an important place in the narrative, just as he does in my own evolution as a scholar and activist.

Notes

[1]   See Erving Goffman, *Stigma: Notes on the Management of Spoiled Identity* (Englewood Cliffs, NJ: Prentice-Hall, 1963); Laud Humphreys, *Tearoom Trade: Impersonal Sex in Public Places* (New York: Aldine Publishing Company, 1970); Howard S. Becker, *Outsiders: Studies in the Sociology of Deviance* (New York: The Free Press, 1963).

[2]   See, for example, my latest book, *The Genocidal Mind: Sociological and Sexual Perspectives* (Lanham, MD: University Press of America, 2006).

[3]   Mary Anne Warren, *Gendercide: The Implications of Sex Selection* (Totowa, NJ: Rowman & Littlefield, 1985); Adam Jones, ed., *Gendercide and Genocide* (Nashville, TN: Vanderbilt University Press, 2004).

[4]   Dale Gutzman's play on Hirschfeld is called *Scenes of Love and Death in the Third Reich*. Gutzman is the former associate director of the Odessa Russian Drama Theater, and presently director of the Off the Wall Theater Company in Milwaukee, where the play was performed in April and May of 2005.

[5]   Magnus Hirschfeld, *Sexual Anomalies: The Origins, Nature, and Treatment of Sexual Disorders* (New York: Emerson Books, Inc., 1956).

[6]   See Robert J. Kiss, "Queer Traditions in German Cinema," in Tim Bergfelder, Erica Carter, and Deniz Gokturk, eds., *The German Cinema Book* (London: British Film Institute Publications, 2002), pp. 48–56.

Marie Uchytilová and Jiří V. Hampl, Monument to the Child Victims of War

The Multiple Meanings of Lidice

Atenea Acevedo

Translated from the Spanish by Margaret Schroeder

The Monument to the Child Victims of War, by sculptor Marie Uchytilová and her husband Jiří V. Hampl, is a grouping of bronze statues, slightly larger than lifesize, of 82 children. The monument represents a milestone in my life: a turning point in my decision to become a human rights activist.

Ironically, the first time I saw the words "Lidice" and "genocide" associated was at a teenagers' party. About half a dozen of us used to go to the country house of a good friend in Cuernavaca, where we would drink and play dominoes until we dropped. On one morning after, when everyone else was sleeping off their bacchanalia, I found myself unable to rest. Wandering around the living room looking for something to read, I came across a white, hardcover book. The cover showed an engraving of a woman, her face contorted with sobs. From the book's contents I learned the history of Lidice, a mining town in what was then Czechoslovakia. The Nazis had tried to wipe it off the map on June 10, 1942, in retaliation for the assassination of Reinhard Heydrich.

Heydrich had been appointed governor of Bohemia and Moravia in September 1941, and tasked with suppressing the antifascist resistance. He took to his duties with such zeal that the Czech government in exile, headed by Edvard Beneš, decided, with Winston Churchill's support, to organize an assassination plan named Operation Anthropoid. A team of Czech soldiers, trained by the British army, parachuted into Czechoslovakia and successfully carried out their mission. But the consequences were fatal not only for Heydrich, but for the approximately 500 villagers of Lidice. The men were shot, and most of the women transported to the Ravensbrück concentration camp. The majority of the children were probably gassed at the Chelmno death camp. A few were adopted by German families and "Aryanized."

In 1996, academic and personal motives brought me to Prague for graduate studies. As soon as I could, I boarded a rundown suburban bus with

Two views of the Lidice monument (courtesy Jason C. Holt, www.livingprague.com).

Libor, my first Czech friend, and quickly traversed the 20 kilometers to Lidice. The town had been rebuilt a short distance from its original location. The old schoolyard and other public areas were outlined with stones and marked with commemorative plaques. An expanse of pine forest surrounded the area; but in spite of the green grass and trees, it smelled like a desert. We visited the small museum and watched the silent film made of the massacre that was later used as evidence in the Nuremberg trials.

Beyond a rose garden in full autumn bloom, I thought I saw a group of people. But there were no other visitors in Lidice that afternoon. Drawing closer, I saw the 75 statues that Marie Uchytilová had laboriously begun to erect in 1969—first in plaster, then in bronze. She was unable to finish the memorial commemorating the 82 dead children, hindered by a lack of funds and then stopped by her sudden death in 1989. Her husband, Jiří Hampl, sought private support and continued the sculpture. The monument was finally completed in 2000. Childish figures; toddlers so small they can hardly stand alone, holding the hand of an older sister or friend. Half-grown adolescents, their play abandoned, faces caught between loss and despair. The artist had thought of calling the group "The Children of Lidice," but then she realized that her sculptures reflected the inestimable loneliness of all children who suddenly understand they will never return home.

I, too, had lost my innocence. Before Lidice, I had toured the barracks of Auschwitz-Birkenau; seen the dark, narrow path to the execution wall at Terezin; visited Warsaw and its terrible monument to the boy soldier. I had read the history of Lidice. But nothing had prepared me for the lifelike pain in the children's faces, sorrowful enough to melt cold bronze. I recognized that both evil and solidarity are part of the human condition. I am haunted by the realization that I, too, am capable of yielding to cruelty, a potential that is as surely a part of me as my desire to render visible the forgotten and the marginalized. This knowledge, an ever-present companion during my stay in Prague, is a defining aspect of my commitment to social change.

At the age of 16, half drunk, I had discovered that the name of one of the neighborhoods in my hometown, Mexico City—San Jerónimo Lídice—was a hand held out to another country that would, a decade later, become an integral part of my own history.

Günter Grass, *The Tin Drum* (*Die Blechtrommel*) (1959)

A Boy Who Refused to Grow Up, and One Who Did

Michael Hayse

The end of the 1970s and beginning of the 1980s was a minor watershed in Holocaust awareness that coincided with my own coming of age. I graduated from high school in Kentucky and spent a year working before heading off to Dartmouth College in 1980. At around the same time, Holocaust deniers grew more vocal and visible, prompting many more Holocaust survivors to add their testimonies to the growing memoir literature. Despite its shortcomings, the docudrama miniseries *The Holocaust* aired in 1978. I watched all the episodes, but remained critically, even emotionally, somewhat detached—perhaps influenced more by the cool critical reception in the media than by any sensibilities of my own.

Around the same time, the Holocaust Commission recommended the creation of a US Holocaust Memorial Museum, a project approved by Congress in 1980. I knew of the Third Reich and the Holocaust, but had no deep interest or understanding—that is, until I picked up and read *The Tin Drum*, by the postwar German author Günter Grass.[1] Coincidentally, it was the same year that Völker Schlöndorff's film adaptation of the epic novel was released; I was able to view it at the local art-house cinema within months of reading the book.[2]

The Tin Drum was originally published in Germany in 1959 as *Die Blechtrommel*, but was quite new to me even twenty years later. It was the first of three installments in Grass's so-called "Danzig Trilogy," which also includes the novella *Cat and Mouse* [*Katz und Maus*], and the full-length novel *Dog Years* [*Hundejahre*], first published in 1961 and 1963, respectively.

The Tin Drum is not really about the Holocaust, but rather about German society in the 1930s and 1940s. It is an odd, allegorical piece of fiction, but one that, for me at that moment, added complexity, nuance, and biting satire to my otherwise simplistic notions of the Nazi dictatorship.

The main character is the precocious Oskar Mazerath, born in 1924 in Danzig (today the Polish city of Gdansk). As a young boy, Oskar refuses

Günter Grass addresses American students, Munich, 1968 (courtesy the Junior Year in Munich program, Wayne State University, Detroit, Michigan).

to keep growing, having become aware of the corrupt and decadent society he inhabits. His own family is racked by lower-middle-class hypocrisy, infidelity, and political opportunism. In one of the most unique and memorable passages, his mother commits suicide by overdosing on pickled herring.

Throughout the Third Reich, Oskar's constant companion is a toy tin drum. He beats it to drown out the noise around him, but also to subvert the doings of "adult" society. In one of the novel's central scenes, he plays counterpoint to a Nazi marching song during a militaristic parade, causing the soldiers to lose their martial rhythm and cohesion. It is a momentary victory. Not until the defeat of the Nazis, and the expulsion of Germans—including Oskar and his remaining family—from Danzig, does the stunted protagonist will himself to resume growing.

It is fair to ask how this quirky, critically acclaimed, and best-selling piece of fiction could have influenced anyone, let alone a college-bound Kentucky boy, to study the Third Reich and the Holocaust. It was not as if a light suddenly went on, and I realized what I wanted to do with my life. In fact, I still imagined myself studying law. However, the characters were deliciously flawed, and portrayed as muddling through: some as enthusiastic supporters of the Nazis; others as simply following the political winds. Oskar narrates the moment when he is handed a picture of Beethoven removed from the wall to make way for a portrait of Hitler. Oskar's father, Alfred, is a Nazi Party member who dies when the Russians arrive: he chokes on his Nazi Party pin while attempting to hide his political affiliation. Even Oskar is a sort of anti-hero: annoyingly self-assured, self-centered, and often cruelly vengeful. While he serves as the "conscience" of the novel, he is mostly silent during the Third Reich, except for his drum and a glass-shattering shriek. Clearly, the Third Reich demonstrated that conscience without action is unacceptable. Beyond the plot, seen from "below" (i.e., Oskar's level), German society is portrayed as materialistic, debauched, and self-absorbed. This fictional world, drawn from Grass's own experiences in Danzig during this period, piqued my interest, and made me want to learn more.

My mother was a German immigrant who married my father when he was stationed in Europe in the late 1950s. But I had never learned German, and had only once visited relatives for a brief trip when I was thirteen. Now particularly curious, I dove into German language studies from the very first semester in college. Ironically, one of the books assigned was *Cat and Mouse*, and I waded through *Dog Years* the following summer. As my interest in German literature and society turned more toward the historical context, I switched majors from comparative literature to history.

Günter Grass became one of the leading voices of conscience in postwar German society, actively engaging in political controversies with progressive stances. In a sense, he practiced the humanist call to action that he preached through his fiction. He openly campaigned for the moderate-left Social Democratic Party in several elections, until he publicly resigned in protest over the Party's support for a tightening of German asylum laws in 1993. Grass was active in antinuclear and antiwar movements. He long headed the German PEN society of writers, and was awarded the Nobel Prize for Literature in 1999.

In 2006, however, with the publication of his memoirs about his wartime youth imminent, Grass disclosed publicly for the first time that he had served in the Waffen SS as a youth draftee during the war. The media in Germany and elsewhere criticized him for having kept silent about such an important issue for so long, especially since his protracted silence seemed at odds with his earlier calls for Germans to face up to the Nazi past. Some even demanded that his Nobel Prize be revoked or returned. Grass defended himself in part by pointing out that he never participated in any war crimes, and that his public engagement was driven by a sense of shame over his wartime actions.

It is unclear what the long term ramifications of these revelations will be. Regardless, one of the biggest ironies is that Grass's writing and public life in the past four decades have helped to transform German society into a culture capable of acknowledging the burden of the Nazi legacy. When *The Tin Drum* was published in 1959, an author's service in the Waffen SS would not have generated the controversy that it rightly does today.

Notes

[1]   I do not know what English translation I read, but as far as I can tell, the only one in print at the time was Günter Grass, *The Tin Drum*, trans. Ralph Mannheim (London: Seckert and Warburg, 1962).

[2]   *The Tin Drum*, dir. Völker Schlöndorff (Germany, 1979). I have fond memories of the historic palatial cinema, the Kentucky Theater in Lexington, having worked there for most of my high-school years.

Hans Peter Richter, *Mon Ami Frédéric* (1963)

A Tale of Two Children

Diane F. Afoumado

Eleven years old. It was about my age when I chanced to read *Mon Ami Frédéric*, by Hans Peter Richter.

The book tells a simple story. During the mid-twenties, two young boys are born at almost the same time; only a week separates them. Both are German, but one (Frédéric Schneider) is Jewish, while the narrator is not. (we do not know his name, for he is supposed to be the author himself.)

At first, it seems that nothing can separate these two children. They are raised in the same country; they live in the same building; they go to the same school; they play together; they share almost everything. But historical events will intervene, and put a decisive end to this innocent friendship.

At the story's outset, we are in 1925. Germany is dealing with its terrible economic and political crisis after World War One. The father of the narrator has difficulty finding a job, and experiences great hardships in fulfilling his duties as both husband and father. But soon, the rise of Nazism will bring radical changes. People who join the Nazi Party will be able to find their place in the new society organized according to the Nazi scheme.

Grownups are not the only ones whose lives will be changed. From the moment of the Nazi ascendancy, the lives of the two young boys will cease to have much in common. In the narrator's family, things improve: his father finds a job, thanks to his enrolment into the Nazi Party; soon, the narrator will belong to the Hitler Youth Movement, and make new friends there.

On the Schneiders' side, life has taken a different and much darker course. Frédéric experiences humiliations at school because he is Jewish. Slowly, he comes to feel he no longer belongs in the "German community." His father loses his job, and the owner of the building where they live tries to evict them. Little by little, their life-space narrows, until it encompasses almost nothing beyond the three of them. Frédéric must give up school, and struggles simply to survive as his family descends into penury.

The narrator's father advises Mr. Schneider to leave Germany, but this he refuses, because he is German and proud of it—even if the Nazis have decided to the contrary. To him, the Nazi period is just a bad spell that will pass, that *must* pass. But life becomes completely unbearable for Jews, and his wife is unable to survive these harsh conditions.

Frédéric realizes he is losing everything. His mother has died. His friend, the narrator, has begun to behave differently toward him. He no longer has the right to go to school. His father has been denounced by the building's owner for hiding a rabbi in his apartment, and arrested by the Gestapo. Now Frédéric finds himself alone in a terrifying world.

In 1942, during an Allied bombing raid over Germany, Frédéric seeks refuge in a shelter below the building where he once lived. But because he is Jewish, the people in the shelter deny him entry. When the alert ends, the narrator's family discovers Frédéric dead on the front steps of their building. The owner of the building kicks the body, as if being dead for a Jew is not enough.

Through the eyes of the narrator, and through the increasing persecutions of the Jews as inflicted upon the Schneider family, we observe the world growing more crazy by the day. We feel almost as powerless as the Jewish characters in the novel.

For me, this classic book opened the professional path I would take at university and beyond. It expanded upon the answers I had received when I questioned my parents about our family origins. Inside the family circle, I had heard stories about the Holocaust, but perhaps not the ones the reader of this essay expects. The stories of the persecution of Jews throughout history had always interested me, and in the late 1990s, I learned that a distant great-uncle of my father had been deported from France to Auschwitz in the first convoy, on March 27, 1942. But our family's background was far more complicated, so I also heard sharply different stories.

My father was born in Cairo immediately following World War Two. He and his parents had to leave the country when Gamel Abdul Nasser took power. They emigrated to France, and other members of the family to diverse countries and continents around the world. I always heard about how my grandfather had lost his job, and was forced to leave Egypt and abandon everything. On my father's side, our family was "just" uprooted; but I found an echo of this experience in *Mon Ami Frédéric*, when Frédéric's father refuses to leave Germany because it was also his country.

Then there was my mother's side of the family. She was born on July 14, 1943—the anniversary of the French Revolution!—in the midst of war, to a French mother and a father who was a soldier in the German *Wehrmacht*.

Because my parents love reading, I was raised among hundreds of books, many of which concerned World War Two and the Holocaust. But it was not until I read *Mon Ami Frédéric* that I was able to formulate more pertinent questions about the fate of the Jewish people in the 1930s and '40s. From the moment my curiosity was piqued, the desire to learn more was insatiable. I thought that by reading more books, I would uncover the reasons underlying the Holocaust, and figure out how human beings had been able to commit such atrocities against other human beings. When I entered the university, my academic research quickly focused on this period. When I had the opportunity to conduct my first real research, for a Master's of Modern History, I chose to study anti-semitic propaganda in France during World War Two, examining posters and exhibitions in an effort to understand the mechanism of race-hatred that had led to the Holocaust. That was a start.

It is no exaggeration to say that if I had not read *Mon Ami Frédéric* as a teenager, I would not now be working for the United States Holocaust Memorial Museum, or have worked for France's Commission for the Study of the Seizure of Properties Belonging to Jewish People, the Commission for the Compensation of Victims of Spoliation, and the Holocaust Memorial in Paris. This makes me wonder whether, and to what extent, the choices we make in our life are truly "our own." What I do know is that after more than fifteen years studying the Holocaust, I cherish this book and its lessons more than ever.

The Attic and the Imagination

Jina Moore

It begins, really, with a bad cliché. A couple of them. It begins, in fact, with, "It all began with the diary of Anne Frank . . ." But that isn't this story. This story begins with chicken soup.

It might have been my third day of being sick and home from school; my sixth meal of chicken soup; and, undoubtedly, the last straw for my mother, whose relentless efforts to entertain me had become tiresome even to her. So she put a video in the player: a recording she'd made of a recent TV movie called *The Attic: The Hiding of Anne Frank*.

I watched the movie a few times in a row. What was this "Holland"? This war? These scary-sounding accents, and those yellow stars everyone wore? What in the world was a "Jew"? And did anyone know what happened to the diary they saved from the empty attic at the end of the movie?

My mother handed me a copy of *The Diary of a Young Girl*, and I felt worlds collide. The people who had seemed so real and yet so inaccessible on TV were suddenly there for me to encounter again and again, in the intimacy that is the voice of a diarist—one who'd written when she was not much older than I was then.

I was hooked.

It's difficult for me now, roughly twenty years later, to remember what so struck me about the book. I remember being excited that I shared with Anne a love for mythology and languages and literature. Even at eight, I wanted to be a writer—and a year after reading the diary, I would win my first literary prize, for an essay titled: "If I Could Be Anyone In the World I Would Be Anne Frank." Mostly, I remember feeling unconsciously as Anne had: that discovering a diary—her diary—had brought me my first real friend.

In this case, it was an older friend, and therefore a wiser one, from whose extra years I could learn a great deal about life and what I should do with it. I should, for example, learn ping-pong, a sport I'd never heard of, but which must be good if Anne wrote about it so enthusiastically in the days before she went into hiding. I should eat a lot of ice cream. I should probably prepare myself to not get along too well with my mother—something that confused me a great deal when, as a teenager, I sheepishly admitted to my own diary that I actually *liked* my mom.

I wrote as much, and more, to Miep Gies in the summer of my twelfth year. Despite "the Anne Frank thing," as my friends called it, I was also a relatively normal kid, with the same enthusiasm for movie stars that my diarist role-model had had. After a summer of unanswered letters to the Tom Cruises of the day, it dawned on me that sending a letter to an author's publisher was probably no harder than sending a letter to a movie star's studio. So I typed up a gushing two-page epistle to the woman who had hid Anne Frank, and sent it off care of Simon and Schuster, who'd published Miep Gies's *Anne Frank Remembered*.

The reply I received a few months later, in broken English tapped out on a cursive typewriter, changed my life. I showed it to a teacher, who asked me to give a talk about Anne Frank to her English class. Because they were also my peers, I did extra research to impress them. I made notecards out of what I already knew: who had been in hiding; where they were all from; what the most important experiences of the war were, through the eyes of those in the attic. But I was missing some crucial information: what happened to each of them after the sentence, "Anne's diary ends here."

I wrote down the names of the camps that other books said members of the group had died in: Auschwitz, Bergen-Belsen, Neuengamme, Theresienstadt. I wrote down Westerbork, where they had all been interned together.

When I pulled out the relevant encyclopedia volumes, I discovered a meticulously connected geography of

"Anne Frank Grave Marker," 1989.
Doug and Mike Starn.
See Color Plate III

horror. "Germans persecuting Jews" did not mean pulling teenagers out of attics and sending them away, after which they died (from what—heartbreak at leaving home? Adolescent solitude? Nazi bullets?—a twelve-year-old could only guess). These were camps as big as cities, arranged in hierarchies—transit, labor, death—from which people weren't meant to return. They were places you had to board trains to, trains that someone had to schedule, another had to conduct, another to receive. They were places that became camps, but hadn't they been normal places before? They were places that one group of people sent another to die in, while a yet larger group of people, who must have known about it—Miep had known about it, hadn't she?—let them go.

After I finished the entry about Auschwitz, I cross-referenced "DEATH CAMP" and found a table. "TREBLINKA—800,000—1942–1943." I dropped the book in shock. Eight hundred thousand people killed, in barely a year! I left the book on the floor, walked to my room, and cried for hours, unable to understand how that one word and those few digits could signify the end of so many people.

I'd always felt that I knew Anne Frank. Now I felt that I really knew, for the first time, what had happened to her and her family. With that one number—smaller than six million, which I couldn't understand, but bigger than any number I'd ever used to represent anything—I began to understand, emotionally and cognitively, the scale and complexity of this horror.

The moment led me to an obsession with the Holocaust that lasted nearly a dozen years. I'd read a hundred books about it before college. In high school, I spent weekends with Holocaust survivors, carefully recording in my diary stories they told me, and helped start a statewide Holocaust education commission. I crafted a major around Holocaust historiography and literature during my undergrad. I ran Holocaust and genocide education programs on campus. After a moving class on reconciliation, I took up the idea of genocide more generally, of its prevention, and all the debates this entails—over the Security Council, over peacekeeping and the responsibility to protect, over political will and its absence. But nothing I've seen in any book has seared me as deeply as in that moment when I first felt the desolate magnitude of what those yellow stars, those days in the attic, those strange-sounding camps really meant.

If originally I had grown attached to Anne Frank's diary because I'd found a girl who felt like an outsider, who even in the most improbable cir-cumstances wrote about ordinary things, I stayed attached to it for another reason. It taught me to imagine what the world could have been like if I'd been born a different person. In the years when I was still naïve enough to write about my longing to be Anne Frank, this simply meant coping with the eccentricities of living in secret. In the years after I discovered Treblinka, it meant something bigger, something I later learned had a name: witnessing.

These days, I hear it called something else: the "moral imagination," a kind of political will at the micro level. Why didn't ordinary Americans call their congressmen and demand an end to the Rwandan genocide? They *lacked moral imagination.* Why didn't American Jewish leader Felix Frankfurter believe the Polish escapee Jan Karski, when Karski personally recounted death scenes from Belzec? Frankfurter *lacked moral imagination.*

As a writer, this idea has always struck me as strangely redundant. It seems impossible to have imagination without empathy, and vice-versa. It doesn't surprise me when people are moved by human suffering on an incomprehensible scale; it surprises me when they aren't.

But then, I grew up being asked why I did this funny "Holocaust thing," and why I had an odd obsession with Anne Frank. Now I'm asked why I do journalism in distant post-conflict zones—why that is the only thing that makes sense to me. The answer, in turn—like all real answers—makes sense only after a story. It is a long story, one that begins with a cliché, and with chicken soup.

My imagination begins in an attic in Amsterdam.

Gotthold Ephraim Lessing, *Nathan the Wise* (1779)

Lessing's Wisdom

Viktoria Hertling

I remember friends of my mother visiting us in Cologne after the war. They came from Argentina, spoke German fluently, knew my hometown well—and yet they no longer lived there. That puzzled me. But since I was only nine at the time, I knew none of the circumstances that had forced the Steinbergs, who were Jewish, to leave. I also did not know that twenty years earlier, in 1935, my mother had made several trips to Switzerland on their behalf to deposit money into bank accounts. This enabled them to start a new life in South America.

Topics such as German fascism and the Holocaust only entered my conscious mind four years later with the shocking events of December 25, 1959. On that day, the majestic building of Cologne's synagogue in Roon Street was defaced with swastikas and anti-Semitic slogans. This building—destroyed during the Nazis' November 1938 pogrom, known as *Kristallnacht*—had only recently been reconstructed and reconsecrated. The two right-wing offenders also vandalized an anti-fascist memorial in the inner city. The vandalism provoked outrage in the local as well the international press. It even triggered stern responses from the United Nations and the World Jewish Congress. And it certainly was an important subject in my own family.

West Germany had been a democratic country since 1949. Yet many of the reinstated civil servants—teachers included—quietly adhered to the ideological principles of Nazi Germany. My girls' high school in Cologne was no exception.

One of my teachers, however, was different. In January 1960, she arranged for us to visit the Cologne synagogue. We even attended Shabbat services. Afterwards, she assigned us the "Ring Parable" from Gotthold Lessing's *Nathan the Wise*. The play takes place in late twelfth-century Jerusalem, during the time of the Third Crusade, with a learned Jewish merchant and a powerful Muslim sultan taking center stage. Saladin, the sultan, intends to trick his Jewish counterpart by forcing him to state which of the three religions—Islam, Christianity or Judaism—is the true one.

"Recha Welcoming Her Father." From an incomplete series of illustrations for
Nathan the Wise, by Maurycy Gottlieb, 1877 (courtesy Wikimedia Commons).

The playwright answers this provocation by having Nathan relate an ancient
parable. For generations, the story goes, a father had passed a special ring to
his favorite son shortly before his death, until there came a father with three
equally beloved sons. Since he wanted each to get this exceptional ring, he
decided to have two duplicates made. When the father saw the copies, even

he could no longer tell the original from the duplicates. But upon the father's death, each of the three sons claimed that his ring was the genuine one.

To us thirteen-year-olds, the defacing of the synagogue and our recent visit there had brought home to us for the first time the legacy of German Nazism. As we learned about the murder of millions of innocent civilians, including the genocide of European Jewry,[1] we became aware of the horrible consequences of a rigid and authoritarian ideology. But how could we young adolescents, living in 1960, find valid guidelines for ethical decision-making in a post-fascist Germany? Especially when—as Lessing's play metaphorically represents—each son so unyieldingly declared his ring to be the only true one?

Earlier in the play, one learns that in years past, Nathan had lost his wife and all his sons in an anti-Jewish pogrom. He then took in an orphaned Christian child, Recha, and raised her as his own. Lessing, one of the foremost representatives of the German Enlightenment, lifts the parable of the ring beyond its original source. Through his character, Nathan, he tells Saladin that instead of quarreling about which religion is true, members of each faith must earn their self-proclaimed notion of exceptionality by individual acts of kindness and benevolence towards those beyond their own group. Overwhelmed by Nathan's humanism, Saladin, a Muslim, not only relinquishes his unfounded prejudice towards a Jew, but asks for his friendship. Nathan, of course, accepts.

Almost overnight, words such as respect, tolerance, human kindness, and open-mindedness became part of our conscious vocabulary. The visit to a defaced synagogue and Lessing's message sparked our awareness, and allowed us to practice a new humanism in our daily lives. We learned to understand the importance of honoring a variety of opinions with regard to rigid claims of absolute truth. Lessing's message provided me early on with important tools for recognizing and confronting all kinds of commonly-held prejudices. It helped me to cultivate a sense of empathy, compassion, and social justice. It began the process of training my critical perception of ideological and political processes and analyzing the root causes of organized violence. Today, I am more convinced than ever that our respect for other human beings is deepened by opposing all forms of hate-mongering and intolerance, and by honoring the victims of massacres and genocides everywhere.

Notes

[1]   In 1959, the word Holocaust was not yet used. Instead, my teacher referred to the events of the Shoah as *Völkermord* (genocide) or *Judenvernichtung* (murder of the Jews).

Or-Sarua Synagogue, Vienna

Not the Holocaust Memorial

Pam Maclean

Photographed here are the excavated foundations of the Or-Sarua synagogue in Vienna. The synagogue had been one of the largest in medieval Europe and the center of a thriving Jewish community, until its destruction during the intense persecution of Jews in 1420–21. Returning from an abortive attempt to suppress a Hussite rebellion in Moravia, Duke Albrecht V took out his frustration by arresting and torturing "wealthy" Jews whom he alleged financed the Hussites. Jewish property was confiscated, and poorer Jews were placed on a rudderless boat on the Danube and left to drown en route to Hungary. Other Jews who refused to convert were burnt alive in a field outside of Vienna.

At the height of the persecution, eighty Jews, including women and children, are said to have taken refuge in the synagogue under the leadership of Rabbi Jona. After several days under siege by the local population, the rabbi set the synagogue alight, consummating a Masadaesque act of mass suicide. The ruined synagogue was demolished and its stones used to build an annex to the University of Vienna. In 1451, just thirty years after their catastrophic expulsion, Jews returned to Vienna under Habsburg protection.

I accessed the archaeological site via the basement of the "Mizrachi" house, located on the north-eastern corner of the historic Judenplatz in Vienna, where a secondary campus of the Jewish Museum of Vienna was established in 2000. Models of the synagogue and other medieval Jewish buildings are displayed in the museum, as are artifacts from the period. A video describes the main features of medieval Jewish life, but does not detail the specific circumstances of the synagogue's destruction.

My 2005 encounter with these ruins occurred a week after I had attended a conference in Berlin on genocide, so it is hardly surprising that my subterranean viewing of its skeletal remains affected me so strongly. In the semi-darkness, the subtle lighting used to delineate the main areas of the synagogue, including the pulpit (*bima*), evoked a sense of loss and emptiness far more profound than I have felt in the "purpose-built" Holocaust memorials I visited previously or subsequently—hence my decision to discuss this image

The Or-Sarua synagogue, Vienna (courtesy Rod Maclean).

here. Initially, I expected the emotional impact of my visit would be at the forefront of this essay. However, as I started some background reading (see the bibliographic note), I found myself propelled on an unanticipated journey of reflection on the memory politics of a site whose history, spanning over six centuries, I had not understood when I was there. Hence, the following comments unpack broader issues surrounding a site where the semiotics of genocide appears overdetermined.

As already indicated, and somewhat perversely, the historical context of the synagogue's destruction is marginal to the museum display. Although the genocidal narrative can be accessed via an interactive computer terminal (which I did not find at the time), the museum's exhibition is primarily engaged with Jewish life in medieval Vienna, not its annihilation. Regardless, the ruins themselves spoke to me of genocide.

The archaeological excavation of the synagogue was a direct result of the project Simon Wiesenthal initiated in late 1994, with the cooperation of the Vienna city council, to construct a memorial to Austrian Jews murdered in the Holocaust. The Judenplatz was acknowledged to be the logical place for such a monument, and in summer 1995 archaeological investigations were launched to locate the remains of the synagogue, in preparation for the memorial's installation. The site, including the *bima* still covered in ash, was far more extensive than anticipated, with implications for the location of the Holocaust memorial.

A jury of eminent architects organized an international competition to select a memorial design, and in January 1996 British sculptor Rachel Whiteread's vision of an enclosed, inaccessible, and "nameless" library, constructed out of concrete and consisting of inverted books, proved successful. The plan was to open the memorial later that year, on November 9 (the anniversary of *Kristallnacht* in 1938). Then the controversy began in earnest. The radical design itself proved polarizing on both aesthetic and political grounds. Local residents challenged the scale of the monument in the historic square, and raised other trivial objections that smacked of anti-semitism. Divisions emerged within the Jewish community itself, with some arguing that the synagogue ruins constituted a sufficient memorial to the Holocaust.

The project became so politicized that the Viennese council called for its suspension to enable a "pause for reflection." This lasted over a year, until in 1998 a compromise was finally reached among the various interest groups. The proposed site of the Holocaust monument was slightly shifted so that it would not stand above the *bima*. Approval was given to open a museum focusing on medieval Jewish life and providing access to the synagogue foundations. The Vienna city council guaranteed financial support for both projects. Six years after Wiesenthal's original proposal, the memorial and museum opened in October 2000.

Despite this compromise, Whiteread's monument is not immediately recognizable as a Holocaust memorial. Yes, the inscriptions at its base pay homage to murdered Austrian Jews and the sites of their extermination. On an intellectual level, the eternal exclusion of Jews from "the book" acts as a powerful metaphor for both their physical and cultural annihilation. The dimensions of the enclosed structure, the doors of which are permanently "locked," may be reminiscent of crematoria—but in contrast to the site of the Or-Sarua synagogue, the memorial lacks an intrinsic symbolic relationship to genocide, and this arguably undermines its commemorative function.

Whiteread's monument provoked extensive academic discussion of the issue of Holocaust memorialization. In January 1997, during the "pause," the Jewish Museum of Vienna, together with the Institute for Social Sciences, organized a symposium titled "The Stumbling Block—Monuments, Memorials, Shoah Memory." Its objective was to address issues relating to Holocaust remembrance and the problem of post-Nazi states' engagement with Holocaust memory. In its permanent exhibition, the Jewish Museum of Vienna had itself attempted to deal in a novel way with the problem of representing the void created by the physical destruction of the prewar world of Austrian Jewry. Forsaking the display of material objects, it mounted a series of holographs that captured a *bricolage* of spectral and fleeting images from an elusive past. The efficacy of this and other memorial strategies was vigorously debated.

My personal experience of visiting the Or-Sarua synagogue suggested to me that no matter how well-intentioned, self-conscious attempts to memorialize genocide—as with the Whiteread monument or the museum's holographs—may be destined to fail under the weight of unrealizable expectations and reliance on a metaphoric artifice that imposes memory from without. Although the ruins of the Or-Sarua synagogue might be considered an "accidental" or even "incidental" monument to the Holocaust, the synagogue's intrinsic and multiple entanglements with Jewish catastrophe render it a paradigmatic memorial to genocide.

Bibliographic Note

For background information on the construction of the Holocaust Memorial in Vienna and the history of the Or-Sarua synagogue, see n.a., ed. *Judenplatz Wien* (Wien: Folio, n.a.); Hannes Sulzenbacher, "Der Parameter. Eine Chronik der Wiener Schoa-Mahnmalsdiskussion," in Jüdisches Museum der Stadt Wien, ed., *Wiener Jahrbuch für Jüdische Geschicht, Kultur & Museumswesen. Über Erinnerung* (Wien: Verlag Christian Brandstätter, 1997–98); Simon Wiesenthal, ed., *Projekt: Judendenplatz Wien. Zur Konstruktion zur Erinnerung* (Wien: Paul Szolnay Verlag, 2000). For an excellent critical review of the Jewish Museum of Vienna's medieval exhibition, see Christian Kniescheck, *Rezension: Ausstellung: Museum Judenplatz zum Mittelalterlichen Judentum (Aussenstelle des Jüdischen Museums Wien)*, H-SOZ-U-KULT (H-NET), 2001, available from http://www.hsozkult.de/rezensio/ausstell/2001/KnCh0601.htm. On broader questions relating to Holocaust memorialization in Vienna and Jewish museological representations, see Margrete Brock-Nannestadt, "Jüdische Museologie. Entwicklungen der Jüdischen Museumsarbeit im Deutsch-Jüdischen Kulturraum," in Jüdisches Museum der Stadt Wien, ed., *Wiener Jahrbuch für Jüdische Geschichte, Kultur und Museumswesen. Jüdische Kultur in Museen und Ausstellungen bis 1938* (Wien: Verlag Christian Brandstätter, 1994–95); Isolde Charim, "Stein des Anstosses," in Jüdisches Museum der Stadt Wien, ed., *Wiener Jahrbuch*, 1997-98; Jeffrey David Feldman, "Die Welt in der Vitrine und die Welt ausserhalb: Die soziale Konstruktion Jüdischer Museumsexponante," in Jüdisches Museum der Stadt Wien, *Wiener Jahrbuch*, 1994–95); Abigail Gillman, "Cultural Awakening and Historical Forgetting: The Architecture of Memory in the Jewish Museum of Vienna and in Rachael Whiteread's 'Nameless Library," *New German Critique*, 93 (Fall 2004); Sabine Offe and Gottfried Fliedl, "Entgleitende Bilder. Über die Daueraustellung des Jüdischen Museums der Stadt Wien," in Jüdisches Museum der Stadt Wien, ed., *Wiener Jahrbuch für Jüdische Geschichte, Kultur und Museumswesen. Kommunikation & Vernichtung. Schauen, Hören, Staunen, Selbermachen* (Wien: Verlag Christian Brandstätter, 2004).

Raul Hilberg, *The Destruction of the European Jews* (1961)

The Processes of Destruction

Joyce Apsel

As an undergraduate at Skidmore College in Saratoga Springs, New York, I majored in history, and took a number of courses in philosophy as well. I was a serious student. Going to college seemed a real privilege: my parents had entered the workforce early to help support their families, and never completed high school. My maternal grandparents came from Poland, and neither could read or write English. My grandmother loved "America," and wanted to become a citizen and vote. She was my first pupil: I tried to teach her English when I was in grammar school. In the end, she learned to sign her name, but not to read or write enough to pass the citizenship test. Of course, during the afternoons we spent together, she became *my* teacher. She taught me about hiding, terrified, from pogroms as a young girl; about my grandfather fleeing army service during World War One; and about how the Nazis had killed most of her brothers and sisters during World War Two. "Gone," she used to say. Her accounts fueled my interest in issues of violence, revolution, and war, especially the two world wars of the twentieth century.

   I took two college classes in European History taught by Dr. Louise Dalby, whose passion for modern history was contagious. Her husband had been a US soldier during World War Two, and was killed on the European front. She left Nebraska for graduate school at Harvard (I was greatly impressed by this, having never known anyone who had attended such an elite institution), writing her Ph.D. thesis on French socialist Léon Blum. Her knowledge of European politics, fascism, and socialism made a powerful impression on me. I chose as my senior thesis topic the Soviet-German Non-Aggression Pact of 1939: a misnomer if ever there was one. The research opened my eyes to the duplicity of interwar European diplomacy on all sides, revealing how two enemies, Communist Russia and Nazi Germany, were drawn into a secret protocol for dividing up Poland and the Baltic states. Many years later, I met Dr. Mary Johnson, a historian and national educator for Facing History and Ourselves (www.facinghistory.org), in a summer seminar on the Holocaust for university teachers conducted by Dr. Lucjan Dobrozynski at Yeshiva University. It turned out we had both attended Skidmore, and she, too, was deeply influenced by Dr. Dalby's instruction.

There were long lists of recommended readings in the European History courses, and when I tired of reading diplomatic history, I turned to the section on Nazism. One day, I came across a volume by Raul Hilberg titled *The Destruction of the European Jews*, first published in 1961. I recalled the stories of a young boy, Sam Rozines, who came to our small town in upstate New York from somewhere in Europe. I had always avoided him. My brother reported Sam's tales about having to drink his own urine, and other grotesque and unbelievable tales; he and his mother were referred to disparagingly as "the refugees."

Hilberg's work was shocking and transforming in a number of ways. It contributed to my decision to study history rather than philosophy at graduate school, and to explore issues of mass violence and genocide. It also impressed upon me the importance of understanding the complex nature of historical phenomena; and, when I became a teacher and Director of Education at the Anne Frank Center USA, to avoid the "not an eye was dry" version of history.[1] It also showed me how to link diaries and testimonies with historical context and processes.

At the outset, I was working on a senior thesis, and was impressed by Hilberg's use of original source material (he would be criticized for relying only on German sources). His detailed documentation of the genocidal process demonstrated how *rationalized* that process had been. In his Preface, Hilberg emphasized that the book's chapters focused on the perpetrators and the "vast organization of the Nazi machinery of destruction and the men who performed important functions in this machine. They . . . reveal the correspondence, memoranda, and conference minutes which were passed from desk to desk as the German bureaucracy made its weighty and drastic decisions to destroy, utterly and completely, the Jews of Europe."[2]

In contrast to popular stereotypes of Hitler as a madman, and of Nazism as an inevitable outgrowth of German history and national character (as reflected in the theories of AJP Taylor and others), Hilberg's work showed how mass murder was built upon earlier historical and institutional precedents. I recall in particular the chart on "Canonical Law and Nazi Measures" in the chapter on precedents. Over the years, I reproduced that chart for students in my courses, along with several on the role of bureaucracy and processes of destruction, including Hilberg's categorization of definition, expropriation, concentration, and annihilation.

Another important element was Hilberg's multidisciplinary approach. He describes the destruction of the Jews as "a process of extremes" that "can serve as a test of social and political theories." His analysis ranges from the psychology of the language the Nazis employed to mask and sanitize their atrocities, to a sociological analysis of how bureaucracies function. He provided me with a new language of victim, perpetrator, and bystander, along with new ways of looking at World War Two—analyzing, for example, the role of the German military and their work alongside the *Einsatzgruppen*, the mobile killing units that slaughtered Jews by the hundreds of thousands on the Eastern Front.

Hilberg's work would be exposed to criticism, from his estimate of the total Jewish death toll—which he placed at just over five million—to his observations on the lack of Jewish physical resistance to anti-semitism, including that of the Nazis. In response, Hilberg stated that his work was only "the first word on a difficult subject," and he would revise aspects of his findings as new sources and interpretations appeared. He did: two further editions of *The Destruction of the European Jews* had appeared by the time of his death in 2007, including a one-volume student edition.

Taking up my first fulltime teaching position, at SUNY New Paltz in the early 1970s, I taught my first course on genocide, calling it "The Destruction of European Jewry" after Hilberg's work. The course began with the Armenian genocide, and focused on the Nazi genocide against the Jews as well as the Roma and Sinti. Over the years, the course would expand to include indigenous peoples and other targeted groups. Tragically, in the final decades of the twentieth century and spilling into the twenty-first, new peoples—from East Timor to Cambodia to Rwanda and Darfur—were added to the list of the targeted and victimized.

Hilberg's work raised profound moral questions about how and why human destructiveness occurs. Alone and in the classroom, I continue to seek answers to these disturbing but compelling issues.

Notes

[1] See Joyce Apsel, "Looking Backward and Forward: Genocide Studies and Teaching about the Armenian Genocide," in Richard G. Hovannisian, ed., *Confronting the Armenian Genocide: Looking Backward, Moving Forward* (New Brunswick, NJ: Transaction Publishers, 2003), p. 194.

[2] Raul Hilberg, *The Destruction of the European Jews* (New York: Quadrangle Books, 1961), preface, p. v.

Ján Kadár and Elmar Klos (dirs.), *The Shop on Main Street* (1965)

The Look of Terror

Robert Skloot

Shortly before the shocking, infinitely sad finale of *The Shop on Main Street*, the 1965 black-and-white film made from Ladislav Grossman's novel, there occurs a moment that deepens all the film's other significances. The moment speaks to the horrors of the past, the implicit unredeemability of the future, and the futility of seeking in existing knowledge the meaning of events for which we are unprepared. It tears at the heart in part because it is created by an actress of luminous expressiveness. In her character's eyes can be read a horror that nonetheless underestimates the catastrophe awaiting her and her people. In the grip of that image, the Holocaust becomes an unforgettable stimulus for study: full of history and humanity, and the destruction of both.

It takes a while to get to that moment. For two hours, we have watched the almost reluctant unfolding of an ordinary man's story: a poor carpenter who yearns for belonging and friendship, and who possesses a small sense of justice that troubles him more than he could explain. To all appearances a figure of simplicity and ignorance, Tono Brtko makes a compact with evil that leads to his destruction—though not in a way that he, or we, could have anticipated. His fascist brother-in-law, who has taken over the administration of their Slovakian town, along with his hectoring wife's fear of poverty, drive him into the company of a grandmotherly, nearly deaf shopowner, with whom he falls into a kind of love. In the relationship of Tono and Rosalie is found the film's heart, and its tragedy.

It helps to know that Mrs. Lautmann is played by Ida Kaminska, the greatest Jewish actress of her era, whose local language is transcended at that terrible moment-to-come by a single word of more universal application. She represents not only a seller of ribbons and buttons, but (and here is why the film is so crushing) an entire life. It is a life deeply rooted in culture and language, in religious observance and interreligious reliance, and it stands on the cusp of annihilation. Rosalie's story is the Jews' story of coexistence and discrimination. The film's first two hours allow us to glimpse a full century of

Ida Kaminska as Mrs. Lautmann in *The Shop on Main Street*
(courtesy Billy Rose Theatre Division, The New York Public Library
for the Performing Arts, Astor, Lenox and Tilden Foundations).

life: satisfied, generous, isolated, and vulnerable to the murderous momentum
of Nazi atrocity.

Tono, too, in Josef Kroner's innocent yet pugnacious performance,
is unprepared for what will befall him. The extended penultimate scene,
underscored with discordant music, shows him confronting a choice that
drink cannot conceal and experience cannot explain. He is at war with
himself, trying to decide if he should save the old woman or betray her.

He casts about for a way of escape, but is trapped by his small goodness and his apprehension of a massive, inescapable evil. The camera follows his eyes to his own destruction, just as moments earlier it had looked into hers (seeing in and through mirrors—windows and glasses are everywhere in the movie).

Mrs. Lautmann's cry of recognition, torn from her by her witness to the town's Jews being rounded up and deported to their deaths, is: "Pogrom!" She interprets what is occurring as best her age and experience permit. But the point of the moment is that the word is wrong in capturing what she sees. She is not witnessing a spasm of violence that will eventually pass. Along with most of the residents of her village, she lacks the imagination to grasp that outside the shop window an episode of exterminatory bloodletting is underway that will remove from the earth a substantial part of the European inheritance.

Not least because of this film, we will not make such a mistake of the imagination again: what is imagined cannot be unimagined. If there are variations in the way the Holocaust unfolded, *The Shop on Main Street* depicts one of its crucial narratives. Today's students are made edgy or bored by the slow pace of the film; they want more of the action and violence (and color) they are used to in the violent new century they have inherited. But long before Mrs. Lautmann's moment of recognition, they know (and I know again, every time I see the film) that in the work of the best artists, we may discover the magnitude of what awaits us in a time of unrestrained evil. And in the horrified look of an aged ribbon-seller, someone who knew too much and too little of both past and future, we can see what was forever lost in the Holocaust.

Elie Wiesel, *The Town beyond the Wall* (1964)

The Role of the Bystander

Fred Grünfeld

I was raised in the Netherlands—where more than 80 percent of Jews were killed in the Shoah—by parents who had survived in hiding. Under such circumstances, the question is not so much when you become interested in genocide, but where you choose to focus your research. In the postwar period, a threefold distinction emerged of perpetrators, victims, bystanders. At first, study focused mainly on the perpetrators, on the one hand, and resistance movements on the other. Beginning in the mid-1960s, however, greater attention began to be devoted to the victims.

My orientation on the role of the bystander was sparked by a story related in Elie Wiesel's 1964 novel, *The Town beyond the Wall*. Wiesel's description of the scene in the Romanian town of Sighet, at the moment in 1944 when Jews were gathered at the marketplace for transport to Auschwitz, made a deep impression on me. Wiesel writes:

> It was right here at the old synagogue. Yes, I remember now. At Saturday. The police had herded all the city's Jews into the building. The house of prayer and meditation had become a depot where families were separated and friends said farewell. Last stop before boarding the death train. A memory came to surface so violently that I felt dizzy. The window, the curtains, the face: in the house across the way. A spring day, sunny, the day of punishment, day of divorce between good and evil. Here, men and women yoked by misery; there, the face that watched them . . .
>
> It was then that I saw him. A face in the window across the way. The curtains hid the rest of him; only his head was visible. It was like a balloon. Bald, flat nose, wide empty eyes. A bland face, banal, bored: no passion ruffled it. I watched it for a long time. It was gazing out, reflecting no pity, no pleasure, no shock, not even anger or interest. Impassive, cold, impersonal. The face was

Elie Wiesel (courtesy United Nations Photo Agency).

indifferent to the spectacle. What? Men are going to die? That's not my fault, is it now? The face is neither Jewish nor anti-Jewish; a simple spectator, that's what it is.

For seven days the great courtyard of the synagogue filled and emptied. He, standing behind the curtains, watched. The police beat women and children; he did not stir. It was no concern of his. He was neither victim nor executioner; a spectator, that's what he was. He wanted to live in peace and quiet.

The story continues as follows: "The others, all the others were he. The third in the triangle. Between victims and executioners there is a mysterious bond: they belong to the same universe; one is the negation of the other. The Germans' logic was clear, comprehensible to the victims. Even evil and madness show a stunted intelligence. But this is not true of the Other. The spectator is entirely beyond us. He sees without being seen. He is there but unnoticed. The footlights hide him. He neither applauds nor hisses; his presence is evasive, and commits him less than his absence might. He says neither yes nor no, and not even maybe. He says nothing. He is there, but he acts as if he were not. Worse: he acts as if the rest of us were not."[1]

Because of Wiesel's work, I came to see the bystander not as a neutral third party, but as the one who facilitated the genocide, by enabling the perpetrator to continue with the atrocities and genocidal acts. It is difficult to clearly separate the role of the bystander from the other two roles; moreover, any role may change over time. In this respect, it is important to distinguish the phases of atrocity: before, during, and after. Often, the so-called "neutral" and "innocent" bystanders during the conflict were later considered to have been important to the perpetration of the atrocities—that is, to have been collaborators. The crucial question then becomes: is there an actual bystander role, or does it disappear afterwards, in hindsight? Does the threefold distinction of perpetrator, victim, and bystander instead become a twofold distinction of (1) perpetrators and collaborators with the perpetrator, and (2) victims and rescuers of victims?[2]

I have developed a working definition of the bystander as the third party who will not act, or attempt to act, in solidarity with the victims of gross human rights violations.[3] This means that the bystander will be viewed after the events as a collaborator. If, on the other hand, he or she eventually acts or attempts to act in solidarity with the victims of gross human rights violations, they may afterwards be considered as rescuers.

Thus, at the outset, these roles are not predetermined; only later is it possible to evaluate their roles in either collaborator or rescuer.

I also was inspired by Wiesel when I wrote: "The easiest way to become or to pretend to be a bystander has always been the lack of knowledge of what is going on or has passed. This ignorance, which is coupled with indifference towards the fate of the victims, is an important explanation for the behavior of various inactive third parties."[4] This ignorance, which can be seen as a necessary condition for becoming a bystander, is deliberately promoted by the perpetrators in order to minimize the risk of producing solidarity of third parties with the victims.

In my definition, as already noted, there is no room for a category of "indifferent" bystander or "ignorant" outsider. Relevant in this regard is that the perpetrators deliberately try to keep the third party ignorant. For instance, 34,294 Dutch Jews were not murdered outright, but first transported to the isolated camp of Sobibor, as a means of obliterating all traces of their mass murder. Information about the atrocities was top secret, and when it was nonetheless distributed, the perpetrators did their utmost to undermine the reliability of the sources.

Perpetrators manipulate bystander ignorance to perpetuate their atrocities: ignorance means inaction, and inaction offers a *carte blanche* for the continuation of those atrocities. In developing this framework, I was inspired and powerfully influenced by the work of Elie Wiesel.

Notes

[1]   All quotes from Elie Wiesel, *The Town beyond the Wall* (New York: Bergen-Belsen Memorial Press, 1964), pp. 149–151.

[2]   See Fred Grünfeld and Anke Huijboom: *The Failure to Prevent Genocide in Rwanda: The Role of Bystanders* (Leiden: Martinus Nijhoff Publishers, 2007).

[3]   Fred Grünfeld, "The Role of the Bystanders in Human Rights Violations," in Fons Coomans *et al.*, eds., *Rendering Justice to the Vulnerable: Liber Amicorum in Honour of Theo van Boven* (The Hague: Kluwer Law International, 2000), pp. 131–143.

[4]   *Ibid.*, p. 141.

Elie Wiesel, *Night* (1958)

"Revisiting Again and Again the Kingdom of Night"

Steven Leonard Jacobs

There is no question that 1986 Nobel Prize winner Elie Wiesel's slender yet terrifying volume *Night* is the most well-known and widely-read volume addressing the Holocaust against the Jews. Its very brevity, together with its spare writing style, allows the horrors it describes to resonate with an awful power perhaps unrivalled in the literature of atrocity. Somewhat like Marc Chagall's phantasmagoric 1938 painting *White Crucifixion*, in which Jesus's loins are wrapped in a *tallit* (Jewish prayer shawl) amidst Jews fleeing their destroyed and burning ghettos, it assaults religiously-raised and religiously-committed Jews and Christians alike, leaving an impression that lingers long after the book has been replaced on its shelf.

One scene more than any other challenges cherished notions of the goodness of religious faith, its ability to heal and give comfort to the afflicted, and its hope and promise for the future. It is the story of the sad-eyed angel:

> One day [at Auschwitz] when we came back from work, we saw three gallows rearing up in the assembly place, three black crows. Roll call. SS all round us, machine guns trained: the traditional ceremony. Three victims in chains—and one of them, the little servant, the sad-eyed angel.
>
> The SS seemed more preoccupied, more disturbed than usual. To hang a young boy in front of thousands of spectators was no light matter. The head of the camp read the verdict. All eyes were on the child. He was lividly pale, almost calm, biting his lips. The gallows threw its shadow over him.
>
> This time the *Lagerkapo* refused to act as executioner. Three SS replaced him.
>
> The three victims mounted together onto the chairs.
>
> The three necks were placed at the same moment in the nooses.

"Long live liberty!" cried the two adults.

But the child was silent.

"Where is God? Where is He?" someone behind me asked.

At a sign from the head of the camp, the three chairs tipped over.

Total silence throughout the camp. On the horizon, the sun was setting.

"Bare your heads!" yelled the head of the camp. His voice was raucous. We were weeping.

"Cover your heads!"

Then the march past began. The two adults were no longer alive. Their tongues hung swollen, blue-tinged. But the third rope was still moving; being so light, the child was still alive . . .

For more than half an hour he stayed there, struggling between life and death, dying in slow agony under our eyes. And we had to look him full in the face. He was still alive when I passed in front of him. His tongue was still red, his eyes were not yet glazed.

Behind me, I heard the same man asking, "Where is God now?"

And I heard a voice within me answer him:

"Where is He? Here He is—He is hanging here on this gallows . . ."

That night the soup tasted of corpses.[1]

For those for whom religious faith is a vestige of a long-dead and better-forgotten past, this passage merely serves as an example of Wiesel's literary mastery. But those who consider religious faith the ground of their being may find that this passage, perhaps as no other, challenges that faith and demands a response. For those, like myself, who are the children of the inherited terror of our parents' nightmare experiences, and whose birth after the Second World War remains an affirmation of both life and Jewish commitment, this passage continues to disturb and traumatize. As someone who is not only an academic but an ordained rabbi, and who has served the American Jewish community in congregational and organizational settings, it serves to remind me of my own late father's loss of faith in God, and the absence of some religious practices in my own youth.

Perhaps reflecting upon this very passage, Wiesel himself is said to have stated on more than one occasion: "After the Holocaust, how can you believe in God; after the Holocaust, how can you not believe in God? After Auschwitz, how can you believe in humanity; after Auschwitz, how can you not believe in humanity?" In engaging with this paradox, he is assuredly not alone.

All genocides challenge their religious victims. Believers, raised to appreciate the essential goodness and value of their own religious traditions, suddenly confront *génocidaires* who make a mockery of everything they hold sacred, and, in so doing, reveal the powerlessness of their belief systems in the face of such monstrous evil. In a world of genocide, the sad-eyed angel is the childlike faith in all of us: in Germany and Europe, in Turkish Armenia, in Rwanda, in Bosnia-Herzegovina, and now in Sudan. His struggling at the end of the rope is our struggle to affirm goodness in a world repetitively predisposed to genocide.

Whether this story of the sad-eyed angel is wholly factual, or a powerful blending of many child-murders by Nazi killers, is almost beside the point. Staring into the abyss of such monstrous evil negates any notion of positive religiosity; diminishes the sacredness and interconnection of all life; and places the God of Judaism, Christianity, and Islam, and the gods of Hinduism and other faiths, on trial—as Wiesel himself has done in literary form elsewhere.[2]

But even to echo the Job of the Torah/Hebrew Bible—"Though He slay me, yet will I trust in Him; but I will argue my ways before Him" (Job 13:15)—is, despite all evidence to the contrary, to affirm God in a godless world. It is to reject the momentary triumph of the génocidaires in favor of the human community; it is to believe, despite everything, that tomorrow will be better than today, because it *must* be. That which Wiesel's sad-eyed angel affirmed with his dying breath, I, as an objective scholar and subjective religionist, seek to affirm with my living breath.

Notes

[1] Elie Wiesel, *Night* (New York: Bantham, 1982), pp. 61–62.

[2] Elie Wiesel, *The Trial of God* (New York: Schocken Books, 1995).

Elie Wiesel, *Night* (1958)

Will Only the Darkness Remain?

John K. Roth

In his classic Holocaust memoir, *Night*, Elie Wiesel describes the deportation of Auschwitz-destined Jews from Sighet, his hometown in Nazi-occupied Hungary, in spring 1944. That railroad journey reduced his world to "a hermetically sealed cattle car."[1] Wiesel recalls "the heat, the thirst, the stench, the lack of air," but emphasizes that these were "nothing compared to [Mrs. Schächter's] screams, which tore us apart. A few more days and all of us would have started to scream."

Books have changed my life. As an undergraduate at Pomona College in the early 1960s, my reading of Albert Camus's novel *The Plague* made a lasting impression by exploring the persistence of evil and the human responsibility to resist it. In 1966, I was moved by Richard L. Rubenstein's *After Auschwitz*, one of the first detailed studies of the religious and philosophical implications of the Holocaust. Later, Raul Hilberg's *Destruction of the European Jews* deepened my understanding of the bureaucratic process that produced Nazi Germany's "Final Solution." These works were all influential in setting me on the path I have followed for more than thirty-five years: a period in which my work as a philosopher focused on the Holocaust, and increasingly on other genocides as well. No book, however, has been more important in my studies of the Holocaust and genocide than *Night*, which I have read and taught more often than any other. Its questions, its details, the silences embedded in its minimalist construction, continue to engage me. So do its screams, which direct my attention not only to the Holocaust, but to the genocides that preceded and followed it.

The screams and silences of genocide alike demand interrogation, and call everything into question. Some belonged to the middle-aged woman whom *Night* identifies only as "a certain Mrs. Schächter," though Wiesel adds that he knew her well. Along with Wiesel and his family, she was imprisoned in a Holocaust cattle car with her ten-year-old son. Her husband and two older boys had been deported earlier. "The separation," says Wiesel, "had totally shattered her . . . Mrs. Schächter had lost her mind." Her disorientation was revealed not only by moans and hysterical screams, but by the visions that provoked them.

Mrs. Schächter could not see outside; but on the third night of the seemingly endless journey, she saw flames in the darkness. "'Jews, listen to me,' she cried, 'I see a fire! I see flames, huge flames!'" At first, the screams led some of the men to peer through the windows that allowed a little air into their cattle-car prison. But they saw no flames. "There was nothing," reports Wiesel, "only the darkness of night."

Some took pity and tried to calm Mrs. Schächter. Others were less kind. Wanting her quiet, they bound, gagged, and even struck her—"blows," Wiesel acknowledges, "that could have been lethal." Meanwhile, he observes, "her son was clinging desperately to her, not uttering a word. He was no longer crying."

Dawn's arrival stilled the bewildered woman. She remained quiet throughout the following day. But the fourth night again brought her screaming visions of fire. The next day, the train stopped at a station. None of Mrs. Schächter's flames were to be seen, but the signs indicated that the train had reached Auschwitz. "Nobody," says Wiesel, "had ever heard that name."

For an afternoon, and into the evening, the train was stationary. But with nightfall, Mrs. Schächter's mad cries resumed. Once more, she was quieted with great difficulty, before the train again began to move—Wiesel says it was about eleven o'clock—taking the rail spur constructed to facilitate the arrival of transports at Birkenau, the Auschwitz killing center. "We had forgotten Mrs. Schächter's existence," Wiesel writes, but "suddenly there was a terrible scream: 'Jews, look! Look at the fire! Look at the flames!'" This time, the scream's report was all too accurate: "We saw flames rising from a tall chimney into a black sky." Lighting up the darkness as they reached skyward from Birkenau's crematorium, these flames turned Jewish lives into smoke and ashes.

With the transport's arrival at Birkenau, the cattle-cars opened, and the prisoners were rousted toward the selection process that determined their fate: murder in a gas chamber, or slave labor that would eventually result in death for most. *Night* relates that Wiesel caught a final glimpse of Mrs. Schächter and the little boy who held her hand. The selection process spared Wiesel and his father Shlomo, but condemned his mother Sarah and his little sister Tzipora, as well as Mrs. Schächter and her son. Along with countless other Jewish children and their mothers, these four were of no use to the Germans. Birkenau's furnaces soon consumed them.

As for Wiesel and his father, their Auschwitz path led them toward a fiery pit in which little children were being incinerated. Wiesel recalls his father's words: "'Do you remember Mrs. Schächter, in the train?'" The immediate response contains no explicit answer to his father's question, but the words that follow are among Wiesel's most powerful:

> Never shall I forget that night, the first night in camp, that turned my life into one long night seven times sealed.
> Never shall I forget that smoke.
> Never shall I forget the small faces of the children whose bodies I saw transformed into smoke under a silent sky.
> Never shall I forget those flames that consumed my faith forever.
> Never shall I forget the nocturnal silence that deprived me for all eternity of the desire to live.
> Never shall I forget those moments that murdered my God and my soul and turned my dreams to ashes.
> Never shall I forget those things, even were I condemned to live as long as God Himself.
> Never.

Studying Wiesel's *Night* for the first time more than three decades ago, I found myself, as a philosopher, tripped up by Holocaust history. I was in my early thirties. My American life was progressing well, and despite the fact that my philosophical interests focused on questions of injustice, suffering, and evil, the Holocaust did not occupy the center of my attention. The experiences that Wiesel reported in *Night*—even his use of words and silences—were remote from my experience. Nevertheless, what happened to Mrs. Schächter and her son, to Elie Wiesel and his family, had occurred during my lifetime. My life, their lives, indeed *all* our lives, were realities of one world. The resulting collisions of consciousness and concern would spur me to learn as much as I could about how and why the Holocaust happened. My studies convinced me that Wiesel was right when he said that "the Holocaust demands interrogation and calls everything into question. Traditional ideas and acquired values, philosophical systems and social theories—all must be revised in the shadow of Birkenau."[2]

Those words, along with others that Wiesel has written since, suggest that his memory of Mrs. Schächter has never left him. Decades after writing *Night*, Wiesel recalled her in his 1995 memoir, *All Rivers Run to the Sea*. "Certain images of the days and nights spent on that train invade my dreams even now," he wrote, "anticipation of danger, fear of the dark; the screams of poor Mrs. Schechter, who, in her delirium, saw flames in the distance; the efforts to make her stop; the terror in her little boy's eyes."[3] Such recollections made him wonder: "And what of human ideals, or of the beauty of innocence or the weight of justice? And what of God in all that? . . . Why all these deaths?"[4]

Questions shape the legacy of the Holocaust and every genocide. Looming large among them is: "What happened to ethics during and after those disasters?" As my career in Holocaust and genocide studies has unfolded, that question has gripped me more and more. Wiesel's *Night* keeps me wondering whether genocide will ever end; whether only the darkness will remain. It also urges me to do what I can to resist genocide, and the indifference that aids and abets it. No interrogation is adequate unless, and until, it moves one to heed the screams and silences of genocide, and to work to mend our wounded world.

Notes

[1] Elie Wiesel, *Night*, trans. Marion Wiesel (New York: Hill and Wang, 2006). *Night* was published first in France in 1958. An English translation appeared in 1960. The memoir was translated anew by Marion Wiesel, the author's spouse, in 2006. All quotations are from pp. 24–34 of this edition.

[2] The statement is from Elie Wiesel's foreword to Harry James Cargas, *Shadows of Auschwitz: A Christian Response to the Holocaust* (New York: Crossroad, 1990), p. ix.

[3] Elie Wiesel, *All Rivers Run to the Sea: Memoirs* (New York: Alfred A. Knopf, 1995), p. 76. In this book, Wiesel spells the woman's name as Schechter.

[4] *Ibid.*, p. 79.

The Holocaust as the Holocaust

Jonathan C. Friedman

I am a historian of the Holocaust for perhaps no other reason than the influence of my father, who has devoted his life to the subject for nearly forty years. Growing up in an academic home, few aspects of my life were untouched by the trappings of scholarship and pedagogy. Whenever I see a manual typewriter, I am transported back to Saturday afternoons in the mid-1970s, when my father would be furiously at work in the basement, preparing yet another manuscript for publication. What was different about his work was clearly its content. How can a ten-year-old not be affected when he or she sees books with pictures of *Einsatzgruppen* killings?[1] I was only eleven when my father showed me a *Life* magazine issue from 1942, with an inset of photographs taken from the Jewish ghettoes depicting horrors that no young child should ever have to see. I developed an interest in music as a sideline, escaping into the world of the oboe, electronic music, and yes, progressive rock. In fact, I briefly considered music as a major at my first college. But there was no question that I was going to pursue academia as a career, and given that, there was no question about the subject matter to which I would devote my life.

For some academicians, the Holocaust is one of many heuristic pursuits: one that should be handled as neutrally as possible, lest it be tarnished by emotions and identity politics. For some theologians and philosophers, the Holocaust was punishment; for others it was a transcendental mystery; and for others still, it was not the end but the beginning of a new chapter in Jewish history. I do not share these views. For me, the writings of Alexander Donat and Primo Levi are foundational. They confirm our isolation in a universe in which only we have the capacity and the moral duty to cherish and safeguard the lives of all individuals.

My home life was not particularly religious. In fact, while we celebrated Jewish holidays, my formative environment was in most respects a secular, interfaith home, full of ecumenism, individual choice, and a healthy skepticism. It's not surprising, given my marginality within the Jewish and Gentile worlds,

Mira Sorvino in *The Grey Zone*.

that much of my research on the Holocaust and Jewish history investigates experiences or groups that either occupy the margins of the traditional narrative, or fall *between* narratives, not fitting neatly into one category or another. And while I owe much of my worldview to my father's passionate, intellectual zeal and commitment to Jewish history and themes such as social justice and compassion (*tzedakah* and *rachmones*—words which my father frequently invokes at the many funerals we have attended over the decades), I am also indebted to my mother's questioning, liberal agnosticism, born of a quiet and tolerant Protestantism, an outlook on life and the universe I perhaps feel closer to. She may not admit it, but she is very much the existentialist, sober in her assessment of how things really are, but mindful of the need to enjoy what we can of our flawed existence. There may be no redemption or meaning in the end; but that doesn't mean there is no such thing as love or happiness. These are what get us through the day. And when one studies the Holocaust, they are all that's left.

In view of all of this, it seems improbable that I would offer the film *The Grey Zone* as the piece of Holocaust representation that I would regard as a watershed for me. I had seen a host of films and read countless books on the Holocaust prior to *Zone's* release in 2002, and yet I felt more profoundly disturbed and emotionally shaken during and after the film than with any prior moviegoing experience. *Schindler's List* had been a moment of epiphany for me, and yet I had difficulty with its trope of redemption—a point of view articulated not only in Spielberg's film, but in a number of other cinematic productions dealing with the Holocaust. *The Grey Zone* did not merely situate itself outside this trend; it thoroughly and remorselessly eviscerated it.

Director Tim Blake Nelson based his initial play on two sources—Primo Levi's 1988 essay, "The Grey Zone," and Miklos Nyiszli's memoir, *Auschwitz: A Doctor's Eyewitness Account*, which chronicles Nyiszli's experiences as a Hungarian Jewish prisoner and conscripted assistant to the camp doctor, Josef Mengele. The film, like the play, operates on various levels. On one, befitting its title, *The Grey Zone* is a tale of moral ambiguity. On another level, the film is an unflinching look into the heart of the Nazi genocidal beast, offering some of the most graphic cinematic depictions of the gassing operation inside Auschwitz. By anchoring the story to a unit of Hungarian Jewish *Sonderkommandos*, one of a number of such units of inmates forced to work in the gas chambers and crematoria until they themselves were gassed, Blake Nelson leads his audience into uncomfortable territory: a place where Jews see, feel, hear, smell, touch, and taste death, remaining victims, yet victims who are also morally compromised—whose work, however coerced, served the Nazi murder program.

At one point, the character of Hoffman, played surprisingly well by comedic actor David Arquette, beats to death a Jewish prisoner in the disrobing room outside the gas chamber—over a watch. After SS guards execute the dead man's hysterical wife, they hand Hoffman the watch, smirking, leaving unsaid what SS *Oberscharführer* Eric Muhsfeldt (played by Harvey Keitel) actually states later on in the film:

> I never fully despised the Jews until I experienced how easily they could be persuaded to do the work here. To do it so well. And to their own people! They'll be dead by week's end, every soul. And we'll replace them with others no different. Do you know how easy that will be?

Allan Corduner, who plays Nyiszli, responds to this multilayered attack by shifting the terms of responsibility back to the Nazis, declaring that *they* are the ones doing the killing.

On another level, the film is a story of resistance, detailing the *Sonderkommando* uprising of October 1944 and the work of the women in the nearby Weichsel Union factory who helped smuggle gunpowder to them. But even here, any trace of hope is extinguished, as the Nazis execute all who participate in the revolt. The film's message resonates in its final lines of dialogue, uttered by a girl who actually survives the gassing, only to be executed by SS Oberscharführer Muhsfeldt:[2]

> After the revolt, half the ovens remain, and we are carried to them together. I catch fire, quickly. The first part of me rises, in dense smoke that mingles with the smoke of others. Then there are the bones, which settle in ash, and these are swept up to be carried to the river. And last, bits of our dust that simply float there, in air, around the working of the new group ... These bits of dust are grey. We settle on their shoes, and on their faces, and in their lungs. And they become so used to us that soon they don't cough, and they don't brush us away. At this point, they are just moving, breathing and moving, like anyone else, still alive in that place. And this is how the work . . . continues.

The storyline involving the girl, played by Kamelia Grigorova, is yet another example of the film's uncompromising approach to redemption. She becomes the focal point for the *Sonderkommando* unit preparing to rise up. In a sense, though, she becomes more important than that act of military resistance, because instead of destroying a thing (the machinery of genocide), the prisoners are saving a person. The girl is particularly central to Hoffman's expiation, and we gain a glimpse of his mental state when he tells her the story of a prisoner whom he helped to murder at the beginning of the film:

> I used to think so much of myself . . . What I'd make of my life. We can't know what we're capable of, any of us. How can you know what you'd do to stay alive, until you're really asked? I know this now. For most of us, the answer . . . is anything. It's so easy to forget who we were before . . . who we'll never be again. There was this old man, he pushed the carts, and on our first day, when we had to burn our own convoy, his wife was brought up on the elevator. Then his daughter . . . and then both his grandchildren. I knew him. We were neighbors. And in 20 minutes, his whole family, and all its future, was gone from this earth. Two weeks later, he took pills and was revived. We smothered him with his own pillow, and now I know why. You can kill yourself. That's the only choice. I want them to save you. I want them to save you more than I want anything. I pray to God we save you.

There is an extraordinary quality to a film about the Holocaust, shot in color, that actually seems more black, white, and gray than *Schindler's List*, which was consciously shot in two tones. Until I see an equally visceral depiction of the Holocaust as the Holocaust, and not as an act of salvation or "beautiful death"—the recent Hungarian film *Fateless* comes close, but its characters and plot are less accessible—I will continue to show *The Grey Zone* to my classes. I will refuse to allow students to retreat into places of clarity and safety, and urge them to confront the consequences of a world of ambiguities: one in which hope is a human construct; where we have only ourselves to blame, and to rely on.

Notes

[1]   *The Einsatzgruppen* were killing squads, composed of members of the SS paramilitary force, that accompanied Nazi armies invading Eastern Poland and the USSR in June 1941. Over the ensuing few months, they were responsible for the mass murder of hundreds of thousands of Jews, as well as Soviet commissars and others in the Nazi-occupied territories. For more information, see Richard Rhodes, *Masters of Death: The SS-Einsatzgruppen and the Invention of the Holocaust* (New York: Knopf, 2002).

[2]   Nelson altered the subplot involving the girl for dramatic effect: according to Nyiszli, she did survive the gassing, but was executed quickly thereafter by Muhsfeldt.

Primo Levi (1919–1987)

Keeping Memory Alive

Henry Maitles

More than sixty years after the genocide of some eleven to twelve million people, the Nazi Holocaust is still very much to the fore in human memory. Literally thousands of books have been written on the experience of the Holocaust, many by eyewitnesses and victims. Virtually all of these works are moving and significant, for the Holocaust is a definitive experience of world history. But in all of this literature, there is little to match the books of Primo Levi, an Italian Jew who survived the Nazi genocide.

From his first work, *If This is a Man*, in 1947, which was surprisingly rejected by publishers at the time and not published until 1958, to his last works, *The Drowned and the Saved* and *Moments of Reprieve*, in 1986, Levi gave us the strongest and most mature eyewitness account of the Holocaust and how it affected both victims and oppressors. He waged his personal battle against the Nazis and their attempt to destroy memory. In so doing, he became a spokeseperson for millions without a voice. Indeed, I perceive Levi as growing more urgent and insistent in the works written almost forty years after *If This is a Man*, as if his experiences of genocide and mass destruction had been ignored by the purveyors of modern conflict: from the Americans in Vietnam, to Pol Pot's Cambodia, to the resurgence of fascist organizations in a Europe that began to display similarities with the era of the 1930s that brought the Nazis to power.

Even on an initial reading of Levi, it is easy to understand why his writing has been so acclaimed. His humanity and spirit of resistance shine through. Whether he is speaking of individual resistance to the Nazis or a collective response, Levi admires and articulates it—even as he realizes its terrible cost, and questions his own ability to take part in it. At the heart of his work lies this contradiction between the need to confront Nazi evil, and the vast powerlessness that the experience of the death camp engendered.

Levi is at his best when he examines symbolic forms of resistance. He describes how the spirit of humanity that the Germans were so keen to destroy nonetheless shone through. It is impossible not to be moved by these examples of courage and goodness in the face of fascist barbarism. These instances of humanity are all the more uplifting when set against the degradation and humiliation constantly inflicted upon the prisoners. Yet Levi does not rely upon a notion of mankind's unstinting nobility. Rather, he describes Nazism's impact on prisoners as "mak[ing] them similar to itself."

Degradation was achieved by stripping prisoners of their clothes, shoes, hair, and even their name, replaced by a number tattooed on their forearm. "It is not possible to sink lower than this," Levi declares in *If This is a Man*. Again and again, he resorts to the analogy of animal existence to make his point. The prisoners, "like animals . . . were confined to the present moment." Levi describes how, after being confined in a grossly overcrowded railway carriage for several days without toilet facilities, Jews squatted wherever they could to defecate. To the Germans watching, it must have seemed that "people like this deserve their fate, just look how they behave. These are not *Menschen*, human beings, but animals, it's clear as the light of day."[1]

Power can corrupt, but so too can powerlessness. The institutional violence of the regime imposed on the prisoners was reflected in the attitudes and actions of the prisoners towards each other. The conditions allowed for little camaraderie among them, and "it was actually zero, indeed negative, with regard to newcomers," who were generally seen as a threat. At the basest level, thefts occurred of small amounts of food and other goods. These often resulted in harsh punishments for the victims, who in the Nazis' eyes were as guilty as the thief. The constant fear of theft, and the punishments meted out to those who committed and suffered it, meant that all daily operations—from washing to eating to sleeping—had to be performed with an incredibly watchful eye over one's possessions. The result was a pervasive atmosphere of distrust.

Levi's summation of survival in the camps is that "the worst survived, that is, the fittest; the best all died." In the upside-down world of the camps, all that could be called good in the outside world, the normal world, was of little use for survival. This was a world in the grip of barbarism, where "the law of the jungle" ruled, and starving prisoners learned to "eat your own bread, and if you can, that of your neighbour."[2]

Even after liberation, the bestial struggle for survival continued. Survivors fought over scraps, denied each other help, and drifted "further from the model of thinking man than the most primitive pigmy or the most vicious sadist." Inmates who managed to endure were left not only degraded, but afflicted by feelings of shame and guilt, of "having failed in terms of human solidarity."[3] Levi movingly describes glimpsing in civilians' eyes a belief that he should somehow have resisted. He returned to these themes in a poem, "The Survivor":

> Stand back, leave me alone, submerged people,
> Go away. I haven't dispossessed anyone,
> I haven't usurped anyone's bread.
> No one died in my place. No one.
> Go back into your mist.
> It's not my fault if I live and breathe,
> Eat, drink, sleep, and put on clothes.[4]

For all the shame and degradation depicted in Levi's writings, however, there are also shining examples of humanity. We rejoice in the resistance of the brave, and despair, along with Levi, as they are sent to their deaths. We grieve with him as he recounts his last meeting with his friend Alberto, whom he cannot save by infecting him with scarlet fever, and who is therefore evacuated from the camp and condemned to death along with 20,000 others.

Levi's writing is sometimes angry, expressing a disbelief that this monstrous crime against humanity could have been carried out within living memory in Central and Eastern Europe. Yet his work is not fundamentally about the past. It is "history" in the grandest sense, full of relevance to the present and carrying vital lessons for the future. When Europe is again afflicted by crisis and the whiff of fascism, though in a fairly minor way compared to the 1930s, Levi declaims: "Never Again." But he is also aware that reasoned argument is sometimes inadequate to combat violent and fascistic tendencies. In the last resort, we must "find the strength to resist . . . The memory of what happened in the heart of Europe, not very long ago, can serve as support and warning."[5] It is vital, therefore, that the memory of the Holocaust be kept alive and in public view, as an object example of what societies in crisis are capable of.

On a personal level, as a Jewish anti-fascist activist in the 1970s, understanding the Holocaust—among whose victims were members of my extended family—was a top priority. Many works sought to explain how the Holocaust had happened, but none provided such meticulous insights into the operations of the death-camp (*Lager*) system as Levi's did. I found myself disagreeing with the breadth of his "grey zone"—the area of moral ambiguity where victimhood shaded into complicity. But the structured degradation and powerlessness that Levi identified *within* that zone gave me a powerful sense of how the Nazis had divided prisoners against each other, the better to rule them and to ensure the "efficient" operation of the camps. Levi's books made me a stronger anti-racist—better able, for example, to confront calls by British neo-fascists for "repatriation" of ethnic minorities by arguing that this was a step on the road to Auschwitz.

For the millions who have read Levi's work, it holds a special fascination. His value lies not just in the power of his writing, his lack of hysterical judgment, and the forcefulness of his ideas. He is also, as a human being, a major tragic figure; his writing makes one feel his death, apparently by his own hand in 1987, as a personal loss. The world is a significantly poorer place without him.

Notes

[1] Primo Levi, *The Drowned and the Saved* (London: Abacus, 1989), pp. 88–89.

[2] Primo Levi, *If This is a Man* (London: Abacus, 1987), p.166.

[3] Primo Levi, *The Drowned and the Saved*, p. 59.

[4] Primo Levi, *Collected Poems*, New Edition (London: Faber & Faber, 1992).

[5] Primo Levi, *If This is a Man*, pp. 396–7.

Binjamin Wilkomirski, *Fragments* (1995)

Identity and Contested Authenticity

Dominik J. Schaller

Now I can see the whole belly. There is a big wound on one side, with something moving in it. I get to my feet, in order to see better. I poke my head forward, and at this moment the wound springs open, the wall of the stomach lifts back, and a huge blood-smeared rat darts down the mound of corpses. Other rats run startled out of the confusion of bodies, heading for open ground. I saw it, I saw it! The dead women are giving birth to rats. [. . .] After a while, I try to get up. I do not know anything anymore. I have forgotten everything. I am a stranger to myself. Who am I? What am I? I touch my legs once and again. I take the rags from my calves and feel the skin. Is it human skin, or do I really have a grey rat skin? Am I a rat or am I a human?[1]

This is a characteristic excerpt from Binjamin Wilkomirski's autobiographical account, *Fragments*, first published in German in 1995. As these lines reveal, the literary quality of the book is rather poor. Disgusting accounts of daily life in Auschwitz and Majdanek pervade the whole book, and are combined with an artificial pathos. Nonetheless, the publication of Wilkomirski's description of his childhood in Nazi concentration camps was a sensation. *Fragments* won several prizes, including the prestigious National Jewish Book Award. Literary critics compared its author to Elie Wiesel and Anne Frank. Daniel Goldhagen, author of the much-debated study *Hitler's Willing Execu-tioners*, praised the book as a masterpiece, and claimed that even Holocaust scholars could learn a great deal from it.[2] Unsurprisingly, *Fragments* soon became an integral part of high-school syllabi, and was added to reading lists at universities. Wilkomirski became a sought-after guest for TV shows and academic conferences, especially in the USA. He was viewed not as an "ordinary" Holocaust survivor, but as a hero who had first escaped the Nazis' attempt to exterminate European Jewry, and then, through his literary report and courageous commitment, had given fellow survivors some of the public attention that had been lacking for decades.

I was a student in high school when I first read Wilkomirski's text. My impression was ambivalent. Although I was convinced neither by the structure of the book nor by the author's language and style, I confess that I was distraught and moved after reading *Fragments*. I did not peruse it as a work of literature, however, but as an interesting source: a report written by a man who had witnessed and survived the horrors of Auschwitz, and who had moved to Switzerland as an orphan after the war ended. *Fragments* was just one of many memoirs and books on the Holocaust that I was reading at the time, and it was far from holding the same significance for me as Primo Levi's works or Paul Celan's poems. It was the artistic and refined way in which these two authors transformed their terrible experiences into literature that fascinated me.

I was about to begin university when Daniel Ganzfried, a Swiss journalist and writer, first cast doubt on the authenticity of *Fragments* and Wilkomirski's identity, in a newspaper article published in August 1998.[3] Although Ganzfried had considerable evidence to buttress his bombshell accusation, he must have felt like a lonely voice crying in the desert. His claim did not meet with unanimous approval. Ganzfried, the son of an Auschwitz survivor and himself the author of a novel on the murder of the Hungarian Jews during World War II that was not as well received as *Fragments*, was accused of seeking publicity by denouncing his more successful competitor.[4]

Whatever motives Ganzfried might have had, though, his doubts were perfectly justified. Further research proved that Binjamin Wilkomirski had indeed invented his whole story. His real name was Bruno Grosjean. He had not been born in Riga, Latvia, but in 1941 in Biel (Switzerland). And he was not a Holocaust survivor. He had spent his youth as a foster child in a well-off family in Zurich. He had visited Auschwitz and Majdanek only as a tourist. *Fragments* was thus nothing but a fake.

Although the facts were now clear, Wilkomirski, his publisher, and many of the reviewers who had celebrated his work had great difficulty acknowledging the truth. The publisher's motives were obvious: *Fragments* had been a highly successful book, and its unexpected exposure as fraudulent threatened serious damage to the reputation of Suhrkamp, one of the finest publishing houses in Germany.

I followed the unmasking of Wilkomirski closely, and I admit I was surprised by the revelations, since I had never doubted the book's authenticity when reading it three years before. But what was more surprising was the fact that many renowned scholars of the Holocaust, and literary critics whom I admired, had fallen for Wilkomirski's false claims as well. How was this possible? There were so many historical flaws and deficiencies in the text: why did most scholars ignore them?

It turned out that the publisher had received evidence about Wilkomirski's true identity as early as 1995. Nevertheless, Suhrkamp decided to publish *Fragments* as an autobiography. I think this labelling represents the crucial point in the affair. Wilkomirski's claim for authenticity, as well as his brutal and bloodthirsty descriptions, overwhelmed most readers, and prevented them from employing their critical faculties. The power of the proclaimed authenticity made historians neglect the methods they normally use in evaluating source material. Literary critics, meanwhile, ignored the poor quality of the text, and praised it as a "must read" solely because of its alleged foundation in reality.

When the Wilkomirski case was intensively discussed and debated in the late 1990s, I did not know that I would become a professional historian examining cases of mass violence. However, the Wilkomirski affair was instructive in many ways. Today, whenever I have to deal with written or oral testimonies, I try to maintain as much objectivity as possible. Of course, this is not as easy as it sounds. Survivors, not only of the Holocaust, possess a certain authority, since they have personally experienced the events that I can only try to reconstruct and analyze through a theoretical lens. Furthermore, they command moral respect, and considerable courage is therefore required to critically evaluate their accounts.

There is another element in the Wilkomirski case that fascinated and perplexed me at the time: the author's motivation. Was he a cold-blooded fraud who exploited the Holocaust for his own prestige and financial benefit? Was he a representative of what Norman Finkelstein has called "the Holocaust industry"?[5] While the latter question can surely be answered in the affirmative, I am not sure whether Wilkomirski was merely an ordinary liar. I had the impression, instead, that he genuinely believed his own story: otherwise, he could not have been so convincing. Bruno Grosjean, alias Binjamin Wilkomirski, thus acquired the identity of a Holocaust survivor. But why did he seek to redefine himself in such a radical way?

Although Wilkomirski grew up in Switzerland, and was not at all affected by the devastation of World War II, he *was* a kind of victim. As an illegitimate child, he had spent time in a children's home before being transferred to foster parents in Zurich. His youth was difficult, and characterized by a constant search for identity and recognition.[6] In the postscript to his book, Wilkomirski declared: "I wrote these fragments of memory to explore myself as well as my earliest childhood: it might have been an attempt to set myself free. I wrote them with the hope that other people . . . would find the necessary support and strength to give voice to their own traumatic childhood memories. In this way, they could learn that there are people who will take them seriously, and who want to listen and to understand."[7]

In a nutshell, Grosjean wanted to be recognized as victim. But since his experience was not sufficiently extraordinary to impress his fellow human beings, he had to invent a new one. As the Auschwitz survivor Binjamin Wilkomirski, he managed to gain the sympathy he had been seeking all his life.

However, the Wilkomirski case is more than just a personal travesty. It made me realize, for the first time, that the Holocaust was no longer perceived as a historical event, but rather as a universal symbol for evil. The Wilkomirski affair showed that the Holocaust has gained a kind of metaphysical quality that paralyzes and blinds many of those who engage with the subject. The thesis of Holocaust "uniqueness," and the corresponding assumption that the Holocaust can never be adequately understood, are outcomes of this questionable tendency—one that threatens to place the events beyond the bounds of historical scholarship. The benevolent reception that *Fragments* received was strong and alarming proof of the intellectual obstacles that sacralization of the Holocaust can create.

Notes

[1] Binjamin Wilkomirski, *Bruchstücke. Aus einer Kindheit 1939–1948* (Frankfurt am Main: Suhrkamp, 1995), p. 81 (my translation).

[2] See, e.g., Katharine Vinder, "Great Art from the Terror," *The Guardian*, 11 February 1998. The Goldhagen quote is on the cover of the German edition of Fragments.

[3] Daniel Ganzfried, "Die geliehene Holocaust-Biographie," *Weltwoche*, 27 August 1998.

[4] Daniel Ganzfried, *Der Absender* (Frankfurt am Main: S. Fischer, 1998).

[5] Norman Finkelstein, *The Holocaust Industry: Reflections on the Exploitation of Jewish Suffering* (London: Verso, 2000).

[6] On Bruno Grosjean's youth, see Stefan Mächler, *Der Fall Wilkomirski. Über die Wahrheit einer Biographie* (Zürich: Pendo, 2000).

[7] Wilkomirski, *Bruchstücke*, p. 143 (my translation).

The Language of Klemperer

Jens Meierhenrich

I

In the beginning, there were letters. The way they stood was stupefying. Erect, bold, strikingly set in Garamond Antiqua. **LTI**. What did this type-face conceal? What lay beneath the acronym printed on this otherwise ordinary-looking book?

LTI, it turned out, was Latin: it stood for *Lingua Tertii Imperii*. Ever the linguist, the author, Victor Klemperer, had invoked the language of the classics as the title of what would become, after his death, an important contribution—perhaps the most important—to our understanding of everyday life (and death) under the Nazi dictatorship.

Klemperer had two main objectives in coining what he referred to as a "fine scholarly abbreviation" in his analysis of the language of the "Third Reich": self-preservation and parody.[1] Given the subversive objective of his wartime undertaking, Klemperer had to obscure the title of his ingenious project, for he could never be sure who might happen upon it. As he confessed in his diary entry for June 9, 1942, collecting words and expressions "is a courageous act and [one] which again and again makes me afraid."[2] All his linguistic data "had to be procured surreptitiously and had to be exploited secretly."[3] In fact, on one occasion, Klemperer's subversion came close to being discovered: he was surprised, while busy collecting new linguistic perversions, by a member of the Gestapo. To Klemperer's relief, the Nazi ripped up the notes without looking at them.

As for parody, LTI was also appropriate, Klemperer reasoned, in view of the Nazi penchant for self-important acronyms—from AEL (*Arbeitserziehungslager*), to BDM (*Bund Deutscher Mädel*), to HKL (*Hauptkampflinie*), to SS (*Schutzstaffel*). Writes Klemperer: "The label LTI first appears in my diary as a playful little piece of parody, almost immediately afterwards as a laconic *aide-mémoire*, like a knot in a handkerchief [. . .]."[4] Those three letters were ideal for mocking the Nazi dictatorship. It was the weapon of a weak, elderly man: his everyday form of resistance, in the parlance of political scientist James Scott.[5]

It was "'cos of certain expressions," says Klemperer, that he eventually published *Lingua Tertii Imperii*, translated in English as *The Language of the Third Reich*. These observations saw the light of day in 1947, shortly after Klemperer had been reinstated as Professor of Romance Languages at the Technische Hochschule Dresden—the post from which the Nazis had ousted him, a German citizen of Jewish faith, in 1935.

What is most significant about *LTI*, and the diary from which it was culled, is what it lacks: a retrospective determinism. Unlike most reflections on National Socialism and the institutions that sustained it—including language—Klemperer's account was not compiled under the influence of the Holocaust.[6] He wrote from within the belly of the behemoth, before the genocidal campaign had reached its zenith, and well before its full dimensions were known. Whenever he doubted the utility of his enterprise ("It's only about a handful of phrases and expressions," he complained at one point), he pushed himself "to always hold on to this: in lingua veritas. Veritas is part of intellectual history; lingua provides a general confirmation of the relevant facts."[7]

What were the "relevant facts" about the Third Reich that its language confirmed? Nazism, in Klemperer's argument, attained prominence not through the speeches of Hitler and Goebbels, "because a lot of this was not even understood by the masses, or it bored them in its endless repetitions"; but rather because the regime's propaganda "permeated the flesh and blood of the people through single words, idioms and sentence structures which were imposed on them in a million repetitions and taken on board mechanically and unconsciously."[8] The best-known example is the term "*Volk*," or "people." Nazi language changed both the value of the term and the frequency of its occurrence. *Volk* gradually took on an exclusionary meaning that it had previously lacked. Noted Klemperer: "The term '*Volk* (people)' is now as customary in spoken and written language as salt at table, everything is spiced with a soupçon of *Volk*: *Volksfest* (festival of the people), *Volksgenosse* (comrade of the people), *Volksgemeinschaft* (community of the people), *volksfremd* (alien to the people), *volksenstammt* (descendent from the people)."[9]

A lesser-known example of the manipulation of language by the Nazi dictatorship is the seemingly uncontroversial verb *organisieren* (to organize). The regime's emphasis on the virtues of organization (*Organisation*) and its distaste for systems (*System*) of any kind is instructive. For Klemperer, the semantic distinction was politically significant: "they don't think systematically with the power of reason, they cull secrets from all that is organic."[10]

Victor Klemperer with students of the Romanisches Institut der Humboldt Universität, Berlin, January 1953 (courtesy German Federal Archive/Wikimedia Commons).

This, of course, is not entirely accurate. What I think Klemperer meant was that the regime, steeped in Romanticism, *pretended* this was so. It sought to replace the notion of a universally valid truth with the concept of organic truth, "which emerges from the blood of a particular race and is only valid for that race."[11] The family of words derived from the Greek *orgao* was highly favored in National Socialism, for it contributed to a sense of belonging that ran deeper than mere membership in the *Volk*. Emotion substituted for reason.

Related is the term that Klemperer believed to be "the word utilized most powerfully and most commonly by the Nazis for emotional effect," namely the seemingly inconspicuous *Erlebnis* (experience).[12] "The LTI deliberately draws everything into the realm of experience," Klemperer contended, in order to contain reason and enlarge the realm of emotion. "Emotion was not itself the be-all and end-all, it was only a means to an end, a step in a particular direction. Emotion had to suppress the intellect and itself surrender to a state of numbing

dullness without any freedom of will or feeling; how else would one have got hold of the necessary crowd of executioners and torturers? What does a perfect group of followers do? It doesn't think, and it doesn't even feel any more—it follows."[13] Interestingly, even Klemperer adopted the usage at times. On June 12, 1943, writing about the impending deportation of members of his Jewish community, he "made use of the regime's euphemistic verbal camouflage, writing in his diary of '*Evakuierung*' [evacuation],"[14] though he was well aware that deportation "means slavery and complete loss of property" at the very least.

Cover of the reissue of Victor Klemperer's *LTI* (courtesy Reclam Verlag, Leipzig).

II

In 1983, Sigmar Polke, one of the most important artists of the postwar generation, honored Klemperer with a painting. Curiously, it took several years for the art community to make sense of the erect, bold, strikingly painted letters that adorned Polke's canvass: LTI. This reflected the fact that *Lingua Tertii Imperii* had been all but ignored in what was then the Federal Republic of Germany, until its publication there in 1963—most likely because the work had acquired canonical status in the German Democratic Republic (despite Klemperer's references to a *Lingua Quarti Imperii*, a condemnation of the language of "really existing socialism" which he found increasingly difficult to distinguish, in its functions and effects, from that of the previous dictatorship).

Deciphering the acronym ceased to be a challenge when Klemperer finally received the broad recognition he deserved—in 1995, thirty-five years after his death, with the publication of the first of three volumes of his diary, *Ich will Zeugnis ablegen bis zum letzten: Tagebücher 1933-1945*. Random House acquired the English-language rights for $550,000, the largest sum ever paid to a German publisher for translation rights. It was about five years before that I had encountered the linguist—and his language—for the first time. It was a formative moment in my intellectual development.

Yet my first encounter with *LTI* was also accompanied by a disturbing realization. I experienced, as the late Jürgen Fuchs put it in a related context, an *"Erschrecken über die eigene Sprache"*—a fright about one's native tongue.[15] Unbeknownst to me, a teenager at the time, the language I spoke—the language in which up to that point I had been most comfortable expressing myself; the language I admired—was still laced with a plethora of words and phrases that had been invented, or given new meaning, by National Socialism in order to bolster the totalitarian regime. Klemperer himself had predicted this in 1947: "[T]he language of the Third Reich is to survive in the form of certain characteristic expressions; they have lodged themselves so deep below the surface that they appear to be becoming a permanent feature of the German language."

Then came the publication of the diaries—the cloth from which *LTI* had been cut. The Holocaust historian Omer Bartov wrote that Klemperer's diary "has the immediacy and the poignancy of unedited notes written in the thick of experience."[16] Klemperer's method was that of the participant observer. By unwittingly deploying this research technique for the entire period of the Nazi dictatorship, Klemperer made, among other things, an invaluable and insufficiently mined contribution to the anthropology of genocide. It is here that Klemperer's work on language and my own intersect.

Unlike Klemperer, my focus is on the language of genocide *per se.* For words can do worse than contribute to the homogenization of peoples; they can incite to kill. This function of language was particularly pronounced in the 1994 genocide in Rwanda, as evidence and testimony presented in the so-called "Media Trial" before the International Criminal Tribunal for Rwanda (ICTR) made abundantly clear.[17] Standing on the shoulders of Klemperer, I have explored the instrumental and expressive use of language across several domains, focusing, *inter alia*, on the perpetration, presentation, and prosecution of genocide. My emphasis in each area is on subjective understandings of genocide in everyday life. As Alexander Hinton remarks, "genocide is always a local process and therefore may be analyzed and understood in important ways through the ethnohistorical lens of anthropology."[18] I have sought to bring into focus previously unfamiliar meaning(s) of genocide—as encoded in the words, idioms, and sentence structures of familiar and unfamiliar cultures. For as Klemperer remarks, "language does not simply write and think for me, it also increasingly dictates my feelings and governs my entire spiritual being the more unquestionably and unconsciously I abandon myself to it."[19]

It was *Lingua Tertii Imperii*, this strange little book, which set me on the path of studying the culture of genocide, in which language plays a vital part. Studying languages of genocide (the use of the plural is deliberate here) is essential, for as Klemperer reminds us, "[w]ords can be like tiny doses of arsenic: they are swallowed unnoticed, appear to have no effect, and then after a little time the toxic reaction sets in after all."[20] Such is the legacy of Klemperer. Clandestinely and indefatigably, this German of Jewish faith recorded the homogenization of language, which in turn was integral to the homogenization—and eventually annihilation—of a people. That was Klemperer's heroism. He bore witness, precise witness. We should strive to do the same.

Notes

[1]   The "Third Reich" was a Nazi neologism. Because it was a part of *LTI*, it appears here, contrary to common usage, in quotation marks. The "Third Reich" ("*Drittes Reich*") was an allusion to the Holy Roman Empire of the German Nation, the "First Reich," and the empire that resulted from German unification in 1871, the "Second Reich." The incessant use of the term "Third Reich" in the course of the Nazi dictatorship was meant to conjure a vision of longevity and destiny, and thus to bestow legitimacy on an otherwise illegitimate regime.

[2] Diary entry for June 9, 1942, in Victor Klemperer, *I Will Bear Witness: A Diary of the Nazi Years, 1942–1945* (New York: Random House, 1999), p. 71.

[3] Victor Klemperer, *The Language of the Third Reich: LTI, Lingua Tertii Imperii: A Philologist's Notebook*, trans. Martin Brady (New York: Continuum, 2002), p. 13.

[4] *Ibid.*, p. 9.

[5] James C. Scott, *Weapons of the Weak: Everyday Forms of Peasant Resistance* (New Haven, CT: Yale University Press, 1985).

[6] Henry Ashby Turner, Jr., "Victor Klemperer's Holocaust," *German Studies Review*, 22: 3 (October 1999), p. 386.

[7] See Klemperer's diary entries for April 2 and 28, 1942, in Klemperer, *I Will Bear Witness*, pp. 35, 46.

[8] Klemperer, *The Language of the Third Reich*, p. 15.

[9] *Ibid.*, p. 30.

[10] *Ibid.*, p. 99.

[11] *Ibid.*

[12] *Ibid.*, p. 244.

[13] *Ibid.*, p. 245.

[14] Diary entry for June 12, 1943, in Klemperer, *I Will Bear Witness*, pp. 237–238; Turner, Jr., "Victor Klemperer's Holocaust," p. 392. Emphasis added.

[15] Jürgen Fuchs, "Das Erschrecken über die eigene Sprache," *Jahrbuch der Deutschen Akademie für Sprache und Dichtung* (1983), pp. 42–53.

[16] Omer Bartov, "The Last German," *The New Republic*, December 28, 1998, p. 35.

[17] *Prosecutor v. Ferdinand Nahimana, Jean-Bosco Barayagwiza, and Hassan Ngeze*, Case No. ICTR-99-52-T, Judgement and Sentence, December 3, 2003.

[18] Alexander Laban Hinton, "The Dark Side of Modernity: Toward an Anthropology of Genocide," in Hinton, ed., *Annihilating Difference: The Anthropology of Genocide* (Berkeley, CA: University of California Press, 2002), p. 3.

[19] Klemperer, *The Language of the Third Reich*, p. 15.

[20] *Ibid.*, pp. 15–16.

Viktor E. Frankl, *Man's Search for Meaning* (1946)

Trauma and Transcendence

William L. Hewitt

I'm going to set this up with a background story that I have seldom recounted and never confided to students in my courses, because I think they would lack points of reference, and I realize there are deep currents of emotion in me that would be exposed by the change in timbre of my voice. I have briefly talked about my past with a few colleagues who have inquired, but my background had little in common with their generally bourgeois and middle-class one, and most seemed skeptical about the tone if not the details of my narrative.

I was the first of five children that my parents had in five years. My alcoholic father had difficulty providing for his rapidly growing family, as evidenced by the fact that we lived in a boxcar that had been sawed in half and fitted with a door and window in the opening. My first conscious recollections from childhood are of terrible arguments between my parents, involving shouting, broken dishes, and physical injuries.

My parents' marriage dissolved, and I went to live with my maternal grandparents. My mother moved away with my next oldest sister in tow, while the three youngest children went into foster care, and were eventually put up for adoption. After forty-five years' separation, we were reunited, but it was not an Oprah-style hugs-and-kisses affair, and not much has transpired in the way of subsequent communication.

My grandparents raised me until I was eleven, managing the best they could with limited resources. My grandfather worked on the railroad, and did maintenance in the apartment house where we lived. When I was eleven, my grandfather contracted lung cancer. I was sent to live with my mother and sister, but my mother had married another alcoholic. We lived in a little apartment over a gas company, with a rear entrance up wooden stairs over a junk yard, so of course the number of friends willing to visit us was strictly limited. My sister and I spent most of the year in foster care, anyway. The older couple we lived with didn't like kids. The woman had an obsession with bowel movements and control, administering frequent laxatives and purgatives. She soon discerned that I had an adverse reaction to Alka-Seltzer, so she took some pleasure in having me drink it frequently and become ill.

After about a year in this situation, we all moved to a small house. I had a bed in the corner of an unfinished basement. My stepfather drank more, and became increasingly violent and psychologically abusive. He worked in a flour mill, and was a powerful man. He would challenge other men in bars to contests of strength, such as tearing the three-inch-thick Denver telephone book in half with one try. His favorite torment for me was making a fist with his thumb protruding, then jabbing me, leaving bruises on my upper torso. My mother commented on the bruising a few times, so he began to concentrate on one area, so that I had only one prominent bruise at any given time. He also liked humiliating me as a kind of inside joke. For example, he would put garbage under my pillow, or under my bedcovers, where I would unexpectedly discover it. Greeting me the following day, he would have a devilish prankster smile on his face.

I took up sports to escape home. As a cross-country and track runner, I was metaphorically and literally trying to run away. I wrestled for one season; I enjoyed the focused anger, but didn't like the occasional physical injury and pain. I'd had enough of that already.

During the winter months, I discovered another escape at the Denver Public Library. Bus fare was cheap, so I spent countless hours there. I read stories about boxers first, fantasizing about taking on my stepfather; however, I realized I couldn't possibly win. I loved Alexandre Dumas's novels, because the characters found themselves in bad situations beyond their control, but persevered and eventually triumphed. *The Count of Monte Cristo*, whose main character is falsely imprisoned and abused, but escapes and exacts vengeance, especially appealed to me.

Around this time, one of my acquaintances from athletics, who attended another high school, asked me to help him improve as a runner. We lived a block apart, but the dividing line for the school districts separated us. He was Jewish—a fact that, when my anti-semitic stepfather discovered it, determined that we would have to "hang out" at his house, not mine. I started investigating my friend's heritage. In the process—I'm not sure how, or what I was investigating—I ran across Viktor Frankl's *Man's Search for Meaning*.

The book explores Frankl's experiences as a Nazi concentration camp inmate, and his psychotherapeutic method of finding meaning and transcendence. After he had lost everything, and endured hunger, cold, exhaustion and the constant threat of being sent to the gas chambers, he concluded that his purpose in life was not merely to survive, but to choose: "Every day, every hour, offered the opportunity to make a decision, a decision which determined whether you would or would not submit to those powers which threatened to rob you of your very self, your inner freedom; which determined whether or not you would become the plaything of circumstance, renouncing freedom and dignity to become molded into the form of the typical inmate."[1]

Frankl made his experiences the basis of a new school of psychotherapy that he called *logotherapy*. Whereas Sigmund Freud's psychoanalysis encouraged introspection to understand our drives and instincts determining our behaviors, Frankl emphasized the freedom that exists, beyond environmental determination and physical privation, to choose ideals and values to shape behaviors.

I didn't fully comprehend what I read, but I couldn't put it aside, and I checked it out of the library many times. I looked into Frankl's background, and realized that his experiences as a concentration camp inmate lent credibility to the truths he propounded. What stayed with me after reading the book was the realization that my stepfather did not define me, any more than my other circumstances did. I'm not sure how much Frankl had to do with it, but I remember making the association in my mind that trauma made life feel so much better in its aftermath. I realize now, of course, the shallowness of my understanding of Frankl, myself, and life's complexity.

Frankl reflects a powerful assumption widely held in western thought: that when the resources of art are focused on traumatic events, something essential can be gleaned about human nature. Frankl's description of his survival amidst apocalyptic destruction inspires, renews, and imparts meaning to the suffering he endured. He concludes, for example, "that *it did not really matter what life expected from us*. We needed to stop asking about the meaning of life, and instead to think of ourselves as those who were being questioned by life—daily and hourly. Our answer must consist, not in talk and meditation, but in right action and in right conduct."[2] The optimistic prescription for self-affirmation and perseverance that I read in Frankl's work sustained me in the face of my troubles.

As much as Frankl resonated with me at that time in my life, however, I recognize that my memory of life events is inevitably distorted. Critics of Frankl similarly point to his myopia and distortions. Lawrence Langer, for example, criticizes him for downplaying the magnitude and destruction of Holocaust. Langer's criticism is used as the basis for a wonderfully insightful analysis by Timothy E. Pytell, who points out that "whether or not Frankl's interpretation is valid, it falsely equates survival with having the proper attitude." Nevertheless, Pytell acknowledges that Frankl's "narrative helped him resolve the psychic turmoil caused by, among other things, the knowledge of how his mother died . . ."[3] His narrative helped me as well in my own time of turmoil.

After reading Frankl, I wanted more of what books had to offer. I sought a college that would accept someone with poor academic preparation and lackluster high-school grades, determined to work my way through if the school let me stay. I saw my stepfather once more during my first semester in college. I don't remember what I said, but I ended up on the kitchen floor. That was the last time I ever saw or heard from him.

Notes

[1] Victor E. Frankl, *Man's Search for Meaning* (Boston, MA: Beacon Press, 1959), p. 66.

[2] *Ibid.*, p. 77.

[3] Timothy E. Pytell, "Redeeming the Unredeemable: Auschwitz and *Man's Search for Meaning*," *Holocaust and Genocide Studies*, 17: 1 (Spring 2003), pp. 101–102.

On Visiting the Auschwitz Museum

Jacques Semelin

At the age of 16, I learned that someday I would no longer see. When would that happen? No-one knew. But my fate was sealed from birth. It was as if a curse had been placed upon me, marking me with a terrible injustice in the middle of my teens.

The prognosis did not prevent me, however, from undertaking a Ph.D. in contemporary history at the Sorbonne. The topic I had chosen was civilian resistance in Nazi-occupied Europe, and I planned to go to Poland to investigate the underground education movement there between 1939 and 1945. So far, nothing out of the ordinary: merely the routine work of a doctoral student trying to make headway on his topic. Except that in that month of July 1985, I noticed that my sight had already declined considerably. I was having more and more trouble reading. And I was fraught with increasing apprehension, not to say anxiety. Was I going to be able to finish and defend my dissertation? After that, what was I to become? Needless to say, my spirits were low.

My wife Lydie and our friend Christian wanted to accompany me on this trip. The three of us had another reason to visit Poland. We wanted to meet activists from the famous Solidarity trade union, which had shaken the foundations of the Communist regime. The people we met in Wroclaw, Warsaw, Dansk and Kraków made our trip extraordinarily rich from a human standpoint.

But then came another encounter that marked me forever. Actually, it wasn't with a person, but with a place—one located not far from Kraków. The visit wasn't initially on our itinerary. But how can you go to Poland without stopping there?

We arrived there late in the day, around 7 p.m. We could glimpse the railroad tracks, which in places ran parallel to the road. The sun was beginning to set. We were surprisingly alone, and an extraordinary leaden

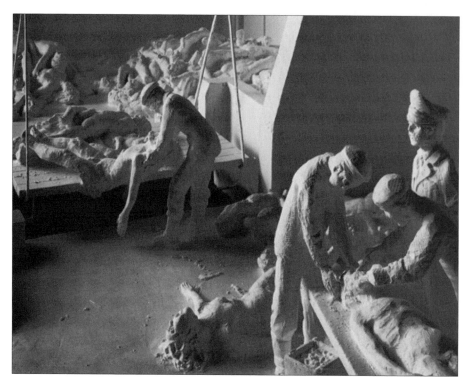

Detail of a scale model of Crematorium II at Auschwitz-Birkenau.
The original, sculpted by Mieczyslaw Stobierski, is in the State Museum
of Auschwitz; this copy is in the permanent exhibition
of the U.S. Holocaust Memorial Museum (courtesy USHMM).

silence reigned. It occurred to me immediately that it was a graveyard
silence, and we were standing before an immense cemetery that for the
most part remained invisible to our eyes. For almost nothing was left, or
so little: only a few barracks.

It was too late to visit the museum. We decided to return the following
morning, after finding lodging for the night.

What a strange experience. Our situation all of a sudden seemed totally
surreal. "You're going to spend the night in Auschwitz?" I repeatedly asked
myself during the evening. "What a crazy idea!" Before we left home, Lydie and
I had watched Claude Lanzmann's film *Shoah*, which had just reached cinema
screens in Paris. It had moved us profoundly. The testimonies of the Polish
farmer, the barber, the locomotive engineer, kept returning to me. And there
we were, at the very place where this industry of death had been organized,
scarcely 40 years earlier. Yet our brief stay at Auschwitz went very well. We
found a charming little hotel, the beds were comfortable, and we had a nice
breakfast . . . all the features of ordinary life.

The next day, however, came the shock. Never mind the already terrifying visit to Auschwitz I, the first camp the Nazis opened in the area, and the place where their first human experiments were conducted. The worst moment was when we approached the glass display cases in the former Block No. 4. Certainly, I couldn't see very much, but I could make out those clumps of hair gone gray with time. And those piles of glasses heaped up any which way. My sight had grown dim, but I nevertheless perceived the suitcases with the owners' names painted in large letters; and those mountains of scrubby old shoes. Not far away, a sign provided details of the victims' national origins. All of Europe seemed to have met at this hell on earth.

How can I explain it? Everything I had already read on the persecution and extermination of European Jews naturally returned to my mind. But it is one thing to grasp history through learning, and quite another to find oneself physically at the very place where a catastrophe occurred, standing before the vestiges that attested to the swallowing-up of hundreds of thousands of human beings—mainly Jews, but also Gypsies, Poles, and Soviet war prisoners. I had no desire to speak, only to meditate. I felt demolished.

Who was I to complain about my fate, compared to everything those unfortunate people had to go through, stripped bare before being herded into the gas chambers? Sure, I could consider myself an innocent victim of the evil that had being silently attacking my eyes from birth. But I had not been beaten, or tortured, or tattooed, or shaven, or starved, or gassed, or burned. By comparison, my own condition suddenly appeared to me as terribly insignificant.

My visit to the Auschwitz Museum thus had an unexpected consequence: It contributed substantially to modifying the way I regarded myself, and the way I continue to do so today. There, I found reasons to fight, instead of complaining. I returned from Auschwitz with a newfound energy, and an even fiercer determination to defy the fate that had been prepared for me.

This new state of mind had an effect on my intellectual pursuits. Of course, I continued to take an interest in the issue of civilian resistance. A good thing, too, because it was the subject of my dissertation! But another research topic came to mind, one that was immense and theoretically impossible to grasp: genocide.

In the autumn, I sought out the historian Leon Poliakov, a pioneer of Holocaust studies in France. He invited me to meet with him at his home in Massy, a Paris suburb. We had a fascinating conversation, and the morning went by far too fast. Poliakov told me about his own research agenda, which led him to the publication of his seminal 1951 work, *Bréviaire de la haine*.[1] He also took an interest in my dissertation topic, and endeavored to help me with it. Finally, he encouraged me to work on genocide, but also to bear in mind a statement that he quoted from the Soviet dissident Alexander Zinoviev: "Since an event has multiple causes, it is impossible to know what the cause of an event is."

As he spoke, I felt I was standing before an old sage who wanted to give his student an aphorism to ponder for the rest of his life. And indeed, I have never forgotten his words. They have illuminated my path as a researcher.

Notes

[1] Published in English as Leon Poliakov, *Harvest of Hate: The Nazi Program for the Destruction of the Jews of Europe* (New York: Schocken Books, 1979).

Judy Ellis Glickman, "Execution Wall, Auschwitz Concentration Camp, Poland" (1990)

At the Wall

Alexander George

A few summers ago, I took an afternoon train from Krakow that followed the setting sun to Oswiecim. It was not a long journey from that civilized city, home to one of Europe's oldest universities. Through the windows of the train, maculated birches shot past. Some of them might have been glimpsed by the doomed through the slats of the cattle cars as they sped towards the ovens. Or perhaps these were the next generation of trees.

At Auschwitz-Birkenau, a few Blocks are now given over to national exhibits by countries whose citizens had been incinerated there. Block 18 is for Hungary. Both my mother and my father were born and raised in Budapest; my father fled the fascists before the war, and my mother fled

Judy Ellis Glickman, "Execution Wall, Auschwitz Concentration Camp, Poland," 1990 (courtesy Judy E. Glickman/Mead Art Museum).

the communists after it. In a dim room of Block 18, dark panels bore the names of the several hundred thousand Hungarian Jews who were gassed here in the summer of 1944. No shortage of namesakes who went up the chimneys and settled as gray ash over the pleasant countryside: . . . *György Endre, György Ervin, György Gábor, György György, György Győző, György Hugo, György Imre, György Jenő, György Jozsef, György Lajos, György Matyas, György Odönné, György Sándor*—and there I was, at eye-level, in small white letters, printed on smooth black paper.

Outside, the grass was knee-high and the heat had dried it to sharp ribbons. Nearby were the ruins of several gas chambers. Yahrzeit candle tins had taken the place of Zyklon B canisters. There was a pond. Not so long ago, it had hissed and steamed with molten human fat. Its surface was still now and umber, like a smoked mirror. I remember a twig splitting underfoot that set off a shower of frogs. They fell like dark hail into the pond. Wildflowers shook madly in the breeze.

Radu Mihaileanu (dir.), *Train of Life* (1998)

"The Wealth of All Humanity"

Donna-Lee Frieze

The use of humor in films about Nazism and the Holocaust is not new. Mel Brooks, Charlie Chaplin, and lately Roberto Benigni have utilized humor and satire to counter the arguably phlegmatic responses to documentary seriousness. Curiously, Radu Mihaileanu's 1998 film *Train de Vie* (*Train of Life*) is often identified as a "Holocaust comedy," but this label is unjust. The film neither laughs at the Holocaust, nor is solely preoccupied with the Holocaust. Rather, Mihaileanu focuses on the vanished world of the *shtetl*, the Eastern European Jewish village with its spirited cultural community, and other victims of the Nazi genocide, the Roma and Sinti. Instead of depictions of the suffering individual, and trains as symbols of certain death, *Train de Vie* highlights the devastating loss of cultural communities to humanity. In this sense, the film's themes are akin to Raphael Lemkin's conceptual understanding of the term "genocide," which includes, among other important elements, the intended destruction of cultural elements of a group. In a 1933 paper in which he outlines his early thoughts on genocide, Lemkin notes that a group's cultural resources are "the wealth of all humanity." In many ways, Mihaileanu's film embodies this original notion of genocide.

Around 1941, the village fool Shlomo announces that the Nazis are in the next village. The *shtetl* community must rally to escape the certain Nazi onslaught. The elders of the village cannot concoct anything more bizarre and brilliant than Shlomo's plan: to build a fake deportation train that will take them to Palestine via the USSR. In order to render the ruse more authentic, some of the villagers disguise themselves as Nazis. The community labors to build a convincing deportation train: tailors design bona fide Nazi uniforms; bakers prepare loads of *challah* (Sabbath bread); cooks preserve too many jars of pickles; cobblers pound nails into the new Nazi boots, while musicians provide the tempo and rhythm integral to the spirit of the working community. Most importantly, the fake Nazis must learn to speak German with a perfect accent, leaving behind the vestiges of their Yiddish inflection. Coaching Mordechai (the fake Nazi) on his accent, the instructor tells him:

Shlomo (Lionel Abelanski) aboard the "train of life" (courtesy Raphael Films).

"Yiddish makes fun of German. It has a sense of humor." Mordechai's innocent response is as heartwarming as it is absurd: "We make fun of their language? Maybe that's why we're at war."

In contrast to many films about genocide, *Train de Vie* combines elements of allegory and fantasy to illuminate the senselessness of the genocidal perpetrator's intentions. By avoiding narrative realism, Mihaileanu works to portray life, not death. Even the film's simple title is revealing: after all, stock images of Holocaust deportation trains are rarely associated with life. And yet the film also has its realistic dimension—albeit not the realism usually associated with the Holocaust and genocide narratives. The culturally rich but financially impoverished community of the Jewish *shtetl*—bickering between neighbors, haranguing among elders, flirting between teenagers, and community support amid poverty—brings a sense of the tangible to a lost world. In order to capture this expanding universe of rural communities, Mihaileanu uses an anamorphic lens, cinematically encompassing "the wealth of all humanity."

The perpetrators of the genocide are rarely seen in the film. Instead we are treated to the antics, confusion, and discomfort of *shtetl* members posing as Nazis. In the lavish front carriage, Mordechai, the reluctant Nazi—a highly respected member of the *shtetl*—acts as the train's commander, while the remaining *shtetl* members are camped in the rear wagons (some turning to communism in an act of rebellion against their "captors"). The ghost train, which does not appear on any German timetables, eventually arouses the suspicions of the real Nazis, and Mordechai finds himself face-to-face with a legitimate *Hauptsturmführer*. Here, Mihaileanu creates an atmosphere of menace: the twilight fog embraces the train, and the rattling wheels reverberate like gunshots. Mordechai escapes this encounter only to later confront someone who appears to be an even more sinister Nazi. Perhaps now, Mordechai's true identity will be exposed? The alarming moment is short-lived when the Nazi is revealed to be just as "authentic" as Mordechai. The Roma and Sinti have also devised a fake deportation transport—not to Palestine, of course, but to India.

When the two groups unite, the film grows increasingly absurd, and also terrifying as it hurtles towards an unexpected but inevitable conclusion. Brewing beneath the surface of the film's celebration of life is the reality of the death camps, and of the Nazis' intention to destroy the essence and very existence of human groups. During my many viewings of *Train de Vie*, it is here, at the end, that I have found my understanding of genocide—what it means to lose "the wealth of all humanity"—most enriched.

Alexander Ramati, *And the Violins Stopped Playing* (1985)

Confronting the *Porrajmos*

Fiona de Londras

For most people, it is difficult to imagine how minimal a role the Holocaust could play in someone's history lessons through twelve years of fulltime primary and secondary education. But in the 1980s and '90s in a country like Ireland—relatively freshly founded,[1] and concerned to use history education to instil patriotism in younger generations—the Holocaust was low on the list of educational priorities. My history textbooks in primary school covered the Holocaust in about three picture-laden pages, and the secondary texts weren't much of an improvement. Therefore, in common with many people of my generation, my formal history education was Ireland-centric, and devoted little attention to the "bigger picture." Not only did we not learn much about the Holocaust in its relation to the Jewish people, but we learned nothing at all about the wide range of other social, ethnic, religious, and political groups targeted by the Nazi genocide. In my formal education, Jews were the sole victims, Germans the sole perpetrators. Nuance was an abandoned virtue.

The inclination to find out more about the Holocaust—and particularly to try to understand "the *why*" of it—was always strong in me. This was perhaps unsurprising, given my history-teaching mother (one of those history teachers, I ought to add, who lamented the propagandizing that then occurred in the history curriculum) and my reading-obsessed father. They introduced me in my teenage years to a variety of resources about the Holocaust, including the book that shaped my interest in genocide: *And the Violins Stopped Playing: A Story of the Gypsy Holocaust*, by Alexander Ramati.[2]

Ramati's book is a fictionalized account of the experiences of Roman Mirga—a Polish Gypsy—his family and his Gypsy clan from 1942 to 1945, as they try to escape the Nazis by leaving Poland, are captured in Hungary, and are dispatched to Auschwitz. It tells how the clan was persuaded by tradition, misplaced trust, and a manipulated *Shero Rom* (clan leader) to stay in their traditional winter-camp until imminent repression forced them to move under the worst possible conditions. Travelling in wintertime in Eastern Europe is treacherous—even more so when Nazis and informants conspire against you. However, the group managed to evade the authorities on numerous occasions. In the end, their capture and deportation to Auschwitz was the product of nothing more than ill-fortune—a cruel reality of so many people's lives under Nazi rule.

The novel, however, tells not only of the cruelty and violence of the Holocaust, but also of the overwhelming power of human emotion. The pride of the *Shero Rom* put his people at risk; others' fears led them to mistrust and inform on the group; the ambition of Josef Mengele, for whom Roman Mirga worked in Auschwitz, caused him to order the killing and dissection of countless children (including many Gypsy children) for experiments; the love of Roman's mother caused her to drop her young daughter through the slats of the train bound for Auschwitz, in the hope that she would run to the nearby house and find shelter there; the defiance of youth caused Roman to fall in love amidst great hardship; and the pervasiveness of violence caused hearts to harden, even when the gas chambers finally swallowed up Roman's father, whose violin-playing in the Nazi-established orchestra had previously accompanied the slaughter of thousands of Jews in Birkenau.

The impact of *And the Violins Stopped Playing* thus derives from Ramati's communication of emotion, in a time when emotion seems so much a luxury as to have hardly been possible. The normalcy of love, sadness, and passion among the family members incarcerated in Auschwitz stands in stark opposition to their chilling experiences there, and the need to harden their hearts in order to survive. It is Ramati's capacity to create an emotional centre for the Auschwitz experience of a young Roman Mirga that makes the novel so poignant.

However, poignancy alone is not sufficient in order for a work to shape one's scholarship on genocide. *And the Violins Stopped Playing* forced me, a teenager with a limited knowledge of the Holocaust, to confront the fact that Jews were not alone in their suffering during the Holocaust. In fact, they were one of many groups exposed to the dehumanizing and destructive malignancy that was Nazism—including not only Gypsies but people with disabilities, communists, homosexuals, and others. Perhaps the numbers were not as great, but the horror for the people involved was no less.

Until reading Ramati's book, I had never heard of the *porrajmos* (the "Gypsy Holocaust"). But I had witnessed high levels of discrimination against members of the so-called "Travelling Community" in Ireland, who are descended from the Roma. They are Ireland's largest minority group, and are systemically discriminated against in practice (although no longer in law).[3] Reading Ramati, I realized that the basic conditions for genocide—discrimination, disgust, feelings of social superiority, hate-based violence—are present in many societies; it is only a sense of order that prevents us, in most cases, from acting on them.

Likewise, when I came to consider the connections between sex, gender, sexual violence, and genocide in my post-graduate research,[4] I automatically reached for my well-worn copy of *And the Violins Stopped Playing*, and reread it to help shape my study and research. I read it anew every year before I teach genocide and international criminal law to my Human Rights Law class. Together we discuss, and I hope work to counteract, the basic societal prejudices against minority groups, recognizing that those prejudices lie at the very heart of mass violence, genocide, and impunity.

Notes

[1]   Ireland became a Free State in 1922; introduced a popularly-approved constitution (*Bunreacht na hÉireann*) in 1937; and declared itself a Republic and left the Commonwealth in 1948–1949.

[2]   Alexander Ramati, *And the Violins Stopped Playing: A Story of the Gypsy Holocaust* (London: Hodder & Stoughton, 1985).

[3]   Membership of the Travelling Community is now one of the "nine grounds" on which discrimination is banned under Irish law. See, e.g., the Employment Equality Act, 1998; the Equal Status Act, 2003. However, members of the Travelling Community still suffer high levels of discrimination, in their everyday lives and in the shaping of government policy. See, e.g., National Consultative Committee on Racism and Interculturalism, *Travellers in Ireland: An Examination of Discrimination and Racism*, 2004; available at http://www.nccri.ie/travellr.html.

[4]   Fiona de Londras, *Genocidal Sexual Violence: Experiences, Perspectives and Legal Responses*; LL.M thesis, University College Cork, Ireland, 2003.

Jackie Farkas (dir.), *The Illustrated Auschwitz* (1992)

There's No Place Like Home

Simone Gigliotti

How is it possible to illustrate Auschwitz? Helene Tichauer, script painter and Auschwitz employee, described doing so in extraordinary detail in her interview with David Boder, held in the Feldafing Displaced Person's camp in 1946.[1] Art Spiegelman did it, too, for his father in *Maus*, mapping the layout of the camp, its barracks and latrines, and arrivals and departures of inmates.[2]

It may seem an impossible task. Auschwitz's otherworldly status as a "kingdom of death" threatens a separation, if not a breach, between survivors and non-survivors, and between witnesses and custodians of memory. How can we reach into history through those who survived it? I confront this question each year when deciding which films to show students in my Holocaust course. And, indeed, there is no shortage of competition for a task that could easily sustain its own atrocity film festival.

Recently, while experiencing a periodic bout of Holocaust fatigue, I decided to be a little provocative, and offer students a montage of "The Survivor Experience." I wanted to explore how we, as a group ostensibly sharing an ethical framework, remember mass death and declare our commitment to survivors in the twenty-first century. My intention was to start with the celebrated, add the subversive, and end with the experimental: Alain Resnais's *Night and Fog*; the "Survivor" episode from Larry David's *Curb Your Enthusiasm*—and Jackie Farkas's *The Illustrated Auschwitz*.

This selection places students in an unusual situation, since their visual preparation for the Holocaust is achieved through exposure to a Hollywood diet of rescue, moral courage, and triumph against the odds. While *Night and Fog* and *Curb Your Enthusiasm* hopefully begin the unraveling of these predispositions, *The Illustrated Auschwitz* seeks to move them to another dimension of representation: into the personalization of history without the recycled images of Holocaust suffering and separations. By selecting this short film, I wanted to share the sensory and representational assault of trauma, and to convey how its director came to approach the Holocaust testimony of Hungarian survivor Zsuzsi Weinstock through the use of Dorothy's search for place and belonging in *The Wizard of Oz*. The juxtaposition of two ostensibly incompatible twentieth-century journeys—the canonical and the iconic—assaults students with a dizzying fusion of blurry images, flashbacks, and unidentifiable voices. In this way, I seek to relive my own first encounter with the film, expecting students to see, feel, and hear it as I did as an undergraduate at the University of Melbourne.

Seeing *The Illustrated Auschwitz* did not first interest me in the Holocaust. I had been oriented, like many students, to the stories, sounds, and images of trauma in innumerable survivor testimonies, and a visual overdose of media. What *The Illustrated Auschwitz* did was raise questions that continue to preoccupy me: how does Holocaust trauma find its way into our world, and why do we find meaning in it? How do spoken, aural, and visual languages function as memory transactions between the body and pain? How did *The Illustrated Auschwitz*, so dependent on the fictional realm for its emotional truth, take custody of Zsuzsi's story and make it real?

Zsuzsi and Dorothy (Judy Garland) are the two heroines of *The Illustrated Auschwitz*. Both were teenagers at the time of the Holocaust, and at the time of making *The Wizard of Oz*. Zsuzsi was stigmatized and designated an outcast by her Jewishness; Garland by her fame. Yet this is really Zsuzsi's story. Farkas takes apart her words, and samples them as incomplete though familiar references to the Auschwitz experience: deportation, arrival, separation from family members and encounter with Josef Mengele. While Zsuzsi's words are the source of moral and historical truth, they need aesthetics and fictionalization to convey a world so often claimed as unknowable to those who were not there. Farkas merges two familiar twentieth-century texts, one horrific, the other affirming. Musings from Dorothy's imaginary journey are underscored by Zsuzsi's response to her forced relocation. Both girls experience the timeless feeling of displacement, but Farkas presents Zsuzsi's trauma as restless, unable to find a firm anchor in historical explanations or objective truths. The film's visual clips, presumably recorded on a Super-8 camera from television, further blur what is told and heard as voices of history and cinema. Images pulsate to Zsuzsi's voiceovers, like a beating heart that increases in rhythm and dangerous excess, until the final scene of an inescapable Holocaust ending: the crematorium chimney.

Reviews of *The Illustrated Auschwitz* have suggested that its flirtation with genre, voice, truth, and trauma symbolizes the longstanding debate about the limits of representation. By rejecting the use of staple archival images, and prioritizing Zsuzsi's spoken words, Farkas has *Shoah*-like pretensions.

But unlike Claude Lanzmann, she has Dorothy's story as counter-narrative, and also as aesthetic surrogate. Farkas suggests that the soul of Holocaust suffering can have an emotional truth in the fictional world: a portable realism that speaks for the victims of history when words are not enough. Dorothy is Zsuzsi's imaginary, emotional proxy who speaks to the agony of being lost on the Yellow Brick Road. But unlike Dorothy, Zsuzsi is homeless at the end of her journey. At liberation, Zsuzsi can just afford to see *The Wizard of Oz* and its conclusive affirmation of "there's no place like home," followed in the credits by the song "Somewhere over the Rainbow." The fictional climax of Dorothy's homecoming cannot compensate for Zsuzsi's devastating loss of her family, but only reinforces it.

It is an understatement to say that I did not manage to convince the class of the virtues of *The Illustrated Auschwitz*. Instead, students pleaded with me to repeat the outrageously funny exchange between a Holocaust survivor and a self-designated "survivor" from *Curb Your Enthusiasm*. But was I too ambitious? On reflection, *The Illustrated Auschwitz* had moved many students to respond as I had. With silence and occasionally blank stares came recognition of a shared experience of understanding, and of *not* understanding—the need to connect with personal stories and questioning of meta-truths about human experiences. In the (unfortunately competitive) world of genocide suffering, we inquired about claims on our responses: why do we direct our grief and ethics towards some victims and not others?

In communicating the abandonment and dislocation of the Holocaust through Zsuzsi's channeling of Dorothy, perhaps the most extraordinary thing about *The Illustrated Auschwitz* is its brevity. At twelve minutes, the film says more about personal suffering than many celebrated feature-length films about the survivor experience. That Farkas has merged the visual and the aural dimensions of fiction and history to produce such a moving memorial to Zsuzsi's story remains a key to my thinking about the Holocaust and memory.

Notes

[1] David P. Boder, Interview with Helene Tichauer, archived at "Voices of the Holocaust," http://voices.iit.edu/frames.asp?path=Interviews/&page=tisch&ext=_t.html. The interview is also available in David P. Boder, *Topical Autobiographies of Displaced People, Recorded Verbatim in Displaced Persons Camps with a Psychological and Anthropological Analysis*, 16 vols. (Chicago, IL: Illinois Institute of Technology, 1957).

[2] See especially the chapter "Auschwitz: Time Flies," in Art Spiegelman, *Maus II: A Survivor's Tale* (London: Penguin, 1992).

Genocide and the Shock Process in Conceptual Art

Stephen C. Feinstein

In 1995, Zbigniew Libera, a Polish artist living in Warsaw, shocked many people unconnected with the art world with the three sets of a conceptual work of art called LEGO Concentration Camp. Each set contained seven boxes of actual LEGO bricks that could be used to construct the concentration camp buildings shown on the box covers. Libera used the logo of the LEGO corporation of Denmark; LEGO tried to file a lawsuit against Libera, but quickly discovered that such use of trademarks is legal for artists in Europe—though not in the United States. When the work was included by the New York Jewish Museum's curator, Norman Kleeblatt, in the spring 2002 exhibition "Mirroring Evil: Nazi Imagery/Recent Art," Holocaust survivors and their children demonstrated outside the museum to protest several works selected for exhibition. In particular, the LEGO Concentration Camp was seen as a kind of blasphemy or negative provocation about the memory and representation of the Holocaust.[1]

Zbigniew Libera, Lego Crematorium.
See Color Plate IV

Each unit of the seven-box set contained the ingredients for a different aspect of a concentration camp. The larger boxes showed the entire camp, with buildings, gallows (one showing an inmate being hanged), and inmates either behind barbed wire or marching in and out of the camp. The guards, in shiny black uniforms, were drawn from the regular LEGO police sets. The inmates, skeletons, came from the LEGO Amazon jungle, pirates, medical, or hospital sets. A second box showed a crematorium belching smoke from three chimneys, with *Sonderkommando*[2] or other inmates carrying a corpse from the gassing room. The smaller boxes depict a guard bludgeoning an inmate, medical experiments, another hanging, and a commandant (Box 6742) who projects the shadow of a five-pointed star. Bedecked with medals and wearing a red hat, he is more reminiscent of a figure from the Soviet Gulag than from the Nazi camp system. Some faces on both inmates and guards are slightly manipulated with paint, making their mouths turn downward in apparent sadness (for the inmates), or upwards in glee or *schadenfreude* (for the guards). The final box is full of personal possessions: the type of debris painted by other artists, and inspired by the vast array of loot collected by the SS in the Kanada warehouses at Auschwitz-Birkenau.[3]

It seems that the public outcry against the exhibition, and against Libera himself, was part of the regular attack against transgressive art in a museum space, when something more traditional is expected. But what is the purpose of conceptual art other than to disturb, especially in an era when genocide still occurs? Libera already had a reputation for pursuing a transgressive edge, especially in conceptual work. He also has a history of studying, from an artistic perspective, the impact of toys in shaping the creations of adults. Holocaust survivors, and some critics, thought that the concentration camp was a creation of German National Socialism. They forgot, it seems, that there were clear precedents in Cuba under the Spanish, and British policies in South Africa during the Boer War—not to mention what Vladimir Lenin constructed after the Russian Revolution.

On the wall of my office, I have color photos of Libera's LEGO creations. Inevitably, they draw curious looks from students. They ask what the works are about, and whether LEGO can really be used to build such models. When I use the images during an art lecture, my audience sometimes reacts with disbelief—partly because of the realistic nature of the boxes, but also, I think, because they sense that the artist has uncovered something that genuinely helps to explain the subject-matter. When I first met Libera and saw his work, it was at a Holocaust conference in Brussels, in a room filled with Holocaust survivors. All grew livid when they saw the projected images of LEGO. The moderator asked Libera to help the audience by explaining what he had created. His only response was: "I am from Poland. I've been poisoned!"[4]

As a contrast with art lacking in subtlety, one might analyze Simon Tyszko's *Suicide Bomber Barbie*, which comes complete with a quote from Noam Chomsky and a specific interpretation: "There is one simple way for the United States to decrease, very significantly, the plague of terror in the world, and that is just to stop supporting and participating in it." In addition, there is an added Soviet-style commentary about how the work "conflates Western commodification with Palestinian desperation." Tyszko's work provides both the question and all the answers about victim and perpetrator, baked in a post-colonialist ideology.[5]

Libera's art, by contrast, has shock value, but is also enigmatic. It needs no didactic statements to be understood or justified; there are always multiple interpretations. One avenue of interpretation might be to note that Adolf Hitler did not have a LEGO set to construct a concentration camp in his childhood—but he did want to be an artist, and his artistic failure changed the twentieth century.

Another line of thought might stress that, through his conceptual art and the LEGO Concentration Camp in particular, Libera has created, since the mid-1980s, a running commentary on the ambitions and consequences of commodification in capitalist culture. If LEGO can actually produce a "Cowboys and Indian Set" with stereotypical views of Native Americans, then why not a concentration camp? The artist's approach provokes both questioning and debate. His work, as much as any literary or historical effort, raises critical questions about whether, and how, representations "on the edge" can help viewers to understand the western culture that produced Auschwitz.[6]

Notes

[1]   An understanding of conceptual and transgressive art seems to have been lost on the editors of the *Encyclopedia of Genocide*, where, after a conventional attribution, an illustration of the LEGO Concentration Camp carries with it a warning of sorts: "Some educators have cautioned strongly against the use of models that may constitute 'gimmicks' that result in a play-like atmosphere rather than real historical understanding." See Israel Charny, ed., *Encyclopedia of Genocide*, Volume 1 (Santa Barbara, CA: ABC-CLIO, 1999), p. 196.

[2]   The *Sonderkommando* at Auschwitz-Birkenau were Jews chosen by the SS to assist inmates about to be gassed in the undressing barracks, and then dispose of their corpses in the crematorium. German SS *Sonderkommando* were also used outside of Auschwitz for "cleansing operations" against Jews and others, hence the translation of "special commando." For an on-line reference see Jacqueline Shields, "Sonderkommando," at the Jewish Virtual Library: http://www.jewishvirtuallibrary. org/jsource/Holocaust/Sonderkommando.html

[3]   For further illustrations of Libera's LEGO Concentration Camp, see the web site for University of Minnesota's Center for Holocaust and Genocide Studies, which exhibited the work in a 1999 exhibition, "Absence/Presence": http://www.chgs. umn.edu/Visual_Artistic_Resources/Absence_Presence/General_Tour_Absence_ Presence/Zbigniew_Libera/zbigniew_libera.html

[4] As heard by the author at the Holocaust and the Contemporary Arts Conference, Fondation Auschwitz, Brussels, 1997.

[5] See the website, "Suicide Bomber Barbie," http://www.theculture.net/barbie/

[6] For more on Libera's work, see Stephen C. Feinstein, "Zbigniew Libera's Lego Concentration Camp: Iconoclasm in Conceptual Art About the Shoah," in *Other Voices: The Journal of Cultural Criticism*, 2: 1 (February 2000), http://www.othervoices.org/2.1/feinstein/auschwitz.html; Roxana Marcoci, "The Antinomes of Censorship: The Case of Zbigniew Libera," in Stephen Feinstein, ed., *Absence/Presence: Critical Essays on the Artistic Memory of the Holocaust* (Syracuse, NY: Syracuse University Press, 2005), pp. 259–270.

Pierre Sauvage (dir.), *Weapons of the Spirit* (1989)

The Moral Capital of the World

Winton Higgins

In March 1944, Pierre Sauvage was born in a German-occupied town in France to a Jewish couple on the run. In 1989, Sauvage released his documentary film, *Weapons of the Spirit*. It traces his attempts to understand how he had survived the Holocaust, which claimed 75,000 French Jewish lives. The political authorities were committed to his destruction; but the poor rural community of five thousand fundamentalist Christians that he had been born into, Le Chambon-sur-Lignon, was even more dedicated to his survival. And not just his, but that of all the five thousand Jews who sought sanctuary there. No-one was turned away; everyone survived.

What went on in the hearts and minds of an entire community to make it the sole example of communal rescue on such a scale in the annals of the Holocaust? The style of rescue only deepens the mystery. The Chambonnais had neither weapons nor organization; as individuals and families, they simply followed an impulse to respond to the needs of strangers, one reinforced by their local Huguenot church. They made no effort to hide their Jewish "guests," who anyway operated Jewish schools in the town and openly observed their customs and rituals. And they certainly made no attempt to hide their repugnance at their Vichy and German overlords.

I teach genocide studies in undergraduate courses in Sydney, and rescuers complete the tableau of any genocide. When the Chambonnais came to my attention, their story beggared belief at first: what sort of people would tempt fate like that, and why didn't the authorities snuff out their unarmed rebellion? Perhaps my lack of insider knowledge of both Jews and Christians was blinding me to something in the relationship? But I was keenly aware of the two millennia of Christian anti-semitism that made the Holocaust possible, and the bleak record of the major Christian churches during the Holocaust itself. By the time I stumbled on Sauvage's film, I knew a great deal about the Holocaust, including the many studies of perpetrators and rescuers. The vast majority of mass killers were "ordinary men," easily recruited, while gentile rescuers of Jews represented a tiny sliver of around 50,000 in an

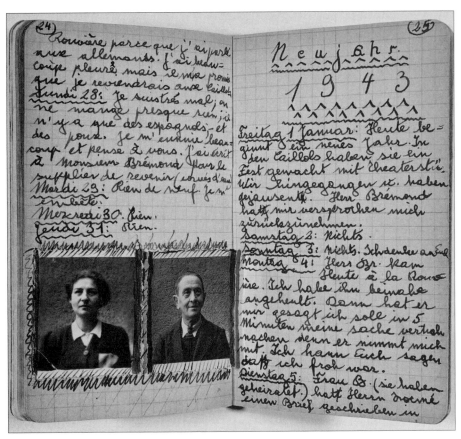

Diary written by Peter Feigl, a Jewish child, during his time
in Le Chambon-sur-Lignon. The photos are of Feigl's parents, who, though he
did not know it at the time, had been deported to the Auschwitz death camp and
murdered there (courtesy United States Holocaust Memorial Museum/Peter Feigl).

overall population of 500 million in German-occupied Europe (that is, about
0.05 per cent). They saved some 250,000 Jews, and in so doing managed, just
barely, to pull our species back from the brink of absolute disgrace.

Rescuers typically plied their arduous and dangerous calling in total
isolation and secrecy, or in clandestine networks. Sociologically speaking,
they had nothing in common: they came from all national, social and
religious backgrounds (including atheism), and in their ranks we even find
fascists, anti-semites, and German soldiers. Their individual stories inspire,
but their small numbers—almost drowned in a sea of bystanderism—only
add to the dispiriting pattern of moral indifference that pervades Holocaust
history. Researching and teaching the Holocaust brought me into contact
with a lot of toxic material. At times, as a result, I experienced bouts of

depression and lethargy. But seeing *Weapons of the Spirit* brought me back to life, and I love showing it to students and other audiences.

Moral indifference doesn't seem to have been an option for the Chambonnais. The day after the Germans clinched victory over France in 1940, Le Chambon's pastor, André Trocmé, told his congregation that their consciences as Christians were about to be sorely tried, and they must "fight back with the weapons of the spirit." That is exactly what they did: theirs is a story of spiritual resistance, the effectiveness of which dwarfs the achievements of more conventional armed resistance.

As Sauvage shows, the resistance had its own irresistible dynamic. Soon the Catholic minority in the area had been drawn into the "conspiracy of goodness." Then it attracted a brilliant, workaholic forger, who churned out false identity papers. It entangled a senior Vichy official who was sent to investigate tip-offs that the area was teeming with Jews. He sat in his hotel room and wrote careful reports back to his superiors, assuring them that there were no Jews present at all. Finally, when the German army occupied the town, the local commander also found it prudent to pretend that Le Chambon's large and visible Jewish population didn't exist. (The locals told the bewildered German soldiers that their "guests" were actually tourists.) Throughout, the authorities realized there was little to be gained by trying to intimidate the fearless, stiff-necked Chambonnais, so they wisely desisted.

Sauvage's research, and the resulting film, leave neither him nor his audience with a cut-and-dried explanation of rescue in general, or what inspired it in Le Chambon in particular. He does not disguise his own continuing perplexity. He lets the Chambonnais themselves speak. Their soft, weather-beaten faces turn uneasily towards the camera, but their shy, self-deprecating answers seem almost calculated to withhold something from us.

Nonetheless, for me, two vital elements seem to unite the Chambonnais with other rescuers in the history of genocide. First, rescuers seem motivated by strong particularistic identities. As the political philosopher Michael Sandel has commented, the love of humanity is a noble sentiment; but most of us live most of the time by more local solidarities. Sometimes those local solidarities foster a moral responsiveness to those beyond their own sharply-defined boundaries—an engagement with the needs of strangers. The Chambonnais are deeply aware of their Huguenot heritage: their ancestors' experience of persecution, as well as the "Good Samaritan" imperative at the heart of their religion. They did not take risks and make sacrifices as citizens of the world, out of an abstract sense of humanitarian duty, but rather had an acute sense of belonging to a particular spiritual community and what they had to do to honor that belonging. For people like me who cleave to more universalistic conceptions of moral obligation, this is a challenging notion indeed.

The second theme I discern in *Weapons of the Spirit* pertains to that most basic of issues: truth and its denial. In the Holocaust, bystanders—especially those who turned their backs on Jews in need of sanctuary—mouthed the standard moral alibis: the Germans are a civilized people, so this can't possibly be happening; these are not my people, so it isn't my problem; and so on. In contrast, the Chambonnais immediately acknowledged the truth and acted upon it: this *is* happening; these people *are* my responsibility, because they're standing right here on my doorstep.

Another, more famous work of art backs up Sauvage on this point. The great existentialist writer, Albert Camus, decided to write an allegory about the German occupation of France in real time, and sought out a quiet rural backwater in which to work on his novel. Of all places, without any idea of what was unfolding there, he chose to rent a room in Le Chambon-sur-Lignon! What he observed on his daily walks left its mark on the classic novel he wrote in the town, *The Plague*. The book deals with a modern town visited by a medieval catastrophe, the Black Death. The town authorities choose the path of denial, while the protagonist, Dr Bernard Rieux, tries to get them to face the calamity. He asserts the starkness and indivisibility of truth as the only basis for responsible action. The point encapsulates something essential to Le Chambon's response to its "guests" and their predicament.

For me, the story of Le Chambon highlights our own moral hazard today in the West, where the art of government depends so unashamedly on spin, euphemism, disinformation, and appeals to the public's baser instincts. In such a cynical political culture, we need regular reminders that a decent, truth-respecting community can stare down apparently unstoppable evil. *Weapons of the Spirit* makes that point unforgettably.

Raphael Lemkin, photographed by Hans Knopf (1951)

"You and I, We Must Change the World"

Helen Bond

I kept staring into his face, hoping to catch a glimpse of the wild-eyed professor who chased reporters through the halls of the United Nations, yelling: *"You and I, we must change the world."*[1] I couldn't find him.

The simple photograph of a balding man in a white shirt, his tie slung to the side, betrayed no hint of the precocious twelve-year-old who asked his mother how Nero could have fed Christians to the lions in front of jeering crowds. With the tip of a Number Two pencil poking out of his shirt pocket, he resembled a corporate executive who had spent a long day in the office, trying to keep shareholders happy. Nothing could have been further from the truth. The man in the picture instead passed endless days haunting the corridors of Congress and the United Nations, making everyone unhappy. The Polish Jew who had lost all of his family in the Holocaust, save one brother, was called a pest who never gave up trying to get people to listen to his tales of "genocide."

Who was this man? What was the source of his obsessive determination? I peered closer at the black-and-white snapshot posted on the Prevent Genocide International web site (www.preventgenocide.org/lemkin). What I couldn't find in the face, I found in the story of Raphael Lemkin: the man who coined the term "genocide" and inspired the United Nations Genocide Convention. It was his dramatic life story, as detailed in Samantha Power's prizewinning book *"A Problem from Hell": America and the Age of Genocide,* that fomented my interest in genocide.

I was not new to the topic. I had read some of Lemkin's work as a doctoral student, while working on a Ph.D. in human rights education. At that point in my development, I didn't understand the complexity or the full barbarity of the "crime without a name." This was the phrase Winston Churchill had used to describe Nazi aggression in occupied Eastern Europe in 1941, before Lemkin had coined his famous term. To an academic, it was just another bloody concept. I came to know genocide best through the power of personal narrative and story.

It was the accounts of Oskar Schindler, Roméo Dallaire, Elie Wiesel, Immaculée Ilibagiza, and Raphael Lemkin, to name just a few, that helped me construct meaning from genocide. Who could resist Ilibagiza's story of survival in her autobiography, *Left to Tell?*[2] Fearing her entire family was dead, the young Tutsi woman hid for 91 days, squeezed in a tiny bathroom with seven other women, while Rwanda was consumed by what Power called the "fastest, most efficient killing spree of the twentieth century."[3] The photographs of Immaculée in her autobiography, as she returned to the bathroom to reflect on her fate, hardly needed words at all.

As for Lemkin, strangely enough it was his profound *ordinariness* in the photographs that made his story even more compelling. He described hearing stories of atrocities against the Jews as a child, and remembered the mental pictures he formed as a result. Lemkin wrote in his unpublished autobiography, *Totally Unofficial Man*: "I could not define history with my childish mind, but I saw it vividly and strongly with my eyes, as a huge torture place of the innocent."[4]

Tell me a story. That is what my "innocents" would ask me when I taught history in a middle school. What they really wanted were pictures, as well as a hero or heroine, and a villain thrown in for good measure. I had to explain to them that things are not that simple, and sometimes people move among several different roles during a state-sponsored conflict. (Consider, for example, John Rabe, the Nazi who was also called the "Oskar Schindler of China" for helping to rescue Chinese from torture and death at the hands of the Japanese occupiers.)[5] Personal narratives serve a critical function in helping people to find meaning in their world. According to Kenyon and Randall, "To be a person is to have a story. More than that, it is to be a story."[6] Bruner argues that a story helps to create engagement on several levels, by enabling us to enter the minds and hearts of the characters and gain deeper meaning.[7] What is left out, we fill in.

Power's book doesn't leave much out. In her text, Lemkin's heroism is critical in maintaining a balance between good and evil. Sandwiched between the Armenian genocide in chapters one and two, and the bloodbath in Cambodia in chapter six, is the story of Lemkin and how he would literally faint from hunger as he chased down delegates at the United Nations. And Lemkin is not the only hero in the fight against genocide who is profiled in Power's work. Beginning in 1967, Senator William D. Proxmire gave a speech

Raphael Lemkin, photographed by Hans Knopf for *Collier's* magazine, 1951.

a day for 19 years, urging Congress to pass the Genocide Convention. Proxmire gave a total of 3,211 speeches before Congress passed an amended version of the law in 1988.

I imagine the moral of Lemkin's story something like this. Once upon a time, the wise men and women of the world adjourned to their councils, to smoke their peace pipes and chant: "Never again . . . never again." Then the wise men and women returned home, with blood on their boots and their hands, as they walked past and sometimes alongside the killers. Still they chanted: "Never again."

Along the way, they met a child whose family would soon be killed. The child pestered them, telling them they were wrong, dead wrong. They paid no attention, and continued their journey. The child grew up, and remembering their insolence, haunted them day and night until a law was passed to make the physical and cultural extermination of a people a crime against humanity. He called it genocide. The man died, and for a long while almost nobody remembered him. Only seven people attended his funeral.

What is so special about Lemkin and his photograph that they served as milestones along my own journey into genocide? The Ute Indians believed that a photograph captured part of the subject's spirit. They often shunned photographers, referring to them as "Shadow Catchers." I was mesmerized by Lemkin's story, and the courage and strength it demonstrated. After reading about beasts masquerading as men in chapter after chapter of Power's book, I needed a Lemkin. I pored over photographs of him as if the camera had somehow captured his spirit.

While I continue to read widely on genocide, I am now most interested in the personal stories and images of genocide. I recently purchased a book that contains the secret diaries and photographs of children who perished in the Holocaust. I viewed the exhibit, "Through the Eyes of Children: The Rwanda Project," which displays pictures taken by Rwandan children with disposable cameras. I am trying to make sense of the "problem from hell," one person at a time. Like the Utes, I feel that personal narratives and photographs may somehow capture the spirit of their subject, one shadow at a time.

Notes

[1] Raphael Lemkin, quoted in Samantha Power, *"A Problem from Hell": America and the Age of Genocide* (New York: Basic Books, 2002), p. 51.

2   Immaculé Ilibagiza, *Left to Tell: Discovering God Amidst the Rwandan Holocaust* (Carlsbad, CA: Hay House, 2006).

3   Power, *"A Problem from Hell,"* p. 334. See also the excerpts from Lemkin's memoir in chapter 1 of this volume.

4   Lemkin quoted in Power, *"A Problem from Hell,"* p. 370.

5   See John Rabe, *The Good Man of Nanking: The Diaries of John Rabe* (New York: Vintage, 2000).

6   Gary M. Kenyon and William L. Randall, *Restorying Our Lives' Personal Growth through Autobiographical Reflection* (Westport, CT: Praeger, 1997), p. 1.

7   Jerome Bruner, *Making Stories: Law, Literature, Life* (New York: Farrar, Straus, and Giroux, 2002).

Eichmann, Mulisch and Me

G. Jan Colijn

As a member of the Dutch post-war generation, I agree with Ian Buruma,[1] who considers the most important event of our adolescence to have been the coverage of the Adolf Eichmann trial, Case 40/61, by Harry Mulisch—a prominent Dutch author, the son of a Jewish mother and an Austrian Nazi sympathizer. Mulisch is an extraordinary writer. You may have read his tour de force, *The Discovery of Heaven*.[2] Each year, I find myself rooting for him to get the Nobel prize in literature. Of all his books that have guided my life, none was more influential than his account of Eichmann's trial, *De Zaak 40/61*.[3] It was my gateway to first grappling with the Holocaust and, much later, with genocide in general.

De Zaak 40/61 was recently published in English by the University of Pennsylvania under the title *Criminal Case 40/61: The Trial of Adolf Eichmann—An Eyewitness Account*, with a perceptive foreword by Debórah Dwork.[4] My Dutch copy hangs in threads, as I reread it many times, not with the "certain pornographic frisson" with which Buruma admits to having read this kind of literature, but because Mulisch dispensed with the Dutch self-image about the war that was based on a false dichotomy of the "good" Dutch vs. the "bad" Germans (and a handful of Dutch collaborators).

In the postwar, rearview moral universe of Dutch mythology, the Dutch created a national narrative of majoritarian and heroic resistance (good) and terrible repression by the German occupiers (bad), marred—but only just—by a few Dutch Nazis and SS volunteers. That self-image was further advanced by the iconic status given to those, such as Miep Gies, who had helped Anne Frank and her family when the Franks went into hiding. Among the poignant questions ignored was why the destruction of Dutch Jewry was so disproportionately calamitous, in comparison with the survivor rates in other occupied Western European countries.

Mulisch's rendering of the trial, and his discourse on Eichmann's persona, had a tremendous influence on my adolescent thinking about the Holocaust, because of a few inter-related themes that emerge in the book (and elsewhere

Adolf Eichmann on trial in Jerusalem, flanked by his Israeli guards
(courtesy Israel Security Agency/Shin Bet).

in his oeuvre). For the first time, I began to understand the extent of Dutch compliance in the deportations; in the betrayal of many hidden Jews; in the roundups; in the abandonment of fellow citizens by all but some 25,000 non-Jewish Dutch men and women who actually tried to help. Here, for the first time, I began to see the parallels between Eichmann, the orderly civil servant, and the Dutch civil service which, with some exceptions, apparently complied with the deportation machinery with few qualms: with professional ease, with a penchant for formalism and a readiness to follow directives. "Orders are orders" was clearly not an exclusively German affliction.

To Mulisch, Eichmann was the prototype of a new, ordinary, modern man—the organization man—doing what was expected of him, never questioning or challenging. Thus, well before I read Graham Greene's *The Quiet American*, Mulisch suggested what I, too, might be capable of: under the wrong circumstances, I could do terrible things. The postwar moral universe of my youth was dealt a severe blow.

As well, I developed an early wariness about the powerful attraction of all closed worldviews and ideologies, not just the Nazi version. The French call it *la puissance d'une idée en marche*. We know the road to hell is paved with good intentions. For those opposed to the salvation of the marching drummer, and for those who can find no place in the utopian endgame of various ideologies, only carnage lies ahead. Mulisch was not the only one, but he was the first, to teach me that terror is neither accidental nor a regrettable byproduct of utopianism: in fact, terror lies at its very core. He opened my eyes to a genocidal canvas of vast complexity and ambiguity. With the division of "good" and "bad" people long abandoned, I have found no easy answers since.

Notes

[1]   Ian Buruma, "I Did Not Know about the Holocaust Then—Growing Up in Holland," in Luc Devoldere, ed., *The Low Countries* (Rekkum: The Flemish Netherlands Foundation/Stichting Ons Erfdeel, 2005), pp. 100–109.

[2]   Harry Mulisch, *The Discovery of Heaven*, trans. Paul Vincent (New York: Viking, 1996).

[3]   Harry Mulisch, *De Zaak 40/61, Een Reportage*, 2nd ed. (Amsterdam: Uitgeverij De Bezige Bij, 1962).

[4]   Harry Mulisch, *Criminal Case 40/61: The Trial of Adolf Eichmann—An Eyewitness Account*, trans. Robert Naborn (Philadelphia, PA: University of Pennsylvania Press, 2005).

Hannah Arendt, *Eichmann in Jerusalem* (1963)

Ugliness and Distance

Eric Gordy

The aesthetic background of the years in which I developed an interest in the world sufficient to examine it in some depth consisted of objects of ironic distancing. A punk song by the Sex Pistols, a group whose transparently engineered popularity was an art project in itself, snarlingly invited people to (not really) enjoy "a cheap holiday in other people's misery."[1] A series of paintings by a formerly reflective and lyrical abstract expressionist, Philip Guston, depicted cartoonish Klansmen with cigars, jaunting in cartoonish little cars, reminiscent of the mustachioed fellow from the *Monopoly* game popping out of their stitched bedsheets.[2] A series of plays by an Argentine psychologist depicted torturers at work, worrying about exceeding the hours for which they are paid, and about what they will be getting when they break for lunch.[3]

These works of art intrigued and attracted me long before I read Hannah Arendt's famous reflection on the Eichmann trial and the "banality of evil."[4] Thematically, they appear to be very similar. There is an ineffectively hidden consciousness of guilt, accompanied by strenuous efforts to employ various strategies of distancing, from the routine to the ironic. Some people might describe the works as engaged; others (perhaps most people) would be inclined to see them as cynical, nihilistic, unfeeling. While I have never felt distant from or unfeeling toward alarming world events (and later, when I worked through Karl Jaspers and his exposition of "metaphysical guilt,"[5] I said to myself: "But of course!"), there was a period, still not concluded, when this kind of art spoke a sort of truth to me—much more than the maudlin, demonstratively empathetic type of work that might be more conventionally characterized as "political."

Arendt's exploration of Eichmann was, of course, a treatment of an individual perpetrator—or, if you prefer, of the self-justifying dynamics of perpetrating institutions. That is to say, it was a study of evil from the point of view of the evildoer. With apologies to the many distinguished scholars who have studied and attempted to explain evildoers and their evil doings, ch

-183-

who followed the Trial -- of whether the accused had a conscience;

yes, he had a conscience, and his conscience functioned in the

expected way for about four weeks, whereafter it began to function

the other way round.

Even during the short weeks when his conscience had normally

functioned it had done its work within rather odd limitations. We

must remember that weeks and months before he was informed of the

Führer-order Eichmann knew of course of the murderous activities

of the Einsatzgruppen in the East, he knew that right behind the

frontlines all Russian functionaries ("Communists"), all Polish

members of the professional classes, and all native Jews were killed

in mass-shootings. Moreover, in July of the same year, a few weeks

before he was called to Heydrich, he had received a memorandum from

Police No.
  1410

some SS-man stationed in the Warthegau telling him of the danger

that "Jews in the coming winter could no longer be fed," and submit-

ting to his consideration "whether it would not be the most humane

solution to kill those Jews who were incapable of work through some

Manuscript page from Hannah Arendt's *Eichmann in Jerusalem*,
as originally published in the *New Yorker* magazine
(courtesy The Hannah Arendt Papers, Library of Congress, Washington, DC).

the subject has always struck me as a dry well. Either the perpetrators' personal characteristics are so unique that no theoretical explanation is possible, or they are responding to conditions so typical that general explanations fail to distinguish the perpetrators from everybody else who arose from the same

Philip Guston, "City Limits" (oil painting, 1969; courtesy
The Museum of Modern Art, New York/Licensed by SCALA/Art Resource, NY).

environment. Just about every actor who has played a "baddie" in a James
Bond film tells interviewers afterward how much fun they had. And why
shouldn't they have fun? Evil is stereotypical, and any decent actor knows
how outlandish a costume to assemble, what facial expressions to mimic,
and how to modulate his or her voice to convey it. Like real evildoers, these
fictional roles are overdetermined: they "write themselves." Every element of
the evil role comes down to depicting the myriad ways in which a perpetrator
differs from everybody else.

And that is the problem. Almost everybody, in fact, is *not* a perpetrator;
but everybody lives, more or less powerlessly, in the world the perpetrators
made. Ernest Renan's often-repeated formulation that the nation is "a community of memory and of forgetting"[6] highlights the degree to which "forgetting" can never really be achieved. Ordinary people in their ordinary lives
participate both in memory and in its obliteration, whether they want to or
not. But not in good faith: when I admire the scenery in a park named after
the people who were killed in order to make it federal property, its history is
there. When I pay extra, because I can, for a home in a school district where

the history of racism is not recreated to foreclose the futures of all those children whose families cannot pay, I participate in the history of slavery and imperialism. But not in the manner of the active racist: more like Guston's cartoon Klansman, who is two-dimensional, propelled by somebody else's bad humor, and unaware.

This is the dimension of living amidst atrocity that I have tried to comprehend in my research, whether on the popular press in Argentina during their last military dictatorship, or on everyday life and the strange conflict between rock 'n' roll and folk cultures in Serbia, while mass deportations and killings were ongoing in Bosnia-Hercegovina and Kosovo. People knew what was happening, unless they were very energetic in pursuing ignorance. And yet they ate lunch, told jokes, entertained themselves, and participated in the whole set of worries and enjoyments that we think of as "ordinary." That has always struck me as the most mystifying contradiction.

This may be why I was never able to find refuge in Marxist theory and its various reformulations, however much I might have wanted to. The good student of German philosophy built an epistemological-political edifice around the perception that people could not live with contradiction. Even early on, it was already clear to me that living with contradiction is probably humans' greatest talent; without it, it would be hard to survive at all. If there was an answer to the mystery of living with evil, it had to lie somewhere inside that complex of evasions which most people recognized as their everyday world.

Theodor Adorno once famously stated that "It is barbaric to write poetry after Auschwitz."[7] Though regularly quoted, the comment raises more questions than it answers, and seems impossible to take as any sort of declaration or instruction. What does he mean by "barbaric," and why is it only here that he pretends the distinction between civilization and barbarism is a neat one? What does he mean by "poetry," and is this an invitation to break the link between art and beauty? Maybe most of all, what does he mean by "after," and is he certain that we have reached that point?

I had to move pretty far beyond adolescence to recognize the posture of my old punk-rock heroes for what it was: a mask crafted by young writers and artists who, much like myself, felt overwhelmed, isolated, bewildered and powerless in an environment in which evil was rapidly normalized and generally accepted, and in which the standard responses had repeatedly proved their bankruptcy. What else was there to do but become a researcher?

Notes

[1]   The Sex Pistols, "Holidays in the Sun," on *Never Mind the Bollocks, Here's the Sex Pistols* (London: Warner/WEA, 1977).

[2]   A selection of the works of Philip Guston in the collection of the Museum of Modern Art is available online at: http://www.moma.org/collection/browse_results.php?criteria=O%3AAD%3AE%3A2419&page_number=1&template_id=6&sort_order=1.

[3]   Eduardo Pavlovsky, *Telarañas* (Buenos Aires: Ediciones Búsqueda, 1976), *El señor Laforgue* (Buenos Aires: Ediciones Búsqueda, 1982), and *El señor Galíndez y Pablo* (Buenos Aires: Ediciones Búsqueda, 1986).

[4]   Hannah Arendt, *Eichmann in Jerusalem: A Report on the Banality of Evil* (New York: Penguin, 2006).

[5]   In *The Question of German Guilt*, trans. E.B. Ashton (New York: Fordham University Press, 2002).

[6]   The reader will expect a citation here. But like everyone else, I have never read Renan, and know only this line.

[7]   The sentence has been rendered differently in various translations. I am relying on the translation provided in the discussion by Elaine Martin, "Re-reading Adorno: The 'After-Auschwitz' Aporia," *Forum*, no. 2 (2006), available at: http://forum.llc.ed.ac.uk/issue2/index.html.

Lost Worlds

Detail of Diego Rivera, "La Gran Tenochtitlán" (courtesy James Kiracofe).

Warning: Here There Be Experts

The missing volume of Ottoman history. Poster by Yervant Herian, www.armeniangenocideposters.org (courtesy Yervant Herian).

The Attic and the Imagination

"Anne Frank Grave Marker," 1989.
Toned ortho film, Plexiglas, wood, glue; 20 x 18 inches. © 2007
Doug and Mike Starn/Artists Rights Society (ARS), New York.
Reproduced with permission of the artists.

Genocide and the Shock Process in Conceptual Art

Zbigniew Libera, Lego Crematorium (courtesy Stephen Feinstein).

Apocalypse Soon

Art Nuko, "Explo" (1986).

The Face of Genocide

A defaced photograph that was found by a Bosnian family when they returned to their home in a suburb of Sarajevo, Bosnia, March 1996 (Ron Haviv/VII).

"Never Again," Again

"The Way Forward," by Ardyn Halter (www.ardynhalter.com).
Stained-glass window in the Genocide Memorial Centre in Gisozi, a suburb
of Kigali, Rwanda. Halter is the son of a survivor of the Auschwitz death
camp (courtesy Ardyn Halter).

Dili on Fire

A September 8, 1999 Landsat 7 ETM+ satellite scene with band assignments RGB 741 (false color representation), showing Dili, capital of East Timor, just days after the results of a pro-independence referendum were announced. The light violet colored pixels represent the focus points of the fires, and the black smoke produced by the fires can be seen streaking southwest across the image. The spatial resolution has been enhanced to 15m using the panchromatic band (courtesy Russell Schimmer/Genocide Studies Program, Yale University).

Gitta Sereny, *Albert Speer: His Battle with Truth* (1995)

Morality, Indifference, and Evil

Ernesto Verdeja

Early in my graduate-school years, I read Gitta Sereny's extraordinary biography, *Albert Speer: His Battle with Truth*. It offered a more complex and disturbing account of perpetrator psychology than any work I had encountered to that point. I'd read a number of perpetrator biographies and social psychological studies on mass violence. Sereny's Speer, however, was a deeper and more troubling character. Her portrait of "Hitler's architect" forced me to reckon with moral indifference to suffering, and how it could serve as a cornerstone of genocide.

Of all the major Nazi war criminals, I found Albert Speer the most enigmatic. Others, of course, evoked their own morbid fascination. Hermann Göring's pompous dress and flamboyant behavior came together so absurdly that he would have been a comical figure, if not for the terrible power he wielded. Adolf Eichmann remains the paradigmatic example of banal evil (if we follow Hannah Arendt's reading): the epitome of the modern bureaucrat whose fixation on rational efficiency blinded him to the human impact of his actions. Speer, however, provided an additional dimension to mass atrocity, one that was missing in many of the standard accounts.

Sereny captured him perfectly when she defined him as neither immoral nor amoral, but "somehow infinitely worse, morally extinguished."[1] As Minister of Armament and Munitions, Speer was so effective at reorganizing the German economy and harmonizing it with the needs of Hitler's war machine that he was probably responsible for extending the war by a year or two. To this end, of course, he relied heavily on slave labor, on prisoners-of-war and Jews, who would be cruelly worked to death.

On the dock at the Nuremberg trials, Speer distanced himself from his fellow defendants and denounced the Nazi regime. He accepted responsibility for Nazi war crimes, while adamantly denying knowledge of the Holocaust. He claimed he had not been present at Himmler's infamous Posen speech in October 1943, when the SS leader made clear his intention to exterminate the Jews (Speer said he left before Himmler spoke). Witnesses corroborated

Albert Speer, on trial at Nuremberg
(courtesy United States Holocaust Memorial Museum).

his denial, and when documentation emerged showing that the July 1944 coup plotters had considered Speer a potential ally, his defense in court was strengthened. His carefully crafted position, part *mea culpa* and part evasion, spared him the noose, which—had the trial judges been consistent—he clearly deserved.

When he was finally released from Spandau prison two decades later, Speer refashioned himself as a symbol of what could happen to "decent" people if they blindly followed their leaders. He published and spoke on the seductions of Hitler, and the need for Germany's youth to resist authoritarian temptations. Nonetheless, he always insisted he had been ignorant about the extermination of the Jews, so any guilt he carried was at most that of *not knowing what he should have known*.

Edmund Burke famously said that evil triumphs when good men do nothing. Speer was not a "good man" in Burke's sense—much as he would have liked to think he was. Though he pleaded ignorance about the extermination camps, as Armaments Minister in the later stages of the war, he *did* know that Germany's prodigious military output was achieved through the pervasive use of slave labor. He even visited one camp (Dora), and witnessed firsthand the human cost of his industrial policy. So what did his ignorance mean for him, and for us?

Shortly before his death, Speer wrote: "To this day I still consider my main guilt to be my tacit acceptance [*Billigung*] of the persecution and the murder of millions of Jews."[2] This highlights the moral boundary between *knowledge* and *acknowledgement*, and how he redrew that boundary for his own ends. Speer knew what was happening to Europe's Jews, but he was unwilling to acknowledge his complicity in the campaign of extermination.

The brilliance of Sereny's account is not that it shows a man who consciously and carefully crafted a pack of lies to escape the hangman. Rather, it is the way she traces the half-truths Speer told himself: dissimulations that were necessary to avoid a complete mental and emotional collapse. By consciously "choosing" not to know the crimes of his regime—that is, by failing to acknowledge the moral and physical catastrophe to which he substantially contributed—Speer found a way to achieve at least some degree of psychological stability. But this came at a great moral cost. The lies and half-truths led, unsurprisingly, to an indifference toward victims that was facilitated by an "instinctual anti-Semitism," as Sereny terms it—typical of many Germans (and Europeans more generally) of his generation.[3]

Speer, of course, was not just another German. He was a member of the Nazi leadership who wielded enormous power, and whose organizational talents gave Nazi terror a longer life than it would otherwise have enjoyed. But Speer's battle with truth highlights an important lesson about behavior during mass violence: one that needs to be repeated, for our own and for future generations. While hatred of an enemy is certainly a prerequisite for genocide, it is the wilful indifference of the majority—the willingness to redraw the moral domain to exclude victims—that makes genocide a reality.

This abrogation of responsibility is itself a moral act. We may avoid thinking through the consequences of our actions, and later plead ignorance; but we cannot escape the moral responsibility that adheres to such complicity.

Notes

[1]   Gitta Sereny, *Albert Speer: His Battle with Truth* (New York: Vintage Books, 1995), p. 10.

[2]   *Ibid.*, p. 707.

[3]   *Ibid.*, p. 91.

Walter Sanning, *The Dissolution
of Eastern European Jewry* (1983)

Journey through Denial

John C. Zimmerman

The Dissolution of Eastern European Jewry will sound to most readers of
this volume like a straightforward historical account of the Holocaust. In
fact, Walter Sanning's book is a work of Holocaust denial that attempts to
"explain" what happened to the Jews of Europe. In short, Sanning argues
that the Jews were not really present in the first place, so could not have
been rounded up and killed. They had emigrated to Palestine or the Americas,
or had been sequestered in the eastern regions of the Soviet Union. The
implication was that the hundreds of thousands that Sanning could not
account for had indeed been murdered—but by Stalin, not Hitler.

I first heard of Holocaust denial in the late 1970s from a news
item about Arthur Butz, author of the best-known work in the genre, *The
Hoax of the Twentieth Century: The Case Against the Presumed Extermination of European Jewry*. Not surprisingly, Butz wrote the introduction to
Sanning's book.

In 1978, I read Butz's book. It was actually the first book I had read
about the Holocaust—a subject about which I knew almost nothing. *The
Hoax* is not well-written, and is somewhat disorganized. Nevertheless, and
quite surprisingly, Butz cited so much evidence that the Holocaust actually
occurred that his account left me with absolutely no doubt about the veracity
of the event. True, he did work to *dismiss* all this evidence, citing this or
that conspiracy theory to explain it away. For instance, he claimed that the
deportations of hundreds of thousands of Hungarian Jews to Auschwitz
from May to July 1944, which was covered extensively in the world press,
never happened. He alleged that the numerous German documents tracing
the progress of the deportations were all forgeries. He argued that only some
minor deportations had taken place. It quickly became apparent that only
someone prone to self-delusion could accept Butz's fanciful arguments.

I thought little about these matters for some years following my
initial reading of Butz. Every now and then, I would run across something

addressing denial in the neo-Nazi publications that I casually monitored. But I had no particular interest in the Holocaust as an academic subject.

In the summer of 1995, however, while visiting Belfast, I heard about a book dealing with Holocaust denial. Upon returning to the US, I visited Princeton University's Firestone Library. The work I'd heard about wasn't there—but I did come across a copy of Sanning's book. I started browsing it, and noticed that a student had made notations in the margins, but was unsuccessful in attempting to refute Sanning's arguments. I also realized that, for my part, I couldn't answer any of them! Sanning had presented a vast array of statistics and data, all of which seemed quite convincing on the surface. Thus did my journey through denial begin.

The remainder of the summer of 1995 was spent in the Firestone Library, the Alexander Library at Rutgers University, and the Jewish Division of the New York Public Library. Upon careful examination of Sanning's sources, as well as a vast range of sources that he simply ignored, it became obvious that he had fabricated nearly all of the information in his book. In fact, there is hardly a reliable statistic in the entire work. There is no mention of concentration camps, or the existence of places like Auschwitz, Belzec, Chelmno, Majdanek, Sobibor and Treblinka—so Sanning did not have to explain what function these places could possibly have served. And there is no mention of the *Einsatzgruppen* death-squads that roamed the Soviet Union and Eastern Poland in 1941–42.

There was, however, a significant difference in Sanning's approach, compared to that of Butz. As noted, instead of ignoring evidence, Butz had worked to dismiss it. At least an objective researcher could realize that the evidence existed. This was not true of Sanning. His strategy, by contrast, was to conceal all evidence that disproved his thesis. Hence, one could say that Butz was an "honest" denier, as deniers go. With Sanning, though, one perceived that deniers were growing more sophisticated. I began to see this new sophistication in other deniers' works. The founding of the *Journal of Historical Review* in the early 1980s, devoted to promoting Holocaust denial and rehabilitating Nazi Germany, was a milestone in the evolution of the denier movement. It introduced a new generation of deniers, and provided an outlet for their views.

My original ambition, to perform a limited analysis of Sanning's data, turned into a five-year research project that comprehensively examined deniers' arguments. I had learned far more about them than could possibly be useful. After the 2000 publication of my book, *Holocaust Denial*,[1] I realized that while I knew a great deal about deniers, I knew much less about the Holocaust per se. The research one undertakes on Holocaust denial is quite different from that of most mainstream historians. One deals with topics such as population movements, cremation efficiency, the lethality of poison gas, and so on, rather than with the motivations of perpetrators and the suffering of victims. It is necessary instead to stick to cold, hard facts.

A major problem the researcher faces when dealing with denial is that there is not much of an outlet for research in this area. Only one paper has been published in an academic journal dealing with the technical claims of deniers.[2] Perhaps this is a good thing. When I began my research into this field, I feared that at some point in the future, denial might spread to the mainstream. In 2002, Fritjof Meyer, who had served as the editor of *Der Spiegel*—Germany's equivalent of *Time* Magazine—wrote an article for a prestigious journal, *Osteuropa*, claiming that the Auschwitz death toll was less than half the 1.1 million that is widely accepted among historians. Examining his article, I saw the same techniques used by Sanning and other deniers. Now, Meyer was not a denier. He acknowledged the existence of gas chambers at Auschwitz and their use to murder human beings *en masse*. But he employed the denier technique of ignoring critical source material that disproved his arguments. The editor of *Osteuropa* informed me that Meyer's article had not been peer-reviewed—something that would be immediately apparent to anyone familiar with the topic. My reply to Meyer appeared in the Summer 2004 issue of the *Journal of Genocide Research*.[3]

Thus it was that my interest in the Holocaust was sparked not by curiosity about the events themselves, but by my insatiable interest in the conspiracy theories of those who sought to deny them. The idea that a worldwide conspiracy of academics, politicians, and Jewish-controlled media could frame innocent Germans for crimes they never committed was preposterous, and therefore irresistible to a debunker like myself.

Notes

[1]   John C. Zimmernan, *Holocaust Denial: Demographics, Testimonies and Ideologies* (Lanham, MD: University Press of America, 2000).

[2]   Dan Keren, Jamie McCarthy, and Harry Mazal, "The Ruins of the Gas Chambers: A Forensic Examination of Crematoriums at Auschwitz I and Auschwitz-Birkenau," *Holocaust and Genocide Studies*, 18: 1 (Spring 2004), pp. 68–103. Many academic articles dealing with denial appear on the website of the Holocaust History Project at http://www/holocaust-history.org.

[3] John C. Zimmerman, "Fritjof Meyer and the Number of Auschwitz Victims: A Critical Analysis," *Journal of Genocide Research*, 6: 2 (2004), pp. 249–66. See also Fransciszek Piper, "Fritjof Meyer, 'Die Zahl der Opfer von Auschwitz. Neue Erkentnisse durch neue Archivfunde,'" at http://www.auschwitz.org.pl/html/eng/aktualnosci/news_big.php?id=563. This is the website of the Auschwitz State Museum; Dr. Piper is the museum's senior researcher, and a world-renowned authority on the death camp.

At Seventeen

Lee Ann Fujii

I was seventeen. The photos were much younger. They were part of a traveling Amnesty International exhibit at a small gallery in Pioneer Square—what was then the hip and edgy section of Seattle. I had read about the show in a tiny blurb in the Arts section, and found my way down to the small space. I was the only one there.

The images did not fail to impress. I had never seen so many skulls, let alone row upon row of cranial bone, neatly stacked. There were photos of other parts of the body (femurs, as I recall); but it was the skulls that left the biggest mark. The head, as one anthropologist has written, is the most symbolically powerful part of the human body, because it is what distinguishes us as individuals. The pictures of the skulls belied this assertion. In death, people looked exactly the same. The skulls were indistinguishable from one another. Men, women, young, old, rich, and poor—they all looked the same.

Despite the horror they recorded, the photos had a beauty to them. Their blown-up proportions intensified the colors and composition. Each photo was attractively framed. Someone had carefully arranged them on the bare brick walls, leaving ample space in between, like so many pieces of precious art. I stared at each one. I don't remember what I thought. I only remember that seeing the images drew me toward, not away from, the reality they depicted. This was long before I knew the name for this kind of fascination with the lurid: pornographic. Had I known, I still would have looked. I wanted to see. I wanted to know. And I wanted to understand.

I did not become a scholar of Cambodia after that experience. I finished college, moved to San Francisco, became an actor. My interest in genocide never waned, however. To satiate my desire to understand, I roved Bay Area bookstores, looking for readings on the topic. One day, I came across Iris Chang's book, *The Rape of Nanking*, which had just come out.[1] I knew nothing about this episode of World War Two. I picked up the book, and turned immediately to the pictures. The grainy black-and-white images with their spartan captions shocked me in a way the Amnesty photos had not.

These were not pictures of the dead, but of the living. Unlike the Amnesty skulls, these photos captured *people*. They were of victims and perpetrators in the moment just before, or just after, killing and torture. The images were so real they seemed *un*real.

At the time, my only outlet for expressing what I had seen was through poetry. I had been workshopping poems for years, writing on many different topics, from basketball to breakups, from jazz to Jesus. I had never written a genocide poem, but after seeing the photos in Iris Chang's book, I wrote this:

Pictures of Nanking

heads sit single file picture perfect faces uniform look they're missing
something hands and feet bayonets everywhere where they shouldn't
be poking into soft live flesh distinguishable in grains of black

and white the man crouches to cover himself a jab light stick until his
body gives the woman tied to a chair for ease of use she is not
a doll or thing for why would a thing slouch or give such a

look two soldiers featured front page they beat the odds 105
to 106 a contest of wills who can kill the most people in a single day a single
head propped like a coconut on sticks cigarette placed for effect a man this one

with torso supported by poles so the thrusts have something
to look forward to a beheading with sword such sport is war camaraderie laughs
all around prisoners buried alive dust to dust how do they breathe

themselves to sleep the woman is naked from the waist down standing
next to the man smiling the woman is naked from the waist
down bayonet where it shouldn't be

protruding from soft live picture
perfect thrust for ease of
sport is how do they

Many years later, I would return to school to study international politics. For my Master's thesis, I wrote about the Rwandan genocide, another case I knew little about when I began the project. I went on to earn a doctorate, and have continued with this line of research to the present.

Through it all, I could never understand why some images or descriptions of killings were more upsetting than others. Then it hit me one day. Pictures of the dead were shocking in the way that pictures of skin diseases in medical textbooks can be shocking. They shock because they represent "things" that we don't see every day. Pictures of the living, however, strike at a much deeper level, precisely because they remind us that genocide targets the living. To see evidence of their having lived—these people with faces, lips, shirts, and pants—and of having lived through the moments of terror that led up to death, was to turn the unfathomable into the imaginable. Suddenly their experiences became real. These were people who knew they were going to die in the most violent way, for the simple reason that they were alive. Finally, I began to understand.

Notes

[1] Iris Chang, *The Rape of Nanking: The Forgotten Holocaust of World War II* (New York: Penguin, 1998).

Beyond Good and Evil

Scott Laderman

I have used *The Killing Fields* in several Vietnam War classes since September 11, 2001. Released in 1984, the film garnered critical praise, won numerous awards, and helped to draw the attention of the American public to the horrific genocide in Cambodia under the Khmer Rouge. I use the film because it is engaging, terrifying, and brutally graphic; its depictions of the genocide under the Pol Pot regime remain the most disturbing, in my view, to have appeared in any Hollywood production.

Yet I also use the film for an altogether different, but equally important, reason. Put simply, *The Killing Fields* offers an important corrective to George W. Bush's ahistorical view of the American past—a view popularized not just by the former president but by countless commentators, politicians, and radio hosts since 2001. It was on September 12 of that year, the day after several hijacked planes crashed into the World Trade Center and the Pentagon, that President Bush pronounced the nation's commitment to what he characterized as a "monumental struggle of good versus evil."[1]

Countless historians cringed at this proclamation, recognizing that history was far too complex to sustain the notion of the United States as unequivocally "good," and that such theological distinctions were probably best left outside the discursive realm of international relations. When the president later insisted that "history has called America and our allies to action, and it is both our responsibility and our privilege to fight freedom's fight,"[2] he left many scholars who actually studied history—including decades of US involvement in Southeast Asia, Latin America, and the Middle East—aghast. Nevertheless, the notion of an unqualified American goodness took hold, and countless students who came of age in the early twenty-first century arrived in college and university classrooms convinced of its legitimacy. As an educator, I seek to disabuse them of such simplistic thinking. *The Killing Fields* has helped me to do so.

The film focuses on the experience during the 1970s of *New York Times* foreign correspondent Sydney Schanberg and, to a lesser extent, that of his

Cambodian colleague, Dith Pran. Schanberg is presented as a fierce critic of American policy in Cambodia. He challenges official explanations, condemns the *realpolitik* that guided American calculations, and laments the tragic consequences of America's actions, especially the harsh realities of Democratic Kampuchea with which Pran must contend after the international press corps flees the country in 1975. In this respect, the film's politics are unabashedly antiwar, offering a rejoinder—though one that is arguably quite mild—to the received wisdom of the United States as an historic force for "good."[3]

Yet what is perhaps most shocking to my students is what *The Killing Fields* does not directly address but graphically, if inadvertently, spotlights: American support for the Khmer Rouge after the Vietnamese overthrow of the Pol Pot regime in the late 1970s. Having witnessed a disturbing cinematic representation of Khmer Rouge atrocities, it seems incomprehensible to many students that the United States would ally itself with the genocidal forces that, together with America's earlier bombing campaign, had brutally ravaged Cambodia. Yet the general contours of this American support are by now reasonably well established. Alarmed that the ouster of the Pol Pot government heralded an expansion of Soviet power in Southeast Asia, Washington, as historian Kenton Clymer wrote, "secretly supported efforts to resuscitate and sustain" the "remaining military forces" of the Khmer Rouge by channeling food aid to their camps along the Thai border, voting in favor of their continued occupation of the Cambodian seat at the United Nations, and backing Chinese and Thai weapons transfers to their guerrilla army.[4] This was not a policy guided by human rights considerations. Rather, it subordinated moral principles to strategic concerns.

To be fair, the extent to which Washington collaborated with Pol Pot's insurgent movement to either topple or cripple the Vietnamese-installed government was not widely recognized when the film was made; it remains not fully known. But in using *The Killing Fields* as a primary document to introduce students to the broader American record in Southeast Asia, the unconscionable collaboration with *génocidaires* that has too often been a feature of American foreign policy helps to reveal the fraudulent cynicism of a political culture in which "we" are deemed unquestionably "good." In this respect, *The Killing Fields* serves a crucial dual purpose. First, it effectively illustrates the horrors inflicted upon the Cambodian people in the 1970s, humanizing a population that was for too many people in the United States a faceless and nameless abstraction, at least when it was on the receiving end of American bombs. Second, the film complicates—nay, demolishes—one of the more pernicious beliefs now rife in American political culture. It demands, even if inadvertently, a more nuanced perspective on US history than contemporary Manichean worldviews allow.

Notes

1   George W. Bush, "Remarks Following a Meeting With the National Security Team," September 12, 2001, *Weekly Compilation of Presidential Documents,* 37: 37 (September 17, 2001), p. 1302.

2   George W. Bush, "Address Before a Joint Session of the Congress on the State of the Union," January 29, 2002; *Weekly Compilation of Presidential Documents*, 38: 5 (February 4, 2002), p. 135.

3   While the film does condemn the American bombing of Cambodia prior to 1975, it regrettably sidesteps a fuller confrontation with the issue of war crimes and national guilt by suggesting that civilian deaths during this period were simply the result of "pilot error" and "computer malfunction." "They screwed up on the coordinates," explains an American embassy official in acknowledging the hundreds of casualties caused by the B–52 bombing of Neak Luong. US responsibility for the deaths of tens of thousands of Cambodian peasants, in other words, appears to have been an unfortunate mistake—not the inevitable and foreseeable consequence of the decision to massively carpet-bomb the Cambodian countryside. For a scholarly treatment of the American campaign, see Ben Kiernan, "The American Bombardment of Kampuchea, 1969–1973," *Vietnam Generation*, 1: 1 (Winter 1989), pp. 4–41

4   Kenton Clymer, "Jimmy Carter, Human Rights, and Cambodia," *Diplomatic History*, 27: 2 (April 2003), pp. 246–247.

Francis Ford Coppola (dir.), *Apocalypse Now* (1979)

The Horror

Stefanie Rixecker

Genocide is a pathology. It concerns the extermination of a people, for whatever reason, "in time of peace or in time of war" (as the UN Genocide Convention phrases it). To understand such a pathology is paradoxically both simple and impossible. How does one person comprehend the mass killing of other humans? Can someone who has not been an eyewitness do more than consume others' accounts, and so be a historical voyeur? Media representations of genocide all have a basic impact—they seem to reach out and sear one's soul. The film, *Apocalypse Now*, had that effect on me when it came out in 1979. Viewing it at the age of twelve was not sensible; neither was it forgettable.

Francis Ford Coppola's film was unusual in many ways. When it was first released (in 70mm format), it had no title or end credits. Instead, audience members received a theatrical-style sheet with details of the film and the cast. In the introduction to that handout, Francis Ford Coppola wrote: "The most important thing I wanted to do in the making of *Apocalypse Now* was to create a film experience that would give its audience a sense of the horror, the madness, the sensuousness, and the moral dilemma of the Vietnam War." Coppola achieved that, and more; he struck to the heart of all wars, and to the heart of darkness.

The cast of characters is not large. There is the Green Beret, Colonel Walter Kurtz, who has lost his mind and set up his own mini-state across the frontier in Cambodia. There are the US top brass in Vietnam who order Captain Willard to undertake a secret mission to eliminate Kurtz's command—to "terminate [him] with extreme prejudice." There is Willard himself, who must embark on a quest to find Kurtz, then witness his madness and use violence to end it.

Willard assembles a patrol-boat crew of young soldiers, none of whom wants to be in Vietnam, and seeks the help of Lieutenant-Colonel Kilgore's "air cavalry" to transport his boat to the mouth of the river. During this part of the journey, the attempt to hold on to home—for instance, by clinging to an obsession with surfing—is juxtaposed with what is supposedly necessary to preserve that home, namely the complete destruction of the enemy as embodied by a village population in Vietnam. The attack on the village has become one of the most iconic scenes in cinema. It begins with the heady roar of the choppers sweeping into the village, a tumult rendered more bizarre by Kilgore's hi-fi infusion of Wagner's "Flight of the Valkyries." After landing to "mop up," Kilgore orders his young soldiers to surf amidst continuing enemy fire. The whole military unit then settles into a beach party, their minds straining for home and working to jettison visions of the mayhem they have caused—all except Kilgore, who famously expounds on the terrible beauty of war:

> Do you smell that? Napalm, son. Nothing else in the world smells like that. I love the smell of napalm in the morning. You know, one time we had a hill bombed, for twelve hours. When it was all over I walked up. We didn't find one of 'em, not one stinkin' dink body. The smell, you know that gasoline smell, the whole hill. Smelled like . . . victory.

Hearing Kilgore's reverie on freshly scorched earth, in a village littered with corpses, one can only wonder how war could ever be "good" or "right." The explicit depiction of civilians being targeted and killed *en masse* means that the specter of genocide is never far away. If everyone is a target, what "rules of war" can exist? This is the purpose of the film: to interrogate the notion that wars can be fought without damage to one's core humanity.

As Willard and his motley crew travel upriver towards Kurtz's compound, Willard reads Kurtz's dossier, trying to understand how a man who was esteemed within the military hierarchy, who was groomed for a top job, who seemed "perfect . . . almost too perfect," could have descended into madness. As Willard works to enter the mind of the enemy he will soon have to face, the young soldiers on the boat confront fear, paranoia, rage, despair, and drug-induced unreality. They are simultaneously warriors and lost children.

Continuing on, Willard and the crew encounter a sampan carrying a Vietnamese family. The patrol-boat captain insists on boarding and searching the vessel. The soldiers' fear rises, and when a woman rushes to clutch something on the sampan, the soldiers lose control and unleash the full fury of their machine guns on the luckless civilians, killing everyone aboard. With the frenzied killing over, one soldier, "Chef," discerns what the woman had lunged to retrieve—not a weapon, but a puppy. An entire family has been murdered because of the soldiers' panic and the woman's affection for a small animal. When one learns that Coppola filmed this scene using South Vietnamese refugees who had escaped their country only two weeks before, the line between the real and the imaginary grows harder to discern.

Apocalypse Now climaxes at Kurtz's compound, where the petty despot is surrounded by Montagnard tribespeople, played by over 250 Ifugao aborigines from the Philippines, where the film was shot. The compound is strewn with dead bodies; it is so hideously realistic in its depravity that my twelve-year-old self tried to counter it by thinking, "It's only a film, it's only a film." But Marlon Brando's depiction of Kurtz allows for no such distancing. Like the Joseph Conrad novella on which *Apocalypse Now* is based, Brando's performance leads us into humankind's *Heart of Darkness*. Kurtz orders the crewman Chef to be murdered, and his severed head dropped in Willard's lap. He then imprisons Willard, before eventually releasing him to serve as an audience for his monologues. In one speech, Kurtz declares that in order to win a war,

> You have to have men who are moral and at the same time who are able to utilize their primordial instincts to kill without feeling, without passion, without judgment. *Without judgment.* Because it's judgment that defeats us.

Kurtz not only tells Willard that he has no right to judge him, he also gradually articulates "the horror"—that which cannot be spoken; the realm where violence and killing is so intense that a new word had to be coined for it: genocide. Trying to explain his passage to that realm, Kurtz declaims:

> It's impossible through words to describe what is necessary to those who do not know what horror means. . . . Horror has a face, and you must make a friend with horror. Horror and moral terror are your friends. If they are not, then they are enemies to be feared. They are truly enemies.

Simultaneously fascinated and repelled, Willard eventually decides to fulfil his mission. He assassinates Kurtz with a machete. The murder is interwoven with images of the sacrificial killing of a water buffalo—apparently a real ritual slaughter by the Ifugao people, which Coppola caught on film.

Kurtz's dying words, "The horror . . . the horror," dissolve into a scene of Willard walking through Kurtz's spartan inner sanctum. There, he comes across a manuscript in which Kurtz has scrawled a handwritten note: *"Drop the bomb; exterminate them all."* Here they are, the final words of Kurtz: war is genocide.

The film ends with Willard exiting Kurtz's compound. When he emerges to face a throng of Kurtz's Montagnard followers, he also confronts the temptation to replace Kurtz as their ruler. Instead, he drops his machete. The tribespeople let their own weapons fall in his wake. Willard leads the sole surviving soldier from the crew back to his boat, and darkness descends as the credits roll (in the 35mm version released later).

The darkness and pathos of *Apocalypse Now* are chilling. This seemingly fictional tale is rendered all too real by the Vietnam War setting. What many do not realize is that its literary source, Conrad's *Heart of Darkness*, is only barely fictional. As Conrad himself wrote, *"Heart of Darkness* is experience . . . pushed a little (and only very little) beyond the actual facts of the case."[1] The book is Conrad's highly personal account of the genocide that Belgium's King Leopold and his minions perpetrated in the Congo during the late 19th century, when the population was decimated to permit the territory to be exploited for its natural resources, especially rubber. So we come full circle. *Apocalypse Now* is about war, and about the US experience in Vietnam. But it is also about the corruption within humans that enables us to perpetrate genocide. And it speaks to the need to understand the darkness and light mingled in all of us.

Notes

[1]   Adam Hochschild, *King Leopold's Ghost: A Story of Greed, Terror and Heroism in Colonial Africa* (Boston, MA: Houghton Mifflin Co., 1998), p. 143.

Apocalypse Soon

Adam Jones

It starts at a peak that few bands have matched, with a squall of guitars and propulsive drumming. And it builds in intensity from there. Midnight Oil's anti-nuclear anthem "Hercules," four-and-a-half minutes of tightly-controlled mayhem, is a crowning moment in the band's career. Over a quarter-century of musical creativity, they rose from the fringes of the Sydney surfing scene to become national icons in Australia—such that lead singer Peter Garrett, a lawyer by training, is now Minister for the Environment, Heritage and the Arts in the present Labour government.

The four-song EP wittily titled *Species Deceases* was released at a crucial moment in the band's evolution. In 1984, they had followed up the groundbreaking *10–9–8–7–6–5–4–3–2–1* with the exciting but uneven *Red Sails in the Sunset*. Garrett, in particular, was becoming a voice of the anti-nuclear and environmental movements in Australia. *Species Deceases* was knocked off in five days at Paradise Studios in Darlinghurst to commemorate the fortieth anniversary of the atomic bombings of Hiroshima and Nagasaki, and to raise money for projects tied to the International Year of Youth. It was also a musical cleansing of the palate after the intricately produced *Red Sails*, returning the band to its roots in hard-driving surf-punk. This back-to-basics approach paved the way for the endeavor that would establish "the Oils" as international stars: a tour of Aboriginal communities in the Australian outback, which inspired their 1986 masterpiece, *Diesel and Dust*, with its enduring odes to Aboriginal dispossession and cultural integrity ("Beds Are Burning," "Warakurna," "The Dead Heart").

Species Deceases came out soon after I returned to Canada from a six-month stay in Australia, where I had fallen in love with the Oils and been mesmerized by the national TV broadcast of their surprise 1985 concert on Goat Island in Sydney harbor. (Excerpts from the show are available on a 1998 DVD release, *20,000 Watt R.S.L.: The Midnight Oil Collection*, which also includes a blazing live version of "Hercules" from 1989.) The months in Australia were formative in my evolution as a political activist. It

Peter Garrett, former lead singer of Midnight Oil, delivers his first speech
in the Australian House of Representatives as Labour MP for Kingsford Smith,
8 December 2004. Garrett is presently Australia's Minister of the Environment
(courtesy www.petergarrett.com.au).

was there that I first read, and corresponded with, Noam Chomsky; and the
blend of anti-imperialism and anti-nuclearism that pervaded Chomsky's
mid-eighties work was very much in the antipodean air as well. In particular,
Australians and New Zealanders were galvanized by French agents' terrorist
bombing of the Greenpeace ship *Rainbow Warrior* in Auckland harbor in

July 1985, which sank the vessel and killed photographer Fernando Pereira. The *Warrior* had been dispatched to monitor French nuclear tests that poisoned atolls, and their human populations, across the South Pacific. Opposition was also strong in Australia to the Reagan administration's nuclear brinksmanship and interventionist wars, which the Oils had pilloried in their hit song "US Forces" (1983).

These themes came together unforgettably on *Species Deceases*, and on "Hercules" in particular. But I wouldn't have known it for a while (the EP was not released in North America for several years) if my Australian girlfriend, Lindsey—well aware of my Oils fixation—hadn't generously bought the cassette and shipped it to me. I played it until the tape stretched, "Hercules" above all. The song has never left my playlist, and it never fails to tingle my spine.

It's hard to capture the power of "Hercules" in cold prose. The Oils could write songs of great gentleness and delicacy, and even at their most aggressive, as here, there is a strongly musical underpinning: a real swing to the playing, and a catchy chorus. The band's identity revolved around the contrast and complementarity of Garrett's staccato, incantatory vocal style, and the rich and subtle instrumentalists: Jim Moginie and Martin Rotsey, who mounted possibly the most cohesive twin-guitar attack in rock history; bassist Peter Gifford, later replaced by Dwayne "Bones" Hillman; and drummer Rob Hirst, whose playing was never more brilliantly tumultuous than on "Hercules." When I met the gregarious Hirst in person, backstage at a late-eighties club show in Hamburg, I asked him about his influences. He immediately mentioned Keith Moon, madcap drummer for The Who. Moon's stamp is all over "Hercules," with Hirst—who cowrote the music with Moginie—propelling the song forward with fills so pulverizing that on the half-dozen occasions I saw him play it live, arms flailing and sculpted biceps bulging, he always appeared to need oxygen after it was over.

After that ferocious opening blast, Hirst and the guitarists pull back, and Garrett steps to the fore with lyrics that are at once harsh and elegiac:

> My life is a valuable thing
> I want to keep it that way, I won't cry . . .

> We give the best we can give
> We won't forget, we can't forgive
> Keep us radioactive free

Strike a bell in Hiroshima Park
You know that we can't see in the dark
We try and we try and we try and we try and we tryyyyyy . . .

Lead vocals, backing harmonies, and crashing instruments coalesce in an apocalyptic chorus:

Why wait for the planes to come
When everybody's got us on the run?
South Pacific carry on (*Pow! Pow! Pow! Pow!*—Hirst's snare drum
                                                hammers the words home),
Here come the Hercules
Here come the submarines
Sinking South Pacific dreams . . .[1]

There's a false ending that merely serves as an entrée to Hirst's most spectacular fill yet. The percussion blends with a ruminative interweaving of guitar lines, and the song closes on a flanging, forward-looking B-major.

The nuclear threat was the first political issue that really consumed me—in 1983, with Pershing missiles about to be dispatched to Western Europe, the largest popular demonstrations in European history set to meet them, and everyone of my generation conscious that we could be vaporized in an omnicidal instant. Around the time *Species Deceases* was released, Vancouver artist Carl Chaplin was working on a chilling series of airbrush paintings which he dubbed "Art

Art Nuko, "Explo" (1986).
See Color Plate V

Nuko." One image was released as a poster to coincide with the city's Expo '86. Titled "Explo," it depicted central Vancouver at ground zero—with much of the familiar landscape disappearing in a thermonuclear fireball, and a mushroom cloud rising to the skies. The poster filled me with dread and a sense of paralysis, as seemingly insuperable threats will. What the Oils accomplished, in their great political anthems, was to counter such paralysis with the irresistible physicality of their music. Whirling about to "Hercules," singing along with that hair-raising chorus, air-drumming maniacally, was sheer catharsis. It left me spent—but also exhilarated, and ready to take on the world. There was no part of me that the song couldn't pick up and toss around like a rag doll; there was no challenge that couldn't be confronted.

Notes

[1] "Hercules" by Midnight Oil, copyright 1985 by Sony Music BMG. See also my 1986 profile of the Oils at http://adamjones.freeservers.com/midnight.htm.

Alejandro Agresti, *The Act in Question* (1993)

The Question of the Act

Lior Zylberman

Translated from the Spanish by Margaret Schroeder

In his documentary on American cinema, Martin Scorsese includes a rather unacademic category: "the director as smuggler."[1] It comprises directors who engage in social criticism and analyze uncomfortable issues in the hidden core of society by relating commonplace stories and themes that enable them to speak of the unspeakable.

The Act in Question, directed by Alejandro Agresti,[2] is in this tradition. Through allegory and hidden symbolism, Agresti transforms the film into a commentary on the Argentine *desaparecidos* (disappeared) and repression during the military dictatorship of 1976–83.

If the film can be singled out as unique in its genre, this is due not only to its formalism, but to the impact it has had on an issue that is the most controversial and difficult to address in Argentine cinema. Many films have attempted a serious treatment of the issue, but Agresti—and this is what lends the film its impact—succeeds through the use of an extended metaphor, the true motives of which are concealed. In short, he acts like a "smuggler." Filmed in his Dutch period, in exquisite black-and-white and in Spanish with Argentine actors, Agresti's film anticipated by ten years the growth of interest in memories, and the examination of the genocide perpetrated by Argentina's last military dictatorship.

What is the story of the film, and its premise? It tells of the rise and fall of the book thief Miguel Quiroga. The story begins when he steals a book on magic and the occult. The book contains the secret to performing "the act in question," which is nothing less than the secret of making anything disappear. Quiroga rises rapidly to fame as a magician. He travels around the world with his magic act, making all sorts of things—and later people—disappear. At the same time, his relationship with books takes a different form. He no longer enjoys reading, but has become obsessed with books. He cannot risk anyone coming across the book with the secret of his magic trick. He searches books and libraries wherever he goes, even to the point of burning them.[3] But it all comes to an end when Quiroga's agent obtains the rights to the original book. He republishes and markets it, betraying Quiroga and causing his downfall.

What does this tragicomedy have to do with the Argentine dictatorship? What is its hidden message? Several scenes throw light on this question. Upon joining the circus, Quiroga is already aware that his trick could be used to make human beings disappear. When Quiroga feels pressured by his boss, he threatens him, and the boss asks whether Quiroga will make *him* disappear.

In the scene where he demonstrates for the first time that he can make a human being—a boy—vanish, an offscreen narrator warns us that "making a human being disappear is no joke."[4] It is at this point, when he cannot bring the boy back from oblivion, that Quiroga's power becomes a weapon. Following the incident, Quiroga flees, and remains hidden for two years, writing. During this time, he develops a relationship with faith, with God, and with the church. From his hiding place, he writes a letter to God, boasting of his ability to make whatever he chooses disappear. He realizes that his power did not actually come from a book. Rather, it was God who gave him the formula, making him a "prophet of the antimaterialist message." He closes his letter by wondering: "Why does everything disappear so easily? Where does it go when it disappears?" Finally, he has understood that "disappearing is nothing; the great 'nuisance'[5] is oblivion."

In this scene, Agresti "smuggles in" the religious justification of the typical military discourse, while at the same time surreptitiously slipping in his own point of view. A later scene, in which Quiroga's agent gives a press conference, alludes to the standard protests of human rights organizations. Although the story takes place in the 1940s, one of the enraged crowd of journalists shouts the Dirty War slogan: "Bring them back alive!"

After two years, Quiroga finally learns how to make people appear. From this point, his worldwide fame begins to grow; he performs his trick before huge audiences. In Spain, Quiroga tells a journalist that his magic trick is nothing but a "process"—a clear allusion to the military dictatorship, which referred to itself as the National Reorganization *Process*. Winking at the camera, Quiroga concludes the interview by claiming that he is the only person in Argentina who can make people disappear . . . "at least for now."

Near the end of the film, Quiroga's agent shows him the book about to be published, which will cost Quiroga his career. Quiroga tells him how difficult it was to keep the secret all those years. At the end, the agent asks, "Do you really think that things disappear?" The image freezes, and the word "disappear" echoes away. The emphasis on the word reminds us that, sooner or later, that which is hidden will be revealed.

Why is this film so important to an examination of the Argentinean dictatorship? Through the use of allegory and double meaning, it manages implicitly to embed the theme of disappearances without referring to them directly. *The Act in Question* teaches us a number of things. At the time the film was made, Argentines were speaking of "reconciliation," of pardoning the generals, of forgetting the past. With his film, Agresti insightfully reminds his audience of the most tragic episode in Argentina's history. Using humor rather than horror, he invites the audience to reflect on "disappearances." The film leaves as indelible an impression as did the horrors of the genocidal dictatorship.

The paradox is that *The Act in Question* was never released commercially in Argentina. We were able to see it thanks to a clandestine edition: a copy of someone else's copy. In 1998, when we first viewed the film, Agresti was a virtually unknown director. He had returned to Argentina for the release of his latest film in Buenos Aires. For Argentine cinema students to see a film of Agresti's from his Dutch period was a real discovery, and a true odyssey. In recent years, it has also been broadcast on cable television, on a channel that plays old Argentine television shows and movies. It has not been released on video or DVD; to the general public, it is still effectively prohibited.

One thing is certain: a single viewing is not sufficient to grasp the film. The viewer needs to watch it several times to absorb its different layers. Argentine cinema has yet to produce the definitive film about the 1976–83 dictatorship, one capable of touching all of us. Meanwhile, *The Act in Question* remains hidden from its wider audience. Decoded, it could perhaps help us to understand better this era of violence. When I have shown the film in my classrooms, it has created an opportunity for students to understand the thematic power and potential of cinema. In the discussions that follow the film, I have realized how deep is the impact of *The Act in Question*, as its viewers begin to comprehend the power of narrative to transmit complex ideas.

Returning to Scorsese's metaphor of the "director as smuggler," Agresti's film itself remains hidden, marginalized. It carries out its task in the shadows, hoping someday to be discovered, studied, and properly appreciated.

Notes

1   Martin Scorsese and Michael Henry Wilson (dirs.), *A Personal Journey with Martin Scorsese Through American Movies* (British Film Institute, 1995).

2   Alejandro Agresti was born in 1961. His body of work is extensive; many of his films were made in the Netherlands, where he took up residence in the late 1980s. *The Act in Question*, a Dutch-Argentine co-production, was filmed in the Netherlands in 1993.

3   One of the characteristics of the Argentine dictatorships was their attacks on culture, often by censoring and burning books.

4   Agresti uses the mildly vulgar slang word, *"joda,"* "joke." The word can also mean a "bother," a "nuisance," an "annoyance."

5   Here the same word *"joda"* is used, which earlier signified "joke."

Jonathan Moller, Photographs from Guatemala

Photography, Memory, and Denial

Marcia Esparza

I first saw Jonathan Moller's photographs in 1998,[1] while I was working for the United Nations Truth Commission in the western highlands of El Quiché department in Guatemala. The Commission's research established that it was in El Quiché that the army and affiliated paramilitary forces committed genocide against Mayan communities. The Commission also established that racism was decisive in shaping the cruelty employed by the Guatemalan army in killing their defenseless victims. The human and material losses were enormous. My work with Mayan survivors and victims involved learning about their communities' history, and their dreams of a better future, for themselves and future generations. We relived the un-speakable traumas they suffered, through their testimonies of massacres, forced disappearances, torture, and rape. Throughout, they exhibited great compassion, and remarkably little desire for revenge.

As intense and devastating as these encounters were, Moller's photographs allowed me to grasp another important aspect. This was the mechanisms by which genocidal violence is reproduced: the collective denial that afflicts observers confronting the reality of mass atrocity. In this sense, these photos are a crucial resource in my efforts to raise consciousness about the slaughter of indigenous peoples in Guatemala and other Latin American countries. While the testimonies I witnessed and recorded for the Truth Commission elicited previously unheard victims' stories, these photos convey the immediacy of mass graves and human remains—the evidence of genocide.

In response to the lack of discussion in US academic circles about genocide committed against indigenous peoples and others in Latin America, in 2001 I founded the Historical Memory Project. It is housed at John Jay College of Criminal Justice in New York, where I teach. The Project promotes awareness of, and discussion about, the legacy of mass violence in the aftermath of the Cold War, together with the ways in which genocide severed—and continues to disrupt—communities' cohesion. It was through my work with memory and the aftermath of war that Moller's photographs came to be exhibited as part of the Project's first conference, held at the College in May 2001.

Since then, I have mounted exhibits of Jonathan Moller's photographs at conferences in Havana, Cuba (2002); Athens, Greece (2004); and Barcelona, Spain (2004). I have also shown them in classes I teach at John Jay College, to help break the silence surrounding violence against indigenous peoples. In all these forums, I have witnessed people's diverse responses to these powerful and disturbing images of human torment.

As a professor of sociology and human rights, I carry these photographs from one classroom to another. In my courses on the history of Latinos and Latinas in the United States, over 80 percent of students are of Latino/a background. Many are second, third, and fourth-generation Puerto Ricans, Dominicans, Salvadorans, and more recently Mexicans and Ecuadorians. Many students engage with the photographs, raising questions and offering insights. Some of the questions deal with their concerns about the roles played by the criminal justice system in holding perpetrators accountable, and the role of the United States in Guatemala's war. But other students remain seemingly unaffected, suggesting they feel some resistance to gaze upon the photographs that confront them. Why, I find myself wondering, aren't more young Latino/a students shaken when they look at images of indigenous peoples' remains tossed into secret graves?

I often show students the photographs that Moller captured of one exhumation in Guatemala—in Nebaj, El Quiché—to illustrate how racism can be lethal for disenfranchised peoples, and to demonstrate the work of forensic science in uncovering crimes committed against them. I display these images with the intention of raising consciousness about racism against minority groups, groups with little political and economic power in their countries.

I also show them in my classes on the international criminal justice system, and my class on "Terror and Truth in Contemporary Latin America." These classes seek to provide students with a basic understanding of human rights law and United Nations conventions, including the Convention on the Prevention and Punishment of Genocide (1948), as well as transitional justice mechanisms such as Truth Commissions. In these classes, some students are of Eastern European descent; some are African Americans; and others are Latinos/as, a more mixed group. All are in their early twenties.

Both in classes and at conferences, I have noticed that as I passed a photo to a student, he or she would glance at it quickly and put it aside—passing it to the next student, who did pretty much the same. Students' responses point to the difficulty we have in acknowledging the side of our humanity that we don't want to recognize: our ability to destroy each other in the name of religious and ideological beliefs, including those of ethnic superiority and inferiority.

What is it about the photographs that seems unbearable? Tattered remains; skeletons of men, women, children, and babies strewn haphazardly alongside cooking pots, plastic mugs and plates, straw mats and hats—the basic possessions of poor indigenous people. The photographs also show the machetes, ropes, and grenades used to quarter and maim people; occasionally death resulted from the removal of vital organs, such as the heart or eyes. Yet they also show Mayan widows and orphans, whose courage and organized resistance leads them to pursue justice, and the full truth of why and how violence came to their communities. If we cannot face the images of the atrocities these people endured, how can we embrace their campaigns of resistance?

Below is one of the first photographs I show in my presentations, which also serves as the logo for the Historical Memory Project. The simplicity of the picture contrasts with its profound meaning. The tiny photograph within the photograph seems heavy in this man's hard-working hands, expressing the weight of memory on genocide's survivors.

I also show this photograph, of an older Ixil woman holding the visual memory of her husband.

I often think that the scientific, forensic components of these pictures will rouse the interest of criminal justice students, especially since many of John Jay's students will graduate in forensic science and forensic psychology. The photographs are material evidence of the crimes they may explore as they become more involved in issues of genocide and mass violence. Often, though, Latino-American students feel too distant from the atrocities committed against the Maya of Guatemalan, or the Mapuches in Chile—even though they are themselves of Latino heritage.

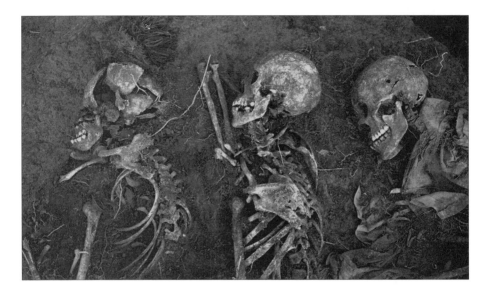

As I show these pictures, I think also about raising awareness of the devastating effects of war upon society, and on children in particular. In the picture below, a young girl becomes an active witness of the militarization and war destruction that will be felt for generations.

How to overcome denial? On the one hand, I believe in exposure to the realities of mass atrocity, as through the work of Jonathan Moller. Photographs can convey the immediacy of violence, but they should be photographs to which students can relate, for example those that derive from their countries of origin. If students could be exposed to their own history of ethnic violence, perhaps they could gradually connect with photographs of the Guatemalan genocide, of indigenous peoples. For example, if students of Colombian descent were exposed to photographs of the country's war, it might then become easier for them to relate to the Guatemalan genocide or other genocides in the region. However, in gauging students' reactions to war photography, I have not sought to evaluate whether students are second, third or fourth generation Hispanic-Americans or Latinos. This fact may be significant in influencing how close they feel to their ethnic heritage, or how distant from it.

Notes

[1]   For six months in 2000-2001, Moller was staff photographer on a Guatemalan forensic anthropology team documenting exhumations of clandestine cemeteries. Moller's photos have won numerous awards, and have been featured in LIFE 2001 *Album: The Year in Pictures*. I thank Jonathan Moller for granting his permission to present the photographs included in this essay. I am indebted to Pierre-Yves Linot for curating the photographs shown in this text, and for his insightful comments on overcoming denial.

Images of Impunity

Victoria Sanford

My two-year-old daughter Valentina and I are walking Jorge to his car. I am recounting Valentina's storytelling to dinner guests the night before—"Jorge lifts me up. He can hold me high." He laughs, and effortlessly raises her to touch a peeling poster two meters above on a lamppost and flowers high up in a tree, both far beyond my reach. He smiles and shakes his head as he says what I have already imagined he is thinking: "She reminds me . . . I remember Claudina Isabel. The memories are bittersweet. I remember her exploring the world and touching new things. And, then it is over. Only God knows why." He gives me the envelope, sealed and wrapped with tape.

I take the envelope to a graphic designer friend who has agreed to scan the contents. When I hand him the envelope, he looks at me quizzically and asks about the sizes of the images. "I haven't found the courage to look at them," I tell him. "I don't know their size. I don't even know if they are useful." Jorge has never looked at these images either. Inside the envelope are crime scene photos from Claudina's murder. They are the first official documentation of her death, and the only photos available for forensic analysis. I need scans of the images to send to forensic anthropologists who are willing to donate their time and skills to offer an expert opinion on the case.

In fact, Jorge has told me he can only look at photos of Claudina when he is with friends, or when he must do so for purposes of a public presentation. But he is referring to photos of his daughter when she was alive. Sometimes, he will ask me, "She was beautiful my little girl, wasn't she?" And the truth is that she was a stunning young woman. I have seen her only in photos and family videos. In these images, she fills whatever space she occupies with life. Her smile is lovely and inviting, not artificial. She is happy and engaged with the world.

Later, my friend brings the scans to my house. He tells me the photos are small. They should have been larger—we had expected eight-by-tens. He gives me the CDs to send to the experts who know how to interpret this material. I know she was killed. I know she was beaten. I believe she was raped. I know she took a bullet through her forehead. I know she had an injury over one of her eyes that looked like it came from a glass or a bottle or a pipe. I know her clothes were in disarray. Her belt was undone. Her sweater was on backwards, and her pants zipper was down. I know all this from reading incomplete forensic reports, from analyses of incomplete forensic reports, and from discussions with lawyers and others without forensic training who have tried to understand the case.

I prepare the packages to send to the forensic anthropologists—one in New York and one in England. I receive a call from Jorge, and we discuss the meeting we will have tomorrow. I tell him the scans are completed. We agree he will retrieve the originals when we meet, in order to return them to their source. He comments: "It is tempting to look at them, no?"

After we finish talking, I summon my courage. The adrenaline runs through my arms to my stomach, making me feel a little nauseous. I open the envelope.

The first photos are taken from a distance. She is lying in the gutter of a trash-strewn street, half her body on the sidewalk. Someone has covered her with a white sheet. Who did this? Her tormentor? The person who called the fire department?

I turn the page. Now the sheet is removed. Her body is twisted. It looks like she is turning to say something—which she is not, because her face is in the gutter. Now I see the open belt and zipper. I see the curve of her waist, her smooth milky skin, her bare belly with a little ring in the navel. Her body still looks alive. I see her sandals and her pink sweater.

I turn the page. Her head has been moved. Her face is covered with a splash of blood from the bullet that entered her forehead. I can't look at the photo long enough to consider the injury to her eye. I notice her mouth is swollen, her lip is split, a dark thread of blood runs from her nose.

I turn the page. I see a close-up of the bullet entry wound. I see gloved hands with blood-covered fingers, manipulating her head to measure the exit wound with a ruler. Her hair is matted with blood. I am unable to look at the measurement. The blood-covered fingers are too much.

Then her sweater is off and spread out in the street. What? I check the first photos again. She was wearing the sweater. Why did they remove it in the street? Now they have taken it off, and left her near-naked upper body lying directly on the bloody pavement. I notice there is not much blood around her, given how bloody her head and face looked. But then I stop looking, overwhelmed. I feel like calling Jorge to ask if he knew they removed her sweater at the crime scene. I stop myself: he doesn't need to imagine this at night. With profound sadness, I realize that, sooner or later, Jorge will have to look at these photos. And I cry.

The last time Claudina communicated with her parents was around 11:45 p.m. on August 12, 2005. Around two in the morning on August 13, her parents were awoken by Zully Moreno, the mother of Claudina's boyfriend, Pedro Samayoa Moreno, who went to their home to inform them that Claudina was in grave danger. Señora Moreno claimed that Claudina called to tell her she was walking home; the call was cut short by Claudina's screams for help. Claudina's parents immediately went to search for their daughter—first at the house where Claudina had attended a party in the nearby neighborhood of Colonia Panorama. Finding no leads there, they began to search the neighborhoods between the party's location and their home.

Desperate, they attempted to file a report at the local police station at around 3 a.m. on August 13. The police, however, refused to take a report, or even listen to the worried parents. They suggested that Claudina had run off with her boyfriend, and that in any case they would not accept any report until Claudina had officially been missing for twenty-four hours. It wasn't until 8:30 in the morning that the police formally received Claudina's parents and classified Claudina Isabel Velasquez Paiz as missing. This was three-and-a-half hours after her lifeless body had been found on Tenth Avenue in Colonia Roosevelt in Zona 11—a neighborhood not more than two miles from the party where she was last seen by friends. But she was not identified until later that day.

In fact, Claudina's case, like those of more than five hundred murdered women in Guatemala in 2005, was dismissed from the moment her cadaver was found. As one official acknowledged: "The crime scene was not developed as it should have been, because of prejudices about the social origin and status of the victim. She was classified as a person whose death did not merit investigation." The first police on the scene determined that Claudina's murder was "not worthy" of investigation, because she had a ring in her belly button and was wearing sandals. In the view of the police, this meant she was a gang member or a prostitute.

But Claudina was not a gang member or a prostitute. She was a 19-year-old law student. She was gregarious and well-liked by her peers. More than five hundred people attended her memorial service. Her father, Jorge Velasquez, did not understand what was happening when several armed officers, in police vests and uniforms, arrived at the memorial service and demanded access to his daughter's cadaver. When Jorge refused, the police threatened to arrest him and his wife. The coffin was removed from the memorial service, and placed in a private room where the police unceremoniously took fingerprints and nail-clippings from the body. When they were finished collecting this material for forensic analysis, they handed Jorge a paper bag, explaining that it contained the clothing Claudina had been wearing at the time she was murdered. "Most families bury the clothing in the coffin," the police explained. In murder cases elsewhere around the world, the clothing would have been part of the evidence held on file.

Jorge remembers, "Claudina Isabel was so loved by everyone. We were so moved by her friends, students from the university. They spoke so highly of her. They loved her. It was oddly satisfying. There is a kind of adrenaline that sets in, and moves you through disaster. The memorial service, in spite of the police disrupting everything, was profoundly moving. We were nearly euphoric. Then, when it was over and we got home, reality knocked us down. The euphoria evaporated. She was gone. She was dead. We would never see her again." And he breaks down in sobs.

I have learned all this, and more, about the case of Claudina Isabel from a 2006 BBC documentary, *Killer's Paradise*, about the feminicide in Guatemala.[1] I have amassed still further details by following the case for the past three years, accompanying Jorge in his quest for justice, and conducting my own research on feminicide, social cleansing, and impunity in Guatemala. A friend and human rights leader first showed me the film in the summer of 2006. He also showed me daily clippings of images of murdered young women from Guatemalan newspapers. I viewed a video montage he had made of television news footage showing the cadavers of young men and women being thrown into the back of police trucks.

This is Guatemala in the twenty-first century, some twenty-five years after the genocide that took the lives of 200,000 Guatemalans. This is impunity unchecked, even after peace accords and a truth commission. This is what happens when the intellectual authors of genocide and their agents of death are not brought to justice. Feminicide and social cleansing are nurtured by, and provide cover for, the same structures of terror that generated genocide.

Notes

[1]   Claudina's murder was just one of the 518 registered murders of women in Guatemala in 2005, and is part of what many now refer to as the Guatemalan feminicide—that is, the killing of more than 2,380 women in the last five years.

A Reluctant Genocide Activist

Thomas J. Nagy

Rather than by exposure to great art, or by witnessing a genocide in progress, I was forced into the role of a genocide activist by a mountain of abstract, technical papers. The key report, a genocide planning document, was buried in a stack of 40,000 declassified papers posted on the Internet by the US Intelligence "community" on the orders of President Clinton. Despite the daunting redactions running through it, I became haunted by an eleven-page Defense Intelligence Agency report, dated January 1991 and blandly titled, "Iraq Water Treatment Vulnerabilities."

In contrast to the stark orders to execute civilians directly, the DIA laid out a more sophisticated, indirect, and public-relations conscious plan: to use economic sanctions to destroy Iraq's ability to produce safe drinking water, and obliterate the entire water system of Iraq in six months.

The document's author or authors precisely identified the tiny range of materials, denial of which to Iraq would be sufficient to generate a tsunami of agony and death among the country's most vulnerable citizens. In addition, the DIA identified the possible countermeasures Iraq might take to supply safe drinking water to its population, and showed why, if the DIA plan were enacted, none could prevent permanent disaster:

> [. . .] 3. FAILING TO SECURE SUPPLIES WILL RESULT IN A SHORTAGE OF PURE DRINKING WATER FOR MUCH OF THE POPULATION. THIS COULD LEAD TO INCREASED INCIDENCES, IF NOT EPIDEMICS, OF DISEASE AND TO CERTAIN PURE-WATER-DEPENDENT INDUSTRIES BECOMING INCAPACITATED, INCLUDING PETRO CHEMICALS, FERTILIZERS, PETROLEUM REFINING, ELECTRONICS, PHARMACEUTICALS, FOOD PRO-CESSING, TEXTILES, CONCRETE CONSTRUCTION, AND THERMAL POWERPLANTS.

4. IRAQ'S OVERALL WATER TREATMENT CAPABILITY WILL SUFFER A SLOW DECLINE, RATHER THAN A PRECIPITOUS HALT, AS DWINDLING SUPPLIES AND CANNIBALIZED PARTS ARE CONCENTRATED AT HIGHER PRIORITY LOCATIONS. ALTHOUGH IRAQ IS ALREADY EXPERIENCING A LOSS OF WATERTREATMENT CAPABILITY, IT PROBABLY WILL TAKE AT LEAST SIX MONTHS (TO JUNE 1991) BEFORE THE SYSTEM IS FULLY DEGRADED.

5. UNLESS WATER TREATMENT SUPPLIES ARE EXEMPTED FROM THE UN SANCTIONS FOR HUMANITARIAN REASONS, NO ADEQUATE SOLUTION EXISTS FOR IRAQ'S WATER PURIFICATION DILEMMA, SINCE NO SUITABLE ALTERNATIVES, INCLUDING LOOTING SUPPLIES FROM KUWAIT, SUFFICIENTLY MEET IRAQI NEEDS.[1]

Additional searching through the DIA's partially declassified documents indicated involvement by its Armed Forces Medical Intelligence Agency, along with predictions about who was most likely to die from this indirect but lethal biological warfare (infants and very young children), and what they would die of (water-borne diseases) if "Iraq Water Treatment Vulnerabilities" were implemented. Further investigation turned up reports documenting implementation of the plan, and the accuracy of the predictions of deaths by age and cause.

What did the unclassified ("open source") literature show? Shortly after America's first invasion of Iraq in 1991, the findings of the Harvard Study Group were published in America's premier medical journal, the *New England Journal of Medicine*. We also have a range of reports by UN study groups, and stories filed by individual journalists. These disparate sources converged on a conclusion that, contrary to international law, the US had destroyed electrical plants and water treatment and distribution infrastructure needed to supply safe drinking water to the people of Iraq. They also agreed that a massive, immediate aid effort was required to prevent an even greater humanitarian disaster than had already occurred. The Harvard Study Group estimated approximately 50,000 Iraq civilians dead as of 1991, and warned of a spread of epidemic disease without immediate rehabilitation of the water system.

For the record, the US government categorically, but without detail or plausible rationale, denied the conclusions of the medical community and UN study groups. Nevertheless, Rep. Henry B. Gonzalez (D-TX) introduced legislation calling for an immediate suspension of the blockade of Iraq, to halt the carnage wreaked by the effects of military bombing.[2] The bombing had served as a multiplier for what one Iraqi teenager referred to as a "silent nuclear bomb that drops into every home and is slowly destroying not only the children but the whole Iraqi nation."[3] It was a reminder that worldwide, structural violence has killed and continues to kill more people than wars and genocides—though it is rarely recognized or studied as genocidal.

What if a single medical doctor at the DIA's Armed Forces Intelligence Agency, or an officer at the DIA, had followed in the tradition of Pentagon Papers whistleblower Daniel Ellsberg, and leaked the truth: that the government's leaders and flacks alike were lying, and the medical journals and other authorities were telling the truth? Would Iraq, the US, and the world have been spared another war, another genocide, the erosion of the US Constitution, the "legalization" of torture, the agony of infants and soldiers alike?

A possible reason why no Ellsberg arose from the DIA's medical or military ranks is that those in the know experienced the same dread I did about condemning my own government's crimes. The first time I prepared a speech for delivery in Canada about America's slow genocide against the Iraqi people, I developed chest pains, and spent an unpleasant half-day being evaluated for a possible coronary. Did any government employees with knowledge of the planned elimination of Iraq's most vulnerable—children under the age of five—likewise experience physical pain when they thought about alerting the media? Or were they all, like Nazi planner Adolf Eichmann, merely "doing their jobs"? Will they share Eichmann's bewilderment if they are ever tried for conspiracy to commit genocide, for complicity in the commission of genocide, for participation in genocide?

Rather than release its own evidence, which corroborated the Harvard Study Group and UN reports, the DIA classified its genocide planning document, as well as its reports on the results of its implementation by sanctions, which blocked the materials needed to rehabilitate Iraq's water system after the 1990–91 Gulf War. The supine US media, acting in the tradition of Turkey and Germany during the extermination of "lesser" peoples, dismissed reports of massive die-offs, and rejected any notion of genocide (except to blame the massive mortality on the Iraqi government that US power had pulverized).

By the time the DIA papers were even partially declassified, the government had had more than half a decade to sell its lie to a compliant Congress and public, which wrapped itself in the same willed ignorance. Only a few years later, a new US administration was laying the groundwork for yet another invasion of Iraq. The casualties of the 2003 conquest continue to mount. They are now nearing one million; these hecatombs of dead join one million other Iraqis, disproportionately the youngest and most vulnerable, who perished in the silent genocide of the 1990s.

This essay is dedicated to the memory of Margaret Hassan, the head of water rehabilitation for Care International in Iraq, who gave her life to halt the slaughter of hundreds of thousands of Iraqi infants and children under the US sanctions regime.

Notes

[1]   To view the articles cited, Google "Iraq Water Treatment Vulnerabilities," "Henry B. Gonzalez A Call to Lift Economic Sanctions Against Iraq," "Mairead Corrigan Maguire Act to Save the Children of Iraq," and "Iraq Water Nagy."

[2]   See Henry B. Gonzalez, "A Call to Lift Economic Sanctions Against Iraq," House of Representatives, 24 June 1991, http://www.fas.org/spp/starwars/congress/1991/h910624g.htm.

[3]   Quoted in Mairead Corrigan Maguire, "Act to Save the Children of Iraq," Nuclear Age Peace Foundation, August 2002, http://www.wagingpeace.org/articles/2002/08/00_maguire_children.htm.

Children's Photos

Daniel H. Magilow

In its December 2006 obituary of Saddam Hussein, The *New York Times* published a photograph of the executed Iraqi dictator as a boy. The image reminded me of a similar photo that helped spark my own interest in Holocaust and genocide studies, and in visual representations of atrocity.

The *Times* image, taken from an identity card or a passport, is faded, blurry, and torn. Saddam is not yet old enough to have grown his trademark moustache and bushy eyebrows. He stares icily into the camera. The corners of his eyes sag slightly. His eyes tempt me to view the photograph as betraying a deep-set fear or anxiety about something infinitely more significant than posing for an identity photo. But I doubt this was the case.

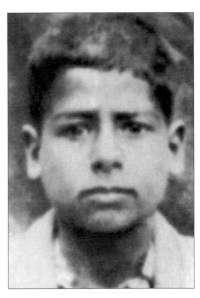

Saddam Hussein

The image of Saddam reminded me of another photograph that I first saw when I was, coincidentally, probably around Saddam's age in the boyhood photo. This second image appeared in a coffee-table book about National Socialism, buried in the shelves of my parents' library. Blurry, overexposed, and surrounded by a halo, Adolf Hitler appears not as a raving orator, supreme leader, or even the avuncular subject of a propaganda portrait. Rather, he is a frightened baby who stares helplessly and ambivalently at the camera. Like the pubescent Saddam, the baby Hitler also lacks the moustache that would become his face's primary signature. Yet his thick, unsightly mop of black hair, unevenly cut, already justifies his later decision to create his physiognomy's second distinct trait: his comb-over to the left.

Others have surely looked at these images and wrestled with a thought experiment: "If you could go back in time to when Hitler (or Saddam, Stalin,

Pol Pot, Idi Amin, or Slobodan Milosevic) was still a child, and kill him, would you do it?" Such ethical questions, and the disjointed temporality of the photographs that provoke them, are in a sense just pointless parlor games. They arise from the photograph's staging of, to cite Roland Barthes, the future anterior tense—the arrested moment that contains a sense of "this will have been." Yet each photograph of the dictator-as-child points to the problems and challenges that one confronts in researching and teaching about the Holocaust and genocide.

Adolf Hitler

Because these images depict evil men before they formed their legacies, before they gave posterity reasons to judge them harshly, they are potent reminders of the fallacies that Marc André Berstein terms "foreshadowing" and "backshadowing." These tendencies to view and judge the past on the basis of *post facto* knowledge present a constant obstacle to responsible interpretation. The child-dictator photographs powerfully demonstrate the need to evaluate cultural materials in their historical specificity, and at the same time to historicize and critically examine the positions from which we interpret them. In light of the radical disparity between these photographs' quotidian appearance and the mass murder they evoke, they demonstrate—as much as any text—the need for interpretive nuance.

When I behold images of dictators as "impressionable" youths, I find myself wondering whether educators can make a difference in young people's lives. Certainly, the photos serve as painful reminders of the consequences of not doing so. These photographs encourage me to view students as unformed subjects whose development must be steered and modulated at critical moments. Still, somehow that mission seems ridiculous. Does it really make sense to ask whether, among my baseball-cap and flip-flop-wearing students, there sits a potential future dictator? Are Holocaust and genocide studies a bulwark against future catastrophe, or is this just a self-serving fantasy that leavens the tedium of grading and undergraduate indifference? The truth probably lies somewhere in the broad territory in between.

Ultimately, for all of the horror they evoke, these images are still family photographs. I almost shudder to think that when I open my own photo albums, I will see photographs just like them. But perhaps that realization can serve as an important reminder. For all of its incomprehensible horrors, genocide remains a cruel fact of human existence. And many of its perpetrators were once photogenic babies, and adolescents yet unformed.

Ron Haviv, photo from "Blood and Honey"

The Face of Genocide

Donna-Lee Frieze

This desecrated photograph can be understood through the concept of the Other, Emmanuel Levinas's distinctive contribution to western philosophy. Always capitalized, the Other is not an alien other who disturbs my freedom, or who is an extension of me. Rather, the Other is the one who is treated ethically, who commands my highest respect, and is apprehended in all their Otherness. This is Levinas's explanation of the ethical: to face the Other is to humanize the Other, and to regard the person as a unique being. Levinas's thesis is, in short, the antithesis of the genocidal perpetrators' assessment of faceless others.

A defaced photograph that was found by a Bosnian family when they returned to their home in a suburb of Sarajevo (Ron Haviv/VII).
See Color Plate VI

These concepts of Other and other are captured in this untitled photograph, tinged with red hues that implicitly signal a bloodbath. Taken sometime before 1996, it is reproduced in Ron Haviv's stunning photographic essay, *Blood and Honey: A Balkan War Journal*. The caption explains how the photograph was all that remained when this Bosnian family returned to their home in Sarajevo: even the windowpanes had been looted.

The photograph is partly located in the realm of everyday life. Someone, perhaps a friend or passer-by, has carefully composed a photograph of a respectably-dressed family standing on the banks of a river in a serene rural setting. Once, this was a normal—or perhaps special—family shot. Now, however, its ordinary aspects have been rendered manifestly dystopic: the faces of the family members have been erased by deliberate scratches.

Why are the faces erased? Why not the entire person? According to Levinas, to define someone by the corporeality of their facial features alone is akin to dehumanization; but the metaphor of *de*facing here is too powerful to overlook. The perpetrators likely do not know the family, but have gazed into a representation of the family's being, and dehumanized it by defacing it. Indeed, the erasure of the faces is a deliberate and empirical act of dehumanization, puncturing the uniqueness of the individual's life. The photograph resonates with the "intent to destroy": to literally and metaphorically "wipe out." It points to acts of genocide extending beyond mass murder, to the destruction of the victim group's identity. In this respect, the photograph is distinct from the conventional images of terror, ethnic cleansing, and genocide.

The obliteration of the face does not only erase facial features: it eliminates facial expressions, which provide clues to the Otherness of the family. I may not be concerned with the color of the family members' eyes or hair, but I am curious about their feelings. Essential to the dehumanization strategies of genocide is the prohibition of a victim's self-expression—unless, of course, it takes the form of terror. However, on closer examination, it is apparent that the perpetrators have not entirely erased the faces. The man's forehead is slightly exposed, as are the chins of the boy and the woman. If it were not for the sketched impalement stakes, it is possible that the expression on the woman's mouth, too, could be discerned.

Impalement as an element of genocide is critically assessed by Linda Boose in her dense and graphic article titled "Crossing the River Drina," in which this photograph is also reproduced. By obliterating the expressions, and (super)imposing stakes on and through the bodies, the perpetrators symbolically attempt to replace a familiar, personal memory with a communal, violent one. The scratches on the faces are strikingly neat, and the impalement stakes too are linear and carefully etched. Both acts of defacing raise questions of memory: both its ownership and its attempted destruction. Erasing heads conveys a desire to remove, or at least control, the victims' thoughts, including their memory acts.

The face of genocide is faceless. This is not because the face of the victimized Other is mysterious or unknowable, but because the ethical relationship between one and the Other is cancelled. The photograph serves as a powerful reminder that, regardless of whether mass killing is involved, genocide always attempts to erase the ethical proximity of Others, seeking to render them faceless and dehumanized.

The Death of "King" Habyarimana

Christopher C. Taylor

One cold October morning in a University of Chicago eatery, while I was drinking tea and watching CNN on the TV monitor, an anthropology graduate student spied me and yelled: "Chris, did you catch what they said earlier about Rwanda?"

"No, I just got here," I replied.

"A force from Uganda just invaded northern Rwanda."

"Must be a Tutsi refugee group."

"Could be," he said, as he took his muffin and coffee and rapidly exited the crowded shop.

That was 1990, and my thoughts raced quickly to my Rwandan friends, Victor and Monique, who had visited me in Chicago in the spring of that year. I worried about their safety. I had talked to Victor a few times about the political situation in Rwanda during his visit, and he told me that things were getting unstable. No-one in Rwanda seemed to think that President Juvénal Habyarimana would be in power much longer, yet no one had any idea about who or what might replace him.

In the months that followed, I learned more about the invasion mounted by Ugandan Army deserters, a group calling itself the Rwandan Patriotic Front (RPF) composed of the sons and daughters of Rwandan refugees who had fled to Uganda in the 1960s and '70s. Many were Tutsi, as they had been the dominant, though minority, group up until 1962; but some RPF supporters were Hutu tired of Habyarimana and his party, the MRND (National Revolutionary Movement for Development), which had been in power since 1973. In subsequent months, I followed what news I could get concerning the progress of the conflict, the various truces that never seemed to hold for very long, and what was happening to my friends there.

In 1993, I had the opportunity to return to Rwanda as an employee of Family Health International, under contract to USAID. I arrived in

Cartoon captioned "Habyarimana will die in March 1994," published in Kangura, December 1993. The dialogue reads: *Kagame*: "On to Kigali." *Habyarimana:* "I've done everything I could to make you Tutsi happy." *Kagame:* "Who asked you?" (Reprinted from Christopher C. Taylor, *Sacrifice as Terror: The Rwandan Genocide of 1994* [Oxford: Berghahn Books, 1999], p. 49).

October 1993, at a moment when most of my Rwandan acquaintances, including Victor and Monique, were still relatively optimistic that the Arusha accords between the RPF and the government of Rwanda would hold, and a coalition government composed of elements from the RPF, the MRND, and several other parties would be in place before the end of 1993.

After my arrival, I witnessed a slow but steady decline in Rwanda's political situation. By January 1994, after a few attempts to install a "broad-based government of transition" had failed, I was beginning to lose hope that a peaceful solution to the political crisis would be found. This sentiment was echoed by most of my Rwandan friends. In sharp contrast, officers at USAID were telling me they still had hope that cooler heads would prevail. One Friday afternoon, I was at my friend Victor's office. His partner, Viateur, said to me: "Chris, if you don't believe things are taking a bad turn here, take a look at this." It was a cartoon printed in the December 1993 issue of *Kangura*, one of the more infamous of Kigali's cheap street magazines. *Kangura* was noted for its support of Hutu extremism.

The cartoon was indeed shocking. It showed Rwandan Patriotic Front leader, Paul Kagame, riding on President Habyarimana's shoulders. Kagame is ordering Habyarimana: "On to Kigali!" while Habyarimana protests, "I've done everything I could to make you Tutsi happy." Kagame replies, "Who asked you?"

That such a cartoon would appear in a Hutu extremist forum, one that up to that point had not been critical of Habyarimana, was a surprise. After all, the political party that Habyarimana had founded, the MRND, was clearly anti-RPF, and its youth wing, the Interahamwe, was notorious for its persecution of Rwandan Tutsi and Hutu moderates. This could only mean that a split was developing among Rwanda's Hutu, with some of them now seeing Habyarimana as a traitor to the cause of Hutu domination. But even more chilling was the caption beneath the cartoon: "Tutsi ingratitude: Habyarimana will die in March 1994." This was the first hint I had seen in Rwanda's media that Habyarimana might be assassinated. Months later, however, I would learn that this had not been the first prediction concerning Habyarimana. About a year before this cartoon appeared in *Kangura*, a Rwandan diviner named Magayane was quoted in the popular media as saying: "Habyarimana will be Rwanda's last Hutu king."

Much of the shock of the image derived from the "cult of personality" that had long surrounded Habyarimana. During my first period of fieldwork in Rwanda in 1983, I quickly became aware of this idolizing of the Rwandan President, reflecting the autocratic nature of his regime. At the time Habyarimana was running for reelection, and MRND party faithful were busy campaigning. There was little chance of his losing the election, though, as he was running unopposed, and the MRND, whose base of support was largely in Habyarimana's home region of northwestern Rwanda, was the country's only authorized political party. Yet the results of the 1983 elections strained the credulity even of sympathetic observers. Habyarimana asked for, and was reported to have won, an incredible 99 percent of the vote. For many years afterward, it seemed as if he and the MRND would hold power forever.

Rwanda was a closely controlled military dictatorship in the 1980s, with very few people daring to raise a dissenting voice. Rarely did one hear a critical word muttered against Habyarimana or the army's tight control over the Rwandan state. Those who did oppose the president, in word or deed, usually found themselves in prison, or "disappeared" under mysterious circumstances. In the capital, Kigali, the presence of army and gendarmerie was pervasive.

Commitment to the government was obligatory. On Saturday mornings, people everywhere in Rwanda would meet to participate in *umuganda*, community service. They would arrive with their shovels and hoes and work at filling in the ruts of dirt roads gouged out by the rain; they would repair municipal buildings; they would plant trees. There was very little complaining. Even most Rwandan Tutsi during the 1980s supported Habyarimana, recalling the violence of 1973 when Habyarimana and the army had intervened to stop the killings of Tutsi, then wrested power from President Grégoire Kayibanda and his Hutu supporters from central Rwanda.

At the time, adulation of Habyarimana was *de rigueur* for Rwandans; it was a key element in the enactment of their *civitas*. Virtually everyone had a portrait of the President hanging on a wall at home, and many wore the MRND party button on their shirt or blouse. On Wednesday afternoons, groups met to practice chants and skits in celebration of the Rwandan state: its overthrow of the Tutsi monarchy, and its rejection of the *ubuhake* cattle contract signifying Hutu servitude to Tutsi. Most of all, they celebrated the figure of the President. Termed *animation*, it did not seem to bother anyone that these Wednesday afternoon get-togethers took people away from their jobs and did nothing to augment the country's gross domestic product. Even songs on the radio seemed to equate Rwanda, its beauty, and its relative prosperity with the person of its President.

To see President Habyarimana now depicted in *Kangura* as a stooge of the RPF rebels was astonishing. And as it turned out, the cartoon's prediction of precisely when Habyarimana would die was not far off the mark. On April 6, 1994, his private plane was shot down near Kigali airport by a shoulder-held surface-to-air missile, killing all aboard, including the President of Burundi. Although Habyarimana's government had been at war for almost four years with the Rwandan Patriotic Front, this event transformed the dynamics of the hostilities from tit-for-tat, attack-reprisal violence into a genocide.

No-one has ever claimed responsibility for killing the president, but the two most credible hypotheses place the responsibility either on Hutu extremist members among Habyarimana's own followers or on members of the RPF. Although I lean in the direction of the Hutu extremist explanation, there is certainly merit to the RPF thesis as well. The death of President Habyarimana could have served the political interests of both groupings. Many of the extremists, for example, were convinced that Habyarimana had grown "soft" on Tutsi, and needed to be replaced by someone more unequivocally "*génocidaire*"—the message conveyed in the cartoon. As for the RPF, they saw the president as an obstructionist who was delaying full implementation of the Arusha Accords and thus preventing their participation in a coalition government.

Although different narratives at the level of political causality can be invoked to explain Habyarimana's assassination, I believe that there was less diversity at the level of the Rwandan cultural imaginary. The prediction by the diviner Magayane, and the cartoon in *Kangura*, showed that something was happening at the cultural level that would produce real-world consequences. In my opinion, the way was being prepared in Rwanda's print media for a revival of "king sacrifice," a tradition with deep roots in the country. At first we see hints of this in the opposition press, with its portrayal of the president as a tyrannical or incompetent "king" that the country would do well to be rid of. Later, even Hutu extremists began to desert him, as the cartoon shows.[1]

For me, the consequences of Habyarimana's assassination would be intensely personal. Shortly after I returned home from work on April 6, I received a phone call from an American Embassy employee whose responsibilities included warning other expatriates when things in Kigali grew dangerous. He warned me to stay at home that evening, as there had been reports that the President's plane had been shot at. He didn't know what kind of weapon had been used, whether the plane had landed safely, or whether anyone had been harmed. I assured him that I and my fiancée, Esperance, who was Tutsi, would not venture out—but also that I thought the reports were just the usual byproducts of the Rwandan rumor mill.

My nonchalance was short-lived. That evening, we retired around 11 o'clock, but were awakened at about 3 in the morning by the sounds of war. Machine-gun fire, small arms, and occasional explosions of grenades, mortars, and artillery rent the air, making further sleep impossible. Later, our house guardian came to the window with his portable radio. On it, they announced the death of President Habyarimana, and advised everyone to stay at home. As ordnance seemed to be exploding close by, we invited the guardian to come inside. He declined. "I've been through this kind of thing before in Zaire, and it usually doesn't last too long," he said. "But I am afraid for my family."

As for the conflict not lasting very long, our house guardian was correct in relative terms. By mid-July, the Rwandan Patriotic Front had taken the city of Kigali, and the remnants of Rwandan government forces had been pushed into Zaire. As for my fiancée and me, we had been evacuated by land convoy to Bujumbura, Burundi, on April 9, 1994. Although we had been forced to leave behind most of our possessions, we and the rest of the American expatriate community had escaped Rwanda with our lives.

But during the three days we spent in Bujumbura, each day brought additional bad news. One evening I learned that my closest friend, Victor, a Tutsi, had been killed, but his wife and children had managed to escape. There was no doubt that a genocide against Tutsi was underway in Rwanda. Only Bill Clinton, French President François Mitterrand, and UN Secretary-General Boutros Boutros-Ghali seemed blind or insensitive to that fact. In the hundred days that it took the RPF to capture the reins of power in Rwanda and stop the genocide, somewhere between 800,000 and one million Rwandan Tutsi were killed. They included my wife's parents and many of our closest friends. Reprisal violence against Hutu after the genocide also claimed tens of thousands of lives.

Today, Rwanda is still living with the consequences of the 1994 genocide. To secure a measure of justice for its victims without exacting the kind of vengeance that would pave the way for the next genocide, locally organized *gacaca* tribunals are underway. It is possible that many perpetrators will get off lightly as a result of *gacaca*; but this is a necessary cost in the country's progress to national reconciliation. It is this process that I plan to study closely in the years to come.

Notes

[1]   For samples of the author's published research on "king sacrifice" in Rwanda, see Christopher C. Taylor, "Fluids and Fractals in Rwanda: Order and Chaos," in Mark Mosko and Fred H. Damon, eds., *Anthropology and Chaos Theory* (Oxford: Berghahn Books, 2005), pp. 136–65; Taylor, "Kings or Presidents? War and the State in Pre- and Post-Genocidal Rwanda," in Bruce Kapferer, ed., *State, Sovereignty, War: Civil Violence in Emerging Global Realities* (Oxford: Berghahn Books, 2004), pp. 125–136; Taylor, "Kings and Chaos in Rwanda: On the Order of Disorder," *Anthropos*, 98 (February 2003), pp. 41–58.

Greg Barker (dir.), *Ghosts of Rwanda* (2004)

A Simple Task

Shayna C. Parekh

First knowledge, then compassion.

I cannot remember the first time I heard this teaching derived from the *Daśavaikālika Sūtra*, a text of the 2600-year-old Jain dharma.[1] I must have been a teenager, because I immediately rebelled, questioning its wisdom and humanity. Surely, nothing could precede compassion.

But the teaching was persistent. Every day, as I walked through Sproul Plaza on the campus of the University of California, Berkeley, I collected flyers and information like a woman possessed. Who was speaking tonight? What documentary was being screened? Where was that group meeting to organize its protest? My four years at Berkeley were nothing short of the living expression of the Jain teaching. I began to meet individuals from around the world, and to appreciate their perspectives: Judge Juan Guzmán of Chile, who presided over the Pinochet trial; Dr. Andreas Toupadakis, a former nuclear scientist turned peace activist; torture survivors of the Falun Gong in China; victims of political persecution in Guatemala. As I was exposed to these issues, something began to stir. First knowledge, then compassion.

Enter Professor Kateri Carmola. Whoever said, "Take the professor, not the class," might have been referring to this young, fiercely committed educator. Professor Carmola crafted her Political Ethics course like a show-don't-tell kindergarten teacher. Learning must be eclectic; all senses must be engaged; we must gain a multifaceted understanding of the problems of the world before we can ever hope to help. We listened, riveted, to the tales of one of the last remaining World War Two Danish resistance fighters; drew original connections between Kant and Shakespeare's Henry VIII; were introduced to the world of theatre with a field trip to see Tony Kushner's *Angels in America*. But our most indelible exposure to knowledge was Professor Carmola's presentation of *Ghosts of Rwanda*, a PBS documentary on the genocide.

The Rwandan genocide had started and ended in 1994, the summer before I entered high school. But watching *Ghosts of Rwanda* in that fecund Berkeley cocoon seven years later, I was effectively learning about the genocide for the first time. Some of the documentary's haunting interviews and footage are as vivid to me today as the day I first viewed them: the bloated bodies carried downstream, some getting caught in inlets; video filmed surreptitiously from above and some distance away, of a human being crumbling under the force of a machete; the dark, deep voice narrating: "By the evening of April 10th, Carl Wilkens was the only American left in Rwanda."

Two other parts of the documentary remain particularly potent. The first is a darkly comedic, bumbling exchange, a lesson in the power of words.

> *CHRISTINE SHELLY, State Department Spokeswoman:* We have every reason to believe that acts of genocide have occurred.
> *REPORTER:* How many acts of genocide does it take to make genocide?
> *CHRISTINE SHELLY:* Allen, that's just not a question that I'm in a position to answer.
> *REPORTER:* Is it true that the—that you have specific guidance not to use the word "genocide" in isolation, but always to preface it with this—with these words "acts of"?
> *CHRISTINE SHELLY:* I have guidance which—which—to which I—which I try to use as best as I can. I'm not—I have—there are formulations that we are using that we are trying to be consistent in our use of. I don't have an absolute categorical prescription against something, but I have the definitions, I have a phraseology which—

A second memorable scene had arguably the most lasting impact. The narrator solemnly describes President Clinton's visit to Rwanda on a pilgrimage of contrition, nearly four years after the genocide. The voice notes that Clinton never left the airport, and the engines of Air Force One never shut down, as the president issued his reflections to a few invited survivors:

> I have come today to pay the respects of my nation to all who suffered and all who perished in the Rwandan genocide. It may seem strange to you here, especially the many of you who lost members of your family, but all over the world, there were people like me, sitting in offices day after day after day, who did not fully appreciate the depth and the speed with which you were being engulfed by this unimaginable terror.

Clinton's admission, repackaged, had been reflected thousands of years earlier. While Clinton was surely exposed to the facts of the genocide, if his statements are to be believed, mere exposure to facts alone does not true knowledge make. What he was missing was a full appreciation, a true under-standing of the "unimaginable terror." Clinton had lacked *this* knowledge; his response lacked compassion. The narrator's parting words would remain a lasting companion: "In his remarks, which were billed as an apology, Clinton did say the US had made mistakes, but he never actually said he was sorry. He met with survivors and heard the human consequences of his policy of non-intervention, and then he left."[2]

The images and lessons of *Ghosts of Rwanda* inspired within me a desire to glean a more detailed understanding of the Rwandan genocide and other atrocities long past. Guided by that ancient teaching, I became particularly interested in the stories of those directly affected, and in sharing those experiences with others. Intrigued by critiques concerning the lack of information, I analyzed media coverage of the Rwandan genocide in the US and the UK as a graduate student at the London School of Economics. I traveled with classmates to Oswiecim, Poland, to witness firsthand the camps of Auschwitz and Birkenau, sharing my photos and video footage with friends and family. I frequented the Imperial War Museum in London, absorbing details about East Timor, Bosnia, and Cambodia, and attended talks and presentations commemorating the anniversary of the Rwandan genocide.

But something was missing.

Almost overnight, I planned a trip to Kigali, Rwanda. It had become clear that to obtain true understanding and knowledge, I had to transcend reading, discussion, and detached analysis. The time had come for immersion with the people and the places that had taken center stage in this genocide.

So, in June 2004—exactly ten years after the genocide, and three years after watching *Ghosts of Rwanda*—I landed in Rwanda. With no agenda except the desire to learn, a friend and I set out with our video camera and notepad. It was only a matter of hours before we came upon the Ntarama church, outside downtown Kigali.

I had done my research before I entered. I knew, in general terms, about the massacre that had taken place there. Most of the guidebooks had warned of blood-stained walls and pock-marked floors. I walked past the tin, dust-covered sign that announced that 5,000 souls had perished in Ntarama, and gave a foreigner's smile to the church's caretaker who opened the rusted gates. Unsure of how to proceed in such a hallowed site, and unable to speak Kinyarwanda, I made my way to the door of the church, guidebooks in hand.

But the guidebooks were out of date.

There, an arm's reach away, on thirty wooden shelves, were the skulls of over 200 victims that had perished in the church that day. One special shelf had been set aside for children. One of the skulls had a dagger protruding.

I was soon joined inside by the others, including our taxi driver, Jean Baptiste, and Dansile, the caretaker. Shocked and desperate for information, Jean Baptiste questioned Dansile—What did she know of the genocide?

Dansile was a survivor. Urged by community leaders to seek sanctuary at Ntarama, Dansile and her family had gathered inside the church, along with hundreds of others. Soon after, they were barricaded inside and massacred. First came the grenades; then men armed with machetes flooded into the church. Lying between two pews, Dansile quickly covered herself with the corpses of those around her. As the killing crews made their way through the church, climbing over the bodies of hundreds of men, women, and children, they passed over Dansile. Before leaving, they placed the decapitated head of one victim on the church's altar. Hours later, in the cover of night, Dansile emerged from the dead; two of her children had been murdered.

We returned daily to collect each piece of Dansile's story, and to answer, however meekly, her questions—Did you know what was happening to us? What did you know? Those who knew—why didn't they help? Why did they just leave? Ultimately, Dansile was conjuring those ancient words: Who had the knowledge, and where was the compassion?

To encounter a survivor's story firsthand is a privilege, and one that carries with it a responsibility to bear witness. When I returned to the States, I shared Dansile's story through talks and articles. As the years passed, and "Never again" capitulated to genocide in Darfur, the obligation I feel to share knowledge and engender compassion has taken on new forms. While a student at Yale Law School, I sought to pass on Professor Carmola's gift of eclectic learning. I co-founded an organization to raise awareness of Darfur, and thousands of students and community members have since been exposed to films—including *Ghosts of Rwanda*—photo exhibits, meetings with world-renowned figures like the ex-child soldier Ishmael Beah, informational panels with Carl Wilkens among others, and intimate classroom discussions.

In the end, if our goal is a world with less suffering, then we must continue to seek, understand, and share the stories of the world's people.

The task, after all, is a simple and unchanging one: First knowledge, then compassion.

Notes

[1] The words of the Sūtra read: *padhamam nānam tao dayā*. Read in context, the teaching may also be understood as *first wisdom, then conduct.*

[2] The particular knowledge that President Clinton acquired through the very experience of interacting with the genocide survivors arguably contributed to his later declaration that he felt a "lifetime responsibility" toward the Rwandan people. Indeed, accepting the prestigious TED Prize in 2007, President Clinton stated that his one wish to change the world was to build a world class health care system in Rwanda, a model for rural health care that could be replicated worldwide. President Clinton has since gone on to establish several health and education projects in Rwanda through the William J. Clinton Foundation. See President Clinton's TED Prize speech at http://www.ted.com/index.php/talks/bill_clinton_on_rebuilding_rwanda.html. President Clinton quoted in Kate Snow, "Bill Clinton's Lifetime Responsibility to Rwanda," ABC News, August 2, 2008, http://abcnews.go.com/GMA/story?id=5502860&page=1

Pablo Picasso, "Guernica" (1937)
Dachau Concentration Camp Memorial Site
Genocide Memorial Centre, Kigali

"Never Again," Again

David J. Simon

My happy middle-class, middle-American childhood afforded mercifully few opportunities to contemplate either evil in the world or the suffering it inflicts. Although my generally progressive primary education was imbued with ethics, morality, and social justice, it wasn't until a family trip to Europe, at age ten, that—via two memorials to suffering—the evil men can do made a searing impression on my psyche.

The first memorial was a work of art: Picasso's enlarged replica of his own "Guernica", which hangs at the Musée Unterlinden in Colmar, France. The dual images of anguished women at the right and left sides of the canvas evoked a deeper pain than I had ever before conceptualized. Yet Picasso's painting also struck me as a weighty retort to the Nazi and fascist airstrikes on the village of Guernica. It was a work of art so powerful that it had laid bare the moral bankruptcy of the perpetrators of the act that inspired it; a work that imbued the victims with a dignity greater than the pain it so evocatively depicted; and one that bookmarked a particularly dark episode of the human experience for future reference and learning.

"The Way Forward,"
by Ardyn Halter.
See Color Plate VII

The second memorial was the Dachau concentration camp outside Munich. The plain evidence of evil, visible in everything from the barracks to the gas chambers, would surely have provoked in me a volatile combination of depression and cognitive dissonance, were it not for the concrete wall located near the camp's exit, emblazoned with the words "Never Again" in five languages. Naively, perhaps—though not inappropriately for a ten-year old—I took great solace in this display. (In fact, I'm fairly certain I bought a postcard of the inscription.) Likewise, I found inspiration in the message on the nearby memorial wall: "May the example of those who were exterminated here between 1933–1945 because they resisted Nazism help to unite the living for the defence of peace and freedom and in respect for their fellow men." As with "Guernica," I took from my tour an injunction to oppose human evil. Indeed, I felt it as part of my own humanity to acknowledge that responsibility—even if it was one which I never envisioned having to act upon. (Curiously, in my own mind, I even conflated the image of "Guernica" with the sculpture above the "Never Again" wall—substituting it for the equally evocative Nandor Glid sculpture that in fact perches menacingly over the inscription.)

The second part of the story is partly one of failure. In 1994, I was a graduate student in political science with a focus on African politics. In April of that year, my peers and professors were in a cautiously celebratory mood as the South African elections—for which some of my mentors had made significant personal sacrifices—approached. The news of mass violence in Rwanda was unsettling, but not, in a literal sense, alarming. I took no steps to challenge American policy, or even to seek a deeper knowledge about the conflict and the country, beyond the stories emanating from National Public Radio and the McNeill-Lehrer News Hour.

A few years later, as I began to teach my own classes, the Rwandan genocide came to be central to how I taught African politics. In it I found examples of identity politics, neopatrimonialism, disengagement (in the form of exile), aid dependency, and global marginality—all wrapped up in an event whose importance as a human tragedy and an embodiment of post-cold war international relations was increasingly evident.

I do not mean to imply that the genocide was merely a subject of pedagogical convenience. In particular, two depictions of the Western (non-)response to the genocide struck a deep personal chord, driving home the fact that through my own inaction in 1994, I had broken the promise I made to myself as a ten-year-old. The first was the scene, depicted in the PBS *Frontline* documentary *The Triumph of Evil* (and later in *Ghosts of Rwanda*), of French and Belgian soldiers evacuating expatriate staff from the Kigali psychiatric hospital surrounded by *interahamwe* militia. A crowd of Rwandans pleads with the gaggle of journalists who have accompanied the soldiers—at first with smiles and charm, then with anguish and despera-tion as they realize there is no plan to evacuate Rwandans, and they are witnessing the passing of their own death sentences. As the camera turned to other journalists, clicking their cameras and scribbling notes, it struck me that these were the eyes with which I had also viewed the events. As victims of the genocide stared plaintively back, those eyes looked and turned away, even when the consequences of doing so could hardly have been more apparent.

The second "image" is a short passage in Samantha Power's *A Problem from Hell*, in which U.S. representative Maxine Waters owns up to her own ignorance about the genocide. "I don't know whether the Hutus or Tutsis were correct," says Waters, "I couldn't tell anybody what I thought they should do."[1] Waters's Los Angeles congressional district adjoins the one in which I had resided (and voted) at the time of the genocide. Perhaps it wouldn't have amounted to much, but I wondered whether a graduate student in African politics, one who had once promised himself to stare down injustice and stand up to evil, might have had some role to play in raising consciousness about an African genocide among the politicians in my own city—the same politicians who would later claim ignorance as their excuse for avoiding meaningful action.

And so Rwanda has become central to my intellectual agenda. By way of a coda, a visit to the genocide memorial in Kigali in 2005 provided two more points of reference for the way I relate to the genocide. The first, the words of a man named Apollon Kabahizi, is an admonition: "When they said 'never again' after the Holocaust, was it meant for some people and not for others?" The second I choose to take as a personal rededication. It reads, in part: ". . . We also remember the events of the past; it is a terrible and unavoidable warning for our future if we do not take active steps to avoid it [happening] all over again."

Notes

[1]   Waters quoted in Samantha Power, *"A Problem from Hell": America and the Age of Genocide* (New York: Harper Perennial, 2002), p. 376.

Dili on Fire

Russell Schimmer

A goal of remote sensing is to positively identify an object for which a unique reflective characteristic can be isolated. How we love things to be unique! Of course, there is always something that competes for our attention. What we analysts dream about are the types of anomalies that, if not perfect, are easily recognizable and discernible amidst the ruckus of irritating "noise"—oh, it's just a patch of snow in the highlands, or a hovering puffy cumulus cloud. Sometimes, only one electromagnetic band is required to achieve this goal; sometimes you need multiple bands in an array of algorithms and logarithms, and crazy applications that keep your mind spinning at night; and sometimes you rely on comparisons with already well-documented examples.

A September 8, 1999
Landsat 7 ETM+ satellite scene
showing Dili burning.
See Color Plate VIII

Now, let us say you are able to isolate the object and find its unique signature. Not only can you recognize it, you can make it plain to others: a positively identified object. In this case, we are speaking of a moment frozen in space and time, establishing irrefutable evidence of a catastrophic human event.

On September 8, 1999, Dili—the capital of the small territory of East Timor at the eastern end of the Indonesian archipelago—was on fire. The billowing smoke was captured on a satellite image from space, some 440 miles above the Earth's surface. But a mere representation of the event is not enough. What does it mean? How does one explain it? What else do we have to help us understand and document the event?

That day, September 8, marked an important moment in the aftermath of the referendum held on East Timorese independence, and the violent transition from Indonesian rule to political autonomy. On September 11, a United Nations Security Council delegation visited East Timor, and reported evidence of mass atrocities, extensive looting, and wanton destruction. The Timorese capital had been burned and ransacked. There was no sign of normal life. The streets were almost completely deserted, apart from stray pigs and dogs. Entire neighborhoods had been reduced to ashes—whole rows of houses burned down.[1] Over the preceding days, eyewitnesses had claimed that anti-independence militants were setting houses alight with gas-spraying hoses. Other witnesses claimed that it was not only difficult to see for all the smoke, but even to breathe.[2] Over 120,000 people had been made refugees; and according to the army's own statistics, only 27 militiamen had been arrested by the force of 15,000 Indonesian soldiers present on the ground.[3] We know all this because a handful of international news agencies and human rights organizations bravely monitored and reported developments.

Almost exactly two years later, the terrorist attack known as "9/11" shocked the world and changed the lives of millions. Hideous in its conception, almost unimaginable in the scale of its execution, it was a massive media event that changed how the world perceived acts of premeditated violence. Moving and still images, live and in color, captured, recorded, and disseminated the event, through thousands of lenses, from thousands of angles, providing a testimony of human suffering. Even from space, the fires at the World Trade Center were far from unnoticed. Possibly not since the invention of still photography and its use to document the American Civil War have media so shaped the public's views of organized violence and atrocity.[4]

What did New York City have in 2001 that Dili in 1999 did not? Does an attempt to answer this question help to explain why the parties most responsible for the destruction in Dili feared no reprisals for their actions? They counted on the fact that the world would hardly notice. Conversely, the architects of 9/11 recognized and incorporated the power of the media as an indispensable component of their vision and scheme. They chose highly visible symbols of the West, targets that would incite world attention and reaction.

Two approaches: the one surreptitious; the other diabolically brazen. But should we judge and measure peoples' and groups' propensity for violence, and the extent of its infliction on others, based on the media attention accorded to it? Is the meaning of violence a function of the interest and awareness level of the audience? Is it thus, at heart, capricious?

In fact, world attention was not as capricious as the perpetrators of the destruction in Timor had expected. Times had changed. The Kosovo crisis was still fresh in people's memories; an international popular movement took to the streets, demanding suppression of the Indonesian-backed militias' campaign of violence. The United Nations briefly considered abandoning the field, but its remaining staff rebelled, and the resolve of the international community stiffened. The US brought sustained pressure to bear on its Indonesian client, and Australia offered to lead an armed intervention force to quell the violence and pave the way for Timorese statehood. Today, the satellite photographs of Dili, and the moment they captured, serve as evidence of the scale of the violence unleashed on the Timorese population—but also of the moment when publics and political leaders were spurred to effective action.

After my remote sensing research with East Timor, I began to wonder what more the environment could tell us by these means. What clues were frozen in time, and over time? What truths could not be hidden or forgotten because they were captured on a picture, on many pictures—the big picture? It became increasingly apparent that there were multiple standard remote-sensing applications that could be used to look back in time at places in the world that had experienced genocide.

In Guatemala, I examined changes in the Ixil Triangle between 1979 and 1986. An entire landscape had altered dramatically in seven years. Small towns had grown into barren nodes denuded of vegetation. In the mountains, where dense forests once had been, more than half the canopy had disappeared. What had happened? In the satellite images, it appeared as though a lava flow had spread across the environment, emanating from a volcano with no conscience or guilt for the destruction it had caused. However, this transformation was not caused by a natural process that man could not control, and had to accept. The "volcano" was in fact successive military regimes, notably under President Efrain Ríos Montt's scorched-earth campaign against the population of the Mayan highlands. In the late 1970s and early 1980s, the military systematically destroyed nearly all the rural settlements surrounding major municipalities in the Ixil Triangle, forcibly centralizing the population. Thousands of in-habitants were able to escape to Mexico. During those same seven years, the images showed villages suddenly emerging on the Mexican side of the border where no sign of habitation had previously existed; roads were carved through a terrain that had been fluid and undisturbed; and the landscape was vividly transformed—a direct result of the eruption of violence taking place just one hundred miles away. It was all plain to see, in a couple of satellite pictures!

Since working on these and similar projects,[5] I have continued to explore and attempt to understand how genocide causes environmental transformation and destruction. Mass atrocities do much more than just scar the landscape, whether rural or urban. They disrupt the ability to extract resources essential to sustaining local and national economies; often, environmental transformation is used as a weapon of genocide, or to obliterate the evidence. In terms of future conflict prevention and resolution, what relevant aspects of an environment—its resources and potential, its inalienable value to populations, the demographic and cultural patterns that arise within it—are key to understanding the environmental aspects of genocide and mass atrocity?

Students and scholars of genocide often begin their inquiries by asking a simple question: *Why?* Attention to the satellite evidence can help to answer that question. It can do so not only by showing physical proof of the violence, but in some cases by pointing to environmental and human-induced stresses that contribute to genocidal outbreaks. More than just capturing a moment in time, spaceborne remote sensing can monitor a location over time. It can potentially detect indications or warnings of increased social tensions due to overpopulation and resource competition, as well as document the systematic marginalization of certain ethnic and cultural groups. However, it can only accomplish these tasks in cooperation with other approaches to genocide studies, as one research tool among others in this interdisciplinary field.

Notes

[1]   Matt Frei, "Dili: Back to Year Zero," BBC World: Asia-Pacific, September 11, 1999.

[2]   Matt Frei, "Eyewitnesses Speak of Timor Devastation," BBC World: Asia-Pacific, September 10, 1999.

[3]   Frei, "Dili: Back to Year Zero."

[4]   See David Friend, *Watching the World Change: The Stories behind the Images of 9/11* (New York: Farrar, Straus & Giroux, 2006).

[5]   For the Guatemala images, and others from the research project, see the website of the Yale Genocide Studies Program at http://www.yale.edu/gsp/maps/.

Tony Kaye (dir.), *American History X* (1998)

Different Kinds of People

Wendy C. Hamblet

When we witness, from our comfortable armchairs, the violence and turmoil that engulf much of the world, we are apt to think of ourselves not as the beneficiaries of history's imperialisms or as shareholders in present-day neocolonialism, but as morally more worthy than the "violent people" who struggle in those conflicts. This purifying projection is paralleled by the way we view marginal people in our homeland: the underclasses of criminals and the homeless. We convince ourselves that these people live their existentially impoverished lives as a result of their moral and indeed substantive impoverishment. They are just "different kinds of people," who act and decide differently than we law-abiding, decent types.

As a scholar and philosopher of violence, I teach Ethics and Morality classes in universities that cater to the middle class of the wealthy West. Such classes generally seek to expose and challenge the ethical assumptions in students' everyday lives. I find from the outset that this task is monumental, since my students' minds are made up in advance about the moral superiority of their lifeworld. How can I challenge these "children of privilege" to examine themselves and their self-affirming assumptions? My students have never known oppression or war, hunger or want of any kind. American wealth grants them not only material prosperity, but the security of ignorance, and a reassuring distance from battles over the world's dwindling resources. America's superpower status, purchased by a military budget running to hundreds of billions of dollars, also buys it the power, if not the right, to play "policeman" for the rest of the world. The young people in my classes believe without a qualm that their country's military presence in 170 nations attests to its innate *moral* superiority.

To teach ethics, I must first upset my students' overly simplistic, unambiguous, and radically polarized worldview. One method I employ is to show them *American History X*. The film, written by David McKenna and directed by Tony Kaye, is appalling from the outset, riddled with shocking language and scandalously violent images. The language and imagery are so

American History X (courtesy Warner Bros. Entertainment Inc.).

alien to the students' (mostly white and middle-class) home lives that, at first, it affirms their sense of themselves as different from "violent people." However, as the film unfolds, they become drawn into its reality, and the distance quickly evaporates.

American History X immerses its audience in the home life of a family that we would readily label "poor white trash." The son, Derek (Edward Norton), head shaved and body branded with swastikas, is the charismatic leader of a local white supremacist group, rallying his motley xenophobic crew into committing racially motivated hate crimes against nonwhite locals. At the outset, Derek's rage and hatred are foreign to the enlightened sensibilities of most viewers, who accordingly find him easy to despise and marginalize. As we learn more about the family's history, though, we begin to realize that its members once had much in common with our own "normal" lives. The father, a fireman, is even a somewhat heroic figure; the children are raised by both parents in a middle-class house in a middle-class neighborhood. They look much like the family next door. But when the father dies fighting a house fire and saving his black American neighbors, the family falls apart. The eldest son, Derek, and his young brother Danny (Edward Furlong), are torn apart by sorrow and rage. They mourn their father's death by targeting the "others" they hold responsible for their loss. Through their racist mentoring by a local supremacist leader, their hate is extended to all their nonwhite neighbors.

The father's death has multiple effects on the family's well-being. It falls into poverty. The mother tries to make a new life for herself and her children, but Derek's rage divides the family, and drives away her prospects for new love and new hope. In her despondency, the mother ultimately falls desperately ill and becomes bedridden; the children are left to raise themselves. Derek's rage spirals out of control. Eventually, in the scene depicted on the previous page, he attacks and brutally murders a black man, an act that sends him to prison.

The racist rage that Derek vents on the screen seems, at first, altogether foreign to an audience accustomed to judging people individually, by their acts and not by their color. Somewhere during the course of the movie, however, we find ourselves drawn into Derek's reality. His neighborhood really *is* beastly; his neighbors *are* dangerous and despicable. As our ears adjust to the guttural language, and our sensibilities to the family's degradation, Derek's violence grows more comprehensible: it seems necessary to his survival. Derek, the swastika-bearing, out-of-control white supremacist, begins to appear more like a hero than a villain. He intelligently explains his mission to his fellow supremacists: he is fighting to save his neighborhood from violent gangs, and to save America from infiltration by morally decadent subgroups. Idealistic and bright, articulate about the cruel realities of his racially fragmented world, Derek gives voice to our refusal to accept the realities of decaying inner-city life in America. We begin to acknowledge that violence is necessary to survival in this diverse world.

Then the black man's murder occurs. The scene, so brutal and horrifying, pulls the audience up short in its identification with the violent hero. We feel shocked to catch ourselves momentarily blinded and in sympathy with this violent young man. But the identification is soon resumed: Derek is dragged off to prison, where the harsh realities of that strange machismo-driven world redouble the need for violence. He sees that only in allying himself with people like him—violent white supremacists—will he have a chance of surviving prison. But, as prison realities unfold, facile identifications are blurred. Derek learns that his new white buddies are not like him at all, not idealistic revolutionaries; they are pragmatic, drug-dealing thugs, crossing even racial lines to make a quick buck.

When Derek questions the status quo, then distances himself from their less idealistic practices, he is targeted by his racial in-group, and brutally raped and beaten in the prison showers. This dramatic event shakes Derek's (and the audience's) sense of reality to its foundations. He begins to realize that bad people come in all colors. His friendship with a black prisoner on laundry detail completes the demolition of the racist worldview, for Derek as well as the film's audience. Derek leaves prison a better man for his experience, and returns to find his family in shambles. Now he must try to repair the damage his hatred, violence, and desertion have caused to his loved ones.

The most challenging of his obligations concerns his younger brother, Danny. Danny has spent the time of Derek's incarceration in another kind of prison, under the spell of the same supremacist group that Derek helped to gain a foothold in their community. Derek finds Danny as he himself once had been—shaven-headed and tattooed, cruising the streets for victims to feed his bigoted hatred. Derek shares with his young brother the prison experiences that overturned his worldview demonizing racial differences. Danny seems to be coming around and breaking free from the supremacist propaganda, when the boy's recent past suddenly catches up with him. In a wrenching scene at the close of the film, Derek embraces a dying Danny on the floor of the high-school bathroom, after the young brother has been brutally shot down by a former "enemy."

When I turn on the lights at the end of this film, there is barely a dry eye in the room. The students express their feelings as though they have just experienced an existential roller-coaster ride. They were anti-racist, then racist, then anti-racist again, in keeping with the twists and turns of this family's history. For a moment, they penitently admit, racism is understandable, a thoroughly comprehensible reaction to living among "different kinds of people." But that facile worldview is turned inside out when they witness the disfigurement that hatred and rage inflict on all kinds of people. They reawaken to a common human experience.

I have watched this film with my classes dozens of times, yet I always fall under its spell along with them. It is easy, in our distance from zones of generalized conflict, to forget that most people reject violence as an aspect of "the good life." To flourish as human beings requires peace and neighborliness, not guns and bombs and war. Few people choose violence as their best option among others, but they are driven to take up arms when their life-world is threatened. Violence is easier in the sickened reactive mode that follows in the wake of suffering, humiliation, want, and despair. One of the most disturbing aspects of the Holocaust is the fact that Adolf Hitler was less a violent anomaly than an "ordinary man," typical of a generation of Germans crushed by the First World War, looking for someone to blame for their country's abjection and degradation.[1] Genocide is a simple, if extreme, extrapolation of the general truth that *American History X* vividly demonstrates: violence is easier and more tempting when we erect stark barriers between ourselves and "alien" others.

Notes

[1] See Christopher R. Browning, *Ordinary Men: Reserve Police Battalion 101 and the Final Solution in Poland* (New York: HarperPerennial, 1993).

"The Enemy We Seek To Destroy"

R. Charli Carpenter

Star Trek, a cultural phenomenon that encompasses the original TV series, five spin-off series, ten feature films, and numerous books, comics, games, magazines, and fan websites, has long been understood by cultural theorists as a political commentary on contemporary world affairs. Those of us who have followed it closely see it above all as a morality play. Episodes routinely discuss timeless issues of what it means to be a person; whether good can triumph over evil; the relationship between emotion and reason; the meaning of free will; and the nature of justice.[1]

As a young person, and later as a budding human rights theorist, I perceived in *Star Trek* a commitment to liberal individualism and a respect for cultural self-determination. In that sense, the "United Federation of Planets"—the cosmopolitan organization that dispatches the Starship *Enterprise* to its distant realms—opposes violations of both individual and group rights. Growing up, the show was a constant touchstone for my emerging ethical and political consciousness. In several episodes, the *Enterprise* encounters planets where genocidal practices are in place. Each case is treated as the outer limit of the non-interference doctrine (the Prime Directive), which might be read as an early articulation of the norm of humanitarian intervention.

Against this background of appreciation for the show's moral universe, I later found myself, somewhat to my surprise, disillusioned by a particular episode, one in which the Federation itself contemplated genocide against an alien collectivist culture.[2] The Borg are a cybernetic race who evolve through assimilating organic species, and their technological distinctiveness, into their own cyber-collective—linking individual "drones" to a single collective consciousness. In the fifth season episode, *I, Borg*, the *Enterprise* encounters the crash site of a Borg scout ship, along with a lone Borg survivor. At the insistence of the doctor, Beverly Crusher, the drone is taken aboard for medical treatment—although the inclination of the other officers is to shoot the drone, since "the collective will come looking for it." (In fact, the Borg have engaged the Federation previously, with the goal of assimilating Earth's entire civilization into their collective. Picard was once abducted by the Borg, which possibly explains his no-holds-barred attitude.)

When the drone recovers consciousness, Captain Picard hatches a plan to introduce an "invasive programming sequence" into the drone's subroutine. When the drone interfaces with the Borg collective, Picard hopes that the computer virus will "infect the entire collective" and "disable their neural network," in effect shutting down their brain, and eliminating them as a threat to the Federation. Over the course of the episode, however, the crew is forced to reconsider this plan, as the Borg drone, now severed from the collective, begins to function as an individual, evoking the sympathy of the crew and respect for his rights.

What immediately struck me about this sequence is that, while the characters eventually come to view harming the *individual* Borg as wrong, the idea of genocide (as a crime against a collective) is never fully critiqued. Most of the officers accept with very little discussion that eradicating the Borg collective as such is an appropriate course of action. Only Dr. Crusher speaks out:

> *LaForge:* If this program works the way I think it will, it will only be a matter of months before the Borg suffer total systems failure.
> *Picard:* Comments?
> *Crusher:* A question. What exactly *is* 'total systems failure?'
> *Data:* The Borg are extremely computer-dependent. A systems failure will destroy them.
> *Crusher:* I just think we should be clear about that. We are talking about annihilating an entire race.
> *Picard:* Which under normal circumstances would be unconscionable. But as I see it, the Borg leave us with little choice . . . They've declared war on our way of life. We are to be assimilated.
> *Crusher:* But even in war, there are rules. You don't kill civilians indiscriminately.
> *Riker:* There are no civilians among the Borg.
> *Picard:* Think of them as a single collective being. There's no one Borg who is more of an individual than your arm or your leg.
> *Crusher:* How convenient.

Crusher is alone in questioning the policy of genocide. Other officers concur with Picard: "We're at war"; "They've attacked us at every encounter." But even Crusher appears implicitly to accept the crew's argument that exterminating the Borg as a collective could be justifiable on grounds of self-defense. Her disagreement focuses on whether exterminating *individual* Borg non-combatants is ethical. She does not concur with Picard's argument that individual drones lack rights. Were collective rights her reference point, Picard's argument about the Borg collective consciousness would not have been "convenient," but would rather underscore the atrociousness of targeting that civilization-defining consciousness.

Subsequent to this scene, the morality of destroying the Borg collective as such is evaded. The ethical debate in the episode (for in *Star Trek*, there always is one) centers only on whether the "invasive program" would violate the rights of Borg drones as individuals. Dr. Crusher does argue on behalf of the Borg prisoner: "When I look at my patient, I don't see a collective consciousness. I see a living, breathing boy who has been hurt and needs our help." But this is reminiscent of protections for wounded prisoners enshrined in humanitarian law. She also continues to question the ethics of "using" an unsuspecting individual to destroy his people, though increasingly the targeting of "the people" is lost in the discussion.

In the end, Crusher's claims are validated as the episode progresses. The drone, now separated from the collective, begins to exhibit individual traits, and becomes increasingly identifiable *as a person*. Thus, while early on Picard had used classic genocidal rhetoric in encouraging his crew not to become too attached to "it,"[3] he eventually comes to view the prisoner as an individual worthy of respect, protection, dignity, and choice. In many respects, the episode is a study in the power of dehumanization to enable atrocity, and of rehumanization to restrain it. But rather than transforming Picard's understanding of the Borg collective, this newfound sensibility simply provides him with a different set of concerns to weigh against the supposed moral viability of genocide. The goal of eradicating the collective continues to hold sway throughout the episode, but it becomes difficult to justify forcing the individual drone to return to the collective like, as Crusher puts it, "some sort of walking bomb."

In fact, it seems that the ability to view the drone as worthy of rights at all is contingent on viewing him as *distinct* from the Borg, rather than as a member of a sentient race that ought not to be exterminated on principle. When Guinan, the ship's bartender and Captain Picard's personal advisor, urges Picard to talk to the prisoner before proceeding with his plan, she couches her concerns in the language of personhood—a concept antithetical to the Borg collective:

> *Guinan:* I need to hear you say you're sure we're doing the right thing.
> *Picard:* Two days ago, you were so upset about the Borg being on this ship you nearly tore the foil out of my hand. Now you're here questioning whether it should be treated as the enemy.
> *Guinan:* No. But when you talk to him face to face, can you honestly say you don't have any doubt?
> *Picard:* I haven't talked to it.
> *Guinan:* Why not?
> *Picard:* I saw no need.
> *Guinan:* If you're going to use this person—
> *Picard:* It's not a person, dammit, it's a Borg!
> *Guinan (firmly):* If you are going to use this person to destroy his race, you should at least look him in the eye once before you do it. Because I'm not sure he is still a Borg.

Ultimately, the debate over whether to deploy the computer virus does not hinge on its status as a genocidal weapon. Instead, what concerns the officers is the ethic of treating an individual as a means to an end—violating the single Borg's individual rights by using him to wipe out his race—rather than whether it is valid to exterminate the race itself. This is perhaps best exemplified by Picard's statement, when he finally concludes that it would be wrong to bring the plan to fruition: "To use him in this manner would be no better than the enemy *we seek to destroy*."[4] Destroying the enemy "as such" is not questioned—only the use of a sentient individual as a tool for this purpose. This is thoroughly inconsistent with the rules of war in liberal international society, as well as the rules of engagement in the *Star Trek* universe. There, one does not seek to destroy one's enemies, but merely to defeat their military forces, and perhaps transform them into allies.

To my mind, the Borg episodes in general, and this one in particular, engage a range of ethical questions relating to the concept of genocide (or *xenocide?*). First, are genocidal strategies appropriate against enemies bent on committing genocide themselves? That is, is genocide justifiable if committed in self-defense? If so, what is the burden of proof for demonstrating that defense against genocide is impossible with less draconian methods?

Second, if an entire society is mobilized (as the Borg arguably are), does treating that society as a military objective constitute genocide, or would it be consistent with the laws of war that permit targeting military objectives? (That is, is it only genocide if the targets are *non*-combatants, or is the reference point the existence of the collective entity itself?) Are the laws of war obsolete when defeating an entire military would, essentially, require the destruction of an entire society? Is destruction of a civilization as such acceptable, even appropriate, if the destruction takes place through non-lethal means and is carried out so as to liberate "oppressed" individuals from a cultural context inimical to their own individual freedoms? And how should a military officer respond, when given a command that could be deemed profoundly unethical?

"I, Borg," and *Star Trek* more generally, offer an opportunity to meditate on these issues. Indeed, as a multimedia phenomenon, *Star Trek* promises (and often delivers) a careful, nuanced grappling with some of the important political problems of our day. In this instance, however, I think the show missed an opportunity to educate viewers about the nature of genocide both as concept and as crime: as something distinct from war, and from questions of individual human rights. Apparently, even the most liberal ethical narrative can accommodate genocidal thinking within certain parameters. This should give us pause.

Notes

[1]   See Richard Hanley, *The Metaphysics of Star Trek* (New York: Perseus Books, 1997).

[2]   One analysis describes the Borg as "the ultimate collectivist threat to the liberal-humanist aspirations of the Federation." See Patrick Thaddeus Jackson and Daniel Nexon, "Representation is Futile? American Anti-Collectivism and the Borg," in Jutta Weldes, ed., *To Seek Out New Worlds: Science Fiction and World Politics* (London: Palgrave MacMillan, 2003, p. 145).

[3]   In a scene in which the engineer, who has befriended the prisoner, expresses doubts about "using him this way," Picard calmly reminds him: "Centuries ago, when laboratory animals were used for experiments, scientists would sometimes become attached to the creatures. This would be a problem if the experiment involved killing them. I would suggest you un-attach yourself from the Borg, Mr. LaForge."

[4]   Emphasis added.

Octavio Paz, *"Hermandad"*

Brotherhood

Alex Hinton

Octavio Paz's poem "Brotherhood" has remained an important source of grounding as I have studied genocide. But not for the reasons you might first think.

> **Brotherhood**
> *Homage to Claudius Ptolemy*
>
> I am a man: little do I last
> And the night is enormous.
> But I look up:
> The stars write.
> Unknowing I understand:
> I too am written,
> And at this very moment
> Someone spell me out.[1]

The title of this brief, elegant poem evokes a broad sense of shared humanity (*hermandad*). But for me at least, the poem, with its back-and-forth between smallness and enormity, being and erasure, the known and the unknown, reaffirms a specific sense of this "brotherhood" that has been so important while studying genocide: humility. I mean this in several ways.

First, there is the humility I have felt in trying to make sense of a devastating and complex phenomenon that has an experiential dimension one can never fully comprehend. Perhaps this is why "Brotherhood" is an "homage to Claudius Ptolemy." As he gazed upon the stars, contemplating the nature of the world, Ptolemy must have experienced a sense of his own smallness against that dark canvas of the night.

Then there is a humility that comes from realizing that the processes taken to the extreme in genocide operate in our lives each day—as we pass by the homeless with averted eyes; as we turn the pages of the newspaper past yet another story about Darfur, or the number of people killed in Iraq; when, enticed by peer pressure, we call someone else "weird" or "strange"; or when we experience that comforting sense of self-inflation that comes at the expense of someone else.

Here, perhaps, is where a sense of humility is most important. For it is precisely the opposite of this sense of humility that so often drives projects of genocide: excessive pride, inflated grandiosity, hubris. Genocidal perpetrators try to write the stars, to transform the world so that it accords with their Manichean vision of good and bad, right and wrong, pure and impure.

Octavio Paz liked to end each of his poetry readings with "Brotherhood." I like to think he did so not just because it is such a magnificent poem, but to remind himself (as he basked in the public gaze), and to remind his audience, of the importance of humility. It is a lesson I try to carry with me, always.

Notes

[1]   Octavio Paz, "Brotherhood" ("Hermandad"), trans. Eliot Weinberger. From Octavio Paz and Eliot Weinberger, *Octavio Paz: Collected Poems* (New Directions Publishing Corp., 1988).

"A Single Child"

Eric Reeves

How does one think about engaging with genocide? If it should become one's life-defining work, how to escape from the ghastly realities that define such work? How to come to terms with the enormity of crimes such as have occurred in the Darfur region of Sudan—and previously in the Nuba Mountains of Kordofan Province, as well as in oil-rich Upper Nile Province? When the numbers of dead reach into millions, when those who have been displaced from their homes number many millions, when suffering seems so endless, how to gain respite? How even to think about the nature of the task?

I have worked full-time as a Sudan researcher, analyst, and advocate for over eight years. These questions are never far from my mind. On most occasions, I have no answers, certainly nothing that gives sufficient peace or solace.

But I try to imagine, as often as I'm able, the single child suffering. Not the vast cauldron of human suffering and destruction that has now spread from Darfur to eastern Chad, and increasingly to the Central African Republic; not the numbing statistics; not the agonizing repetitiveness of the obscene acts and international cowardice that define this first great episode of genocide in the twenty-first century.

It is no accident that the cover of my recent book on Darfur, *A Long Day's Dying*,[1] has as its only image a girl carrying a plastic water vessel—alone, unsure, and terribly vulnerable, even as her task is critical for her survival and the survival of what might remain of her family. She appears to be about ten, and she certainly knows that countless girls her age have been raped, and gang-raped, by the brutal *Janjaweed* militia that serve as such a formidable weapon of destruction and terror for Khartoum's *génocidaires*. The vilest racial epithets typically accompany the acts of rape and murder inflicted upon such innocence.

It is her singularity that was so compelling to me, among the countless photographs that might have been used. Others were more gruesome, more

Darfurese girl (courtesy Paul Jeffrey/The Key Publishing House Inc.).

comprehensive in what they suggested, more shaming. But the image of this young girl seemed perfect, in all ways. Perhaps this response explains why before one audience, which was seeking an explanation of my work, I felt compelled to say the following:

Let me ask that you imagine a place, outside of history or geography, where people of all ages enjoy a magnificent happiness—a rich, sustained, at times ecstatic happiness. I don't have time to give you all the details, but Ursula Le Guin has described this place in her haunting story, "The Ones Who Walk Away from Omelas." What we learn in this story is that the extraordinary happiness of those in Omelas is just as extraordinarily contingent. It depends entirely upon the suffering of a single child, who is confined to a remote basement, denied adequate food, medical attention for her festering sores, and denied, most consequentially, all human companionship.

The people of Omelas know of the child's suffering; indeed, the terms of their happiness are such that they must *know of this suffering, even as they can do nothing about it. Were the child to be rescued, this happiness would end immediately, for everyone. It's not easy to accept, but they do, because their joy depends upon the child's suffering. So, too, do the various impressive cultural achievements that are integral to happiness in Omelas.*

These are the terms, and everyone knows them. When adolescent children

*first learn of these fiercely strict terms, there is regret, sorrow, even rage; yet
eventually they come to accept the arrangement.*

*But quite remarkably, sometimes a young woman or man doesn't accept these
conditions. Sometimes they leave Omelas, each alone. They leave, Le Guin writes,*

> *walking into the darkness, and they do not come back. The place they
> go towards is a place even less imaginable to most of us than the city
> of happiness. I cannot describe it at all. It is possible that it does not
> exist. But they seem to know where they are going, the ones who walk
> away from Omelas.*

*My wish for you is that you never cease to wonder how it is that these young
people know where they are going.*

Notes

[1]   Eric Reeves, *A Long Day's Dying: Critical Moments in the Darfur Genocide*
(Toronto, ON: The Key Publishing House Inc., 2007).

About the Editor

Adam Jones is Associate Professor of Political Science at the University of British Columbia Okanagan. From 2005–07, he was Associate Research Fellow in the Genocide Studies Program at Yale University. He is author or editor of a dozen books, including *Crimes Against Humanity: A Beginner's Guide* (OneWorld Publications, 2008), *Genocide: A Comprehensive Introduction* (Routledge, 2006), *Gendercide and Genocide* (Vanderbilt University Press, 2004), and *Genocide, War Crimes & the West: History and Complicity* (Zed Books, 2004). His scholarly articles on genocide, gender, and human rights have appeared in *Journal of Genocide Research, Review of International Studies, Ethnic and Racial Studies, Journal of Human Rights*, and other publications. He serves as book review editor of *Journal of Genocide Research* and executive director of Gendercide Watch (www.gendercide.org), a Web-based educational initiative that confronts gender-selective atrocities against men and women worldwide. Website: http://adamjones.freeservers.com. Email: adam.jones@ubc.ca

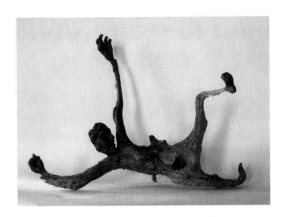

About the Cover

"Fallen," by Susan Clinard (www.clinard.org)
Wood and terracotta, 2003

When humanity falls, it stumbles and crashes down, only to pick itself up and hold on to what it knows to be true: love, and life itself. "Fallen" is a symbolic illustration of the worst atrocity known to humankind: genocide. The figure is caught at the moment in time when reality is turned upside down and gravity itself ceases to exist. Hands clenched, mouth open, toes extended—every essence of this being struggles to stand again. Miraculously, what we find is that, time after time, humanity does indeed rise again and breathe precious life.

My sculptures are about spirituality, destruction, hatred and love. They explore life's continual cycle of tearing down and rebuilding. They are about the duality between the ugly and the beautiful. I cannot see one without the other . . . I ask how it is possible that we have the capabilities to hate, kill, and destroy while others and even the same person can love so deeply, show compassion without limitations, and have faith and hope at all costs. I try to explore these stark dualities in my recent works about "the ugly" and "the beautiful." I try to see all of what life presents to me everyday. Inside this reality my heart and mind travels through utter despair and sheer elation. I am constantly reminded that I am living and am blessed beyond words. I feel the responsibility, as an artist, to reveal truth and remain humble. I want to speak for those who are too frequently forgotten or ignored and to pay honor to fellow creators, musicians, scientists, dancers, and lovers.

– Susan Clinard

About the Contributors

Atenea Acevedo was born and lives in the world that is Mexico City. She holds a bachelor's degree in International Relations with a specialization in Central European studies, a diploma in English-Spanish interpretation and translation, and a diploma in gender and equity relations between women and men. In translation and interpretation, she has found the ideal tools to structure her activism for human rights, gender equality and social change. Email: atenea.acevedo@gmail.com

Diane F. Afoumado is Lead Researcher at the Survivors Registry of the U.S. Holocaust Memorial Museum in Washington, DC. Her publications include *L'affiche antisémite en France sous l'Occupation* (Berg International, 2008), and *Exil Impossible. L'errance des Juifs du paquebot St. Louis* (L'Harmattan, 2005). She contributed to *Repicturing the Second World War: Representations in Film and Television* (Palgrave Macmillan, 2007), and was co-author with Serge Klarsfeld of *La Spoliation dans les camps de province. La documentation française* (2000). She has also published more than twenty articles. Email: dafoumado@ushmm.org

Joyce Apsel teaches in the Liberal Studies Program at New York University and is the 2008–2009 recipient of the NYU Distinguished Teaching Award. She is editor of *Darfur: Genocide Before our Eyes* (Institute for the Study of Genocide, 3rd edn., 2007) and *Teaching about Human Rights* (American Sociological Association, 2005). She is president of the Institute for the Study of Genocide and director of the education project, RightsWorks International. Email: jaa5@nyu.edu

Paul R. Bartrop is an Honorary Fellow in the Faculty of Arts and Education at Deakin University, Melbourne, Australia, and Head of History at Bialik College, Melbourne, teaching subjects in history, international studies, and comparative genocide studies. He has previously been a Scholar-in-Residence at the Martin-Springer Institute for Teaching the Holocaust, Tolerance and Humanitarian Values at Northern Arizona University, and a Visiting Professor at Virginia Commonwealth University. A past president of the Australian Association of Jewish Studies, Dr. Bartrop has published nine books and numerous scholarly articles, mostly in the areas of Holocaust and genocide studies, and has served on the editorial committees of a number of Australian and international periodicals. Email: pbartrop@hotmail.com

Helen Bond is Assistant Professor in the Department of Curriculum and Instruction at Howard University in Washington DC. She is author of "Teaching the Holocaust in the urban classroom," in T. Duboys, ed., *Pathways to the Holocaust* (Sense Publishers, 2008). She also serves as a Human Rights Commissioner appointed by the governor of West Virginia. With a Ph.D in Human Development, her research interests are human rights, teacher education, and development and genocide. Email: helenbond@verizon.net

R. Charli Carpenter is Assistant Professor of Political Science at the University of Massachusetts-Amherst. Her teaching and research interests include national security ethics, transnational advocacy networks, gender and political violence, and comparative genocide studies. She is the author of *"Innocent Women and Children": Gender, Norms and the Protection of Civilians* (Ashgate, 2006), and the editor of *Born of War: Protecting Children of Sexual Violence Survivors in Conflict Zones* (Kumarian Press, 2007). She has also published numerous articles in journals such as *International Organization, International Studies Quarterly, International Feminist Journal of Politics, Security Dialogue* and *Human Rights Quarterly*, and has served as a consultant for the United Nations. Email: charli.carpenter@gmail.com

Ward Churchill is the author of more than 20 books, including *A Little Matter of Genocide: Holocaust and Denial in the Americas, 1492 to the Present* (City Lights, 1997), *On the Justice of Roosting Chickens: Reflections on the Consequences of U.S. Imperial Arrogance and Criminality* (AK Press, 2003), and *Kill the Indian, Save the Man: The Genocidal Impact of American Indian Residential Schools* (City Lights, 2004). Most recently, a jury concluded that he had been illegally fired from his faculty position at the University of Colorado for expressing his political views. It is expected that he will be reinstated as a tenured full professor of American Indian Studies, effective fall semester 2009. Email: wardchurchill@yahoo.com

Sara Cohan serves as Education Director of the Genocide Education Project, a non-profit educational organization that assists educators in teaching about human rights and genocide, particularly the Armenian Genocide. Cohan's background combines research, study, curriculum development and teaching. She was a high school teacher for five years before serving as a research fellow for Teaching Tolerance, a project of the Southern Poverty Law Center. She also studied in Mexico as a recipient of a Fulbright-Hays scholarship. She has written articles and designed educational materials for a variety of organizations. Email: sarac@genocideeducation.org

G. Jan Colijn is Dean of General Studies and Professor of Political Science at The Richard Stockton College of New Jersey. He is co-author, with his late father, of *Ruin's Wheel: A Father on War, A Son on Genocide* (ComteQ, 2006), and author or editor of several other books. His work in Holocaust and genocide education has garnered several awards. Email: Jan.Colijn@stockton.edu

John M. Cox is Assistant Professor of History at Florida Gulf Coast University, where he directs the Center for Judaic, Holocaust, and Human Rights Studies. He is the author of *Circles of Resistance: Jewish, Leftist, and Youth Dissidence in Nazi Germany* (Peter Lang, 2009), and is preparing a book on genocide in the twentieth century. Dr. Cox is also on the editorial board of the Journal of Jewish Studies. Email: jmcox@fgcu.edu

Marcia Esparza is an Assistant Professor in the Criminal Justice department at John Jay College of Criminal Justice. Since 1997, she has undertaken research on state violence and genocide in Guatemala and Chile. She is the co-editor of *State Violence and Genocide in Latin America: The Cold War Years* (Routledge, 2009). She is also Director of the Historical Memory Project, a resource center documenting the history of violence in the western hemisphere. Email: mesparza@jjay.cuny.edu

Stephen C. Feinstein (1943–2008) was Adjunct Professor of History at the University of Minnesota and Director of the Center for Holocaust and Genocide Studies. Among his published edited volumes are *Confronting the Holocaust* (University Press of America, 1998) and *Absence/Presence: Critical Essays on the Artistic Memory of the Holocaust* (Syracuse University Press, 2005). Please see the Preface for further information about Dr. Feinstein.

Jonathan C. Friedman is the Director of Holocaust and Genocide Studies and Associate Professor of History at West Chester University. He is the author of five books, most recently *Performing Difference: Representations of the 'Other' in Film and Theater* (Rowman and Littlefield, 2008), and

Rainbow Jews: Gay and Jewish Identity in the Performing Arts (Rowman and Littlefield, 2007). Email: JFriedman@wcupa.edu

Donna-Lee Frieze is a Research Fellow at the School of History, Heritage and Society, Deakin University, Melbourne. She is collaborating with a team of historians and museologists on a history of the Melbourne Jewish Holocaust Centre. Her teaching and research areas include genocide studies, film, and philosophy. Email: donna-lee.frieze@deakin.edu.au

Lee Ann Fujii is Assistant Professor of Political Science and Program Coordinator of the politics cohort of the Women's Leadership Program at the George Washington University. She is the author of *Killing Neighbors: Webs of Violence in Rwanda* (Cornell University Press, 2009). She has also authored articles on mass killing, ethnicity, and fieldwork challenges in postwar settings. Email: lafujii@gwu.edu

Alexander George is Professor of Philosophy at Amherst College in Amherst, Massachusetts. He is the author of *Philosophies of Mathematics* (with Daniel J. Velleman) (Wiley-Blackwell, 2001), and a collection of humor, *Sense and Nonsensibility* (Fireside, 2004). He has also edited *What Would Socrates Say?* (Random House, 2007), a collection of questions and answers drawn from AskPhilosophers.org, a Web site where philosophers answer questions submitted by the public. He occasionally suffers from chess fever, and maintains the Web forum ChessProblem.net. Email: ageorge@amherst.edu

Simone Gigliotti is a Senior Lecturer in the History Programme at Victoria University, Wellington, New Zealand. She is the co-editor of *The Holocaust: A Reader* (Blackwell Publishing, 2005), and the author of *The Train Journey: Transit, Captivity and Witnessing in the Holocaust* (Berghahn Books, 2009). Email: Simone.Gigliotti@vuw.ac.nz

Eric Gordy is Senior Lecturer in the Department of Social Sciences at the School of Slavonic and East European Studies of University College London, where he is director of the Centre for Southeast European Studies. His research involves culture and politics during and in the wake of the wars of Yugoslav succession; he is the author of *The Culture of Power in Serbia: Nationalism and the Destruction of Alternatives* (Penn State Press, 1999). Email: e.gordy@ucl.ac.uk

Fred Grünfeld is Associate Professor of International Relations and International Organizations at the Faculty of Law of Maastricht University, the Netherlands. At Maastricht University he researches and teaches at the Maastricht Centre for Human Rights and the University College Maastricht. He is also Professor in the Causes of Gross Human Rights Violations at the Centre for Conflict Studies, Faculty of Humanities at Utrecht University. His research is on comparative genocide studies (Rwanda, Srebrenica and Darfur), in particular the failures of third parties to prevent genocide. E-mail: f.grunfeld@ir.unimaas.nl

Wendy C. Hamblet is a Canadian philosopher, and Associate Professor of Liberal Studies at North Carolina A&T State University. She has authored three books on radical violence, including *The Sacred Monstrous: A Reflection on Violence in Human Communities* (Rowman and Littlefield, 2004) and *Savage Constructions: The Myth of African Savagery* (Rowman and Littlefield, 2008), several anthologies, and many articles in peer-refereed international journals. Hamblet is also a practicing Philosophical Counselor and Mediator in public and private sectors. Email: wchamblet@gmail.com

Michael Hayse is Director of the Master of Arts Program in Holocaust and Genocide Studies and Associate Professor of Historical Studies at the Richard Stockton College of New Jersey. He is author of Recasting *West German Elites: Higher Civil Servants, Business Leaders, and Physicians in Hesse between Nazism and Democracy, 1945–1955* (Berghahn Books, 2003). Email: Michael.Hayse@stockton.edu

Viktoria Hertling founded the Center for Holocaust, Genocide & Peace Studies at the University of Nevada, Reno, in 1994, and served as its director until her retirement in 2008. She currently lives in Berlin, Germany. Email: hertling@unr.edu

William L. Hewitt is Professor of History and co-founder of the West Chester University of Pennsylvania Holocaust/Genocide Studies Program. He is the editor of *Defining the Horrific: Readings on Genocide and Holocaust in the Twentieth Century* (Prentice-Hall, 2003). Email: WHewitt@wcupa.edu

Winton Higgins is a Visiting Research Fellow in Cultural Studies at the University of Technology, Sydney. A graduate of the universities of Sydney, Stockholm, and London, he has been a board member of the Australian

Institute for Holocaust and Genocide Studies for the last ten years, and is the author of the Holocaust-themed travel diary, *Journey into Darkness* (Brandl & Schlesinger, 2003). He has also contributed articles to the research series, *Genocide Perspectives*. Email: winton.higgins@uts.edu.au

Alex Hinton is Director of the Center for the Study of Genocide and Human Rights (CGHR) and Associate Professor of Anthropology and Global Affairs at Rutgers University, Newark (http://cghr.newark.rutgers.edu/). He is the author of *Why Did They Kill? Cambodia in the Shadow of Genocide* (University of California Press, 2005), which received the 2008 Stirling Prize, and five edited or co-edited collections, including most recently *Genocide: Truth, Memory, and Representation* (Duke University Press, 2009). E-mail: ahinton@andromeda.rutgers.edu

Steven L. Jacobs holds the Aaron Aronov Endowed Chair of Judaic Studies at the University of Alabama, where he is an Associate Professor of Religious Studies. He is the author, editor, or translator of more than sixteeen books, including his latest, *Confronting Genocide: Judaism, Christianity, Islam* (Lexington Books, 2009). His primary fields of research are biblical interpretation, both Hebrew Bible and New Testament, and the Holocaust and historical and contemporary genocides. He remains active on the executive of the International Association of Genocide Scholars. Email: sjacobs@bama.ua.edu

Adam Jones—see "About the Editor."

Ani Kalayjian holds an honorary Doctor of Science degree from Long Island University (2001), recognizing her 20 years as a pioneering clinical researcher, professor, and administrator at the United Nations. In 2007, she was awarded Columbia University Teacher College's Distinguished Alumni of the Year. She is the author of *Disaster and Mass Trauma* (Vista Publishing, 1995), coeditor of the volume *Forgiveness and Reconciliation* (Springer, 2009), and author of over 40 articles on clinical methods, human rights, trauma, and women's issues. Email: Kalayjiana@aol.com

Nina Krieger is Education Director at the Vancouver Holocaust Education Centre. She studied History at the University of British Columbia and Humanities & Cultural Studies at the London Consortium, a multi-disciplinary graduate program of the University of London, the Architectural Association, the Institute of Contemporary Arts, and the Tate Gallery. She has developed exhibitions, public programs, and education programs at contemporary art galleries and historical museums in the United Kingdom and Canada. Email: ninadkrieger@gmail.com

Scott Laderman is an Assistant Professor of History at the University of Minnesota, Duluth. He is author of *Tours of Vietnam: War, Travel Guides, and Memory* (Duke University Press, 2009). Email: laderman@d.umn.edu

Raphael Lemkin (1900–59) was the pioneer of genocide studies. Born in Poland, he worked as a lawyer in the 1930s on concepts of "barbarity" and "vandalism" to describe, and outlaw, the destruction of ethnic and religious minorities. Fleeing the Nazi invasion of Poland in 1939, he took refuge in the United States, where in 1944 he published *Axis Rule in Occupied Europe* (Carnegie Endowment for International Peace, republished by Lawbook Exchange in 2005). In this work, Lemkin coined the term "genocide," and explored its strategies and consequences in the lands under Nazi occupation. Lemkin spent the immediate postwar years in a relentless campaign to persuade the United Nations to adopt the Convention on the Prevention and Punishment of the Crime of Genocide, which it did in 1948. In 1951, the convention attracted a sufficient number of ratifications to become international law. The final years of Lemkin's life were spent in penury and obscurity, but the modern field of comparative genocide studies has built upon his foundational contribution. His wealth of previously-unpublished writings continue to appear, influencing new generations of scholars and students.

Benjamin Lieberman is Professor of History at Fitchburg State College in Massachusetts. He is the author of *Terrible Fate: Ethnic Cleansing in the Making of Modern Europe* (Ivan R. Dee, 2006). His research focuses on ethnic cleansing and the remaking of border zones. Email: BLieberman@fsc.edu

Fiona de Londras is a member of faculty at the School of Law, University College Dublin, where she is also a member of the Institute of Criminology. She publishes widely on international law and resistance to repressive state action, with a particular focus on counter-terrorism and the judicial role. Her research has appeared in, among other journals, *Modern Law Review, American Journal of International Law* and *Israel Law Review*. Email: fiona.delondras@ucd.ie

Pam Maclean is a Senior Lecturer in History at Deakin University in Victoria, Australia, where she teaches courses in Holocaust and genocide. With Michele Langfield and Dvir Abramovich she has edited and contributed to *Testifying to the Holocaust* (AAJS, 2008), the first systematic study of video testimonies given by survivors to the Jewish Holocaust Centre, Melbourne. She is currently co-ordinating the writing of a history of the Jewish Holocaust Centre in Melbourne. Email: pamela.maclean@deakin.edu.au

Daniel H. Magilow is Assistant Professor of German at the University of Tennessee in Knoxville, Tennessee. He is the editor and translator of *In Her Father's Eyes: A Childhood Extinguished by the Holocaust* (Rutgers University Press, 2008) and the author of numerous articles about the Holocaust, its memorialization, and its representation in visual culture. Email: dmagilow@utk.edu

Henry Maitles is Reader in Education at the University of Strathclyde in Glasgow, Scotland. He was a member of the Scottish Review Group on Education for Citizenship which drew up the proposals now in place in every Scottish school. He teaches about and researches the impact of subjects such as the Holocaust on school students' values and attitudes. He has published sole-authored and edited books, as well as articles in refereed journals and the wider media. Email: h.maitles@strath.ac.uk

Jens Meierhenrich is Assistant Professor of Government and of Social Studies at Harvard University. He is the author of a genocide trilogy, comprising *The Rationality of Genocide*, *The Structure of Genocide*, and *The Culture of Genocide* (all forthcoming from Princeton University Press). He is also preparing, for Oxford University Press, *Genocide: A Reader* and *Genocide: A Very Short Introduction*. He recently published *The Legacies of Law* (Cambridge University Press, 2008). Email: jmeierhenrich@gov.harvard.edu

Jina Moore is an independent reporter and producer who has covered human rights issues in Sierra Leone, Rwanda, the Democratic Republic of Congo, and the US. A regular correspondent for the *Christian Science Monitor*, her work has also appeared in *The Boston Globe*, *Glamour Magazine* and *Best American Science Writing*. Her archive and blog may be found at www.jinamoore.com. Email: jinamoore@gmail.com

Thomas Nagy was a tenured Associate Professor of Expert Systems in Washington, DC. He researches the application of Web 2.0 methods and linguistics to aid doubly exceptional students (both gifted and challenging), and making progressive Web applications more persuasive and easier to use. He is deeply concerned with issues of structural violence, and invites correspondence from those interested in this subject. Email: tom500k@gmail.com

Edward Paulino teaches a wide range of writing-intensive interdisciplinary courses at the John Jay College of Criminal Justice at the City University of New York. His research interests include race, genocide, borders, nation-building, Latin America and the Caribbean, the African diaspora, and New York State history. His research has been supported by the Fulbright Foundation, the National Endowment for the Humanities, the PSC-CUNY Research Foundation, and the New York State Archives. He lives in Brooklyn with his wife and daughter. Email: edpaulino@jjay.cuny.edu

Christopher Powell is Assistant Professor of Sociology at the University of Manitoba in Winnipeg, Canada. He is the author of "What Do Genocides Kill? A Relational Conception of Genocide," published in the *Journal of Genocide Research* in 2007. His current book project, *Civilization and Genocide*, theorizes the relationship between the expansion of western civilization, the conversion of difference into danger, and the practice of genocide. Email: chris_powell@umanitoba.ca

Jack Nusan Porter is the author or editor of such works as *The Jew as Outsider* (University Press of America, 1981), *Genocide and Human Rights* (University Press of America, 1982), *Sexual Politics in Nazi Germany* (Spencer Press, 1995), and *The Genocidal Mind* (University Press of America, 2006). Born in Ukraine in 1944, he is a child Shoah survivor of two Soviet partisans, and was subsequently educated in Jerusalem, at the University of Wisconsin–Milwaukee, and at Northwestern University. Wikipedia page: http://en.wikipedia.org/wiki/Jack_Porter. E-mail: jacknusan@earthlink.net

Eric Reeves is Professor of English Language and Literature at Smith College in Northampton, Massachusetts. He has spent the past ten years working full-time as a Sudan researcher and analyst, publishing extensively both in the US and internationally. He has testified several times before Congress, has lectured widely in academic settings, and has served as a consultant to a number of human rights and humanitarian organizations operating in Sudan. He is author of *A Long Day's Dying: Critical Moments in the Darfur Genocide* (The Key, 2007). Email: ereeves@smith.edu

Stefanie Rixecker is Dean of the Faculty of Environment, Society & Design at Lincoln University in New Zealand. She is Leader of the "Global Justice and Environmental Policy" theme at the Land, Environment and People (LEaP) Research Centre. She is also a member of the advisory board for *Local Environment: The International Journal of Justice and Sustainability* and is Chair of the Governance Board of Amnesty International, Aotearoa, New Zealand. Email: Stefanie.Rixecker@lincoln.ac.nz

John K. Roth is the Edward J. Sexton Professor Emeritus of Philosophy and the Founding Director of the Center for the Study of the Holocaust, Genocide, and Human Rights at Claremont McKenna College. He has published hundreds of articles and reviews, and authored, co-authored, or edited more than forty books, including *Genocide and Human Rights: A Philosophical Guide* (Palgrave Macmillan, 2005); *Ethics During and After the Holocaust: In the Shadow of Birkenau* (Palgrave Macmillan, 2005); and *Anguished Hope: Holocaust Scholars Confront the Palestinian-Israeli Conflict* (Wm. B. Eerdmans, 2008). Email: jroth@cmc.edu

Victoria Sanford is Associate Professor of Anthropology at Lehman College and the Graduate Center, City University of New York. She serves as a Research Associate at Columbia University's Center for International Conflict Resolution and an Affiliated Scholar at Rutgers University's Center for the Study of Genocide and Human Rights. She is the author of four books on Guatemala, including *Buried Secrets: Truth and Human Rights in Guatemala* (Palgrave Macmillan, 2003). As a John Simon Guggenheim Fellow (2009–2010), she is writing *The Land of Pale Hands: Feminicide, Social Cleansing and Impunity in Guatemala*. Email: victoria.sanford@lehman.cuny.edu

William Schabas is Director of the Irish Centre for Human Rights, National University of Ireland, Galway, where he is Professor of Human Rights Law. He is the author of *Genocide in International Law: The Crime of Crimes* (Cambridge University Press, 2nd edition, 2009), and many journal articles on legal aspects of genocide. Professor Schabas was a member of the Sierra Leone Truth and

Reconciliation Commission. He is an Officer of the Order of Canada and Member of the Royal Irish Academy. Email: william.schabas@nuigalway.ie

Dominik J. Schaller is Lecturer and Researcher at the Ruprecht-Karls-University, Heidelberg, Germany. He is editor of the *Journal of Genocide Research* and Executive Secretary of the International Network of Genocide Scholars (INoGS). His main areas of research are the history of mass violence, colonialism, and modern African history. Schaller is the editor of numerous volumes and articles on German colonial rule in Africa, as well as the Armenian and Rwandan genocides. E-mail: dominik.schaller@uni-heidelberg.de

Russell Schimmer is currently a dual-degree J.D.-Ph.D. candidate at the University of Connecticut. His Ph.D. research is on multi-temporal spaceborne remote sensing of environmental change and its applications to monitoring anthropogenic activities, especially the large-scale violence characteristic of genocide. His legal interests are primarily in developing approaches to spaceborne remote sensing obtention and admissibility. He also researches processes of largescale mineral extraction, primarily global copper and gold mining. Email: rschimme@earthlink.net

Jacques Sémelin is Professor of Political Science (Sciences Po Paris, Center for International Research and Studies). He is author of *Purify and Destroy: The Political Uses of Massacre and Genocide* (Columbia University Press, 2007), and founder and editor-in-chief of the online *Encyclopedia of Mass Violence* (Sciences Po, 2008), www.massviolence.org. His text in this volume is excerpted from his autobiography, *J'arrive où je suis étranger*, recently published in French by Le Seuil. Email: semelin@ceri-sciences-po.org

David J. Simon is a Lecturer in the Department of Political Science at Yale University. His research addresses development assistance, post-conflict recovery, and reconciliation, focusing in part on Rwanda. For the past five years, he has taught a seminar entitled "The Rwandan Genocide in Comparative Perspective." Email: david.simon@yale.edu

Robert Skloot retired from forty years of teaching, administrating and stage directing at the University of Wisconsin-Madison in 2008. He is the author and editor of many books and essays about the theater of the Holocaust and genocide, including the two-volume *The Theatre of the Holocaust* (University of Wisconsin Press, 1982, 1999). His one-act play, *If the Whole Body Dies: Raphael Lemkin and the Treaty against Genocide* (Parallel Press, 2006), has been read around the world. Email: rskloot@wisc.edu

Christopher C. Taylor is Professor of Anthropology at the University of Alabama at Birmingham. He is the author of *Sacrifice as Terror: The Rwandan Genocide of 1994* (Berg, 1999). He has also written extensively about traditional medicine in Rwanda, ethnicity, the state, and Rwanda's pre-genocidal media. E-mail: ctaylor@uab.edu

Ernesto Verdeja is Assistant Professor of Political Science and Peace Studies at the University of Notre Dame. His research interests are comparative genocide and theories of justice, forgiveness, and reconciliation. He is the author of the forthcoming *Unchopping A Tree: Reconciliation in the Aftermath of Political Violence* (Temple University Press, 2009). Email: everdeja@nd.edu

Joseph Robert White is research assistant at the Center for Advanced Holocaust Studies, and Adjunct Associate Professor at the University of Maryland University College. He holds a doctorate in Modern European history from the University of Nebraska-Lincoln, and is editor of *The Camps and Ghettos of Germany's Allies, Satellites, and Collaborationist States*, Volume 4 of *The United States Holocaust Memorial Museum Encyclopedia of Camps and Ghettos* (Indiana University Press/USHMM). His articles have appeared in *Holocaust and Genocide Studies*, *Journal of Jewish Identities*, and *Today's Best Military Writing*. Email: historianjoe@yahoo.com

Benjamin Whitmer lives and works in Denver, Colorado with his wife and children. His first novel, *Pike*, is forthcoming from PM Press. Email: benjamin.whitmer@gmail.com

John C. Zimmerman is an Associate Professor in the College of Business at the University of Nevada Las Vegas. He is author of the book *Holocaust Denial: Demographics, Testimonies and Ideologies* (University Press of America, 2000). He has published articles on Pearl Harbor revisionism, the Auschwitz death camp, and radical Islam. Email: john.zimmerman@unlv.edu

Lior Zylberman is currently studying for his Masters in Communication and Culture at the University of Buenos Aires. He is Associate Professor of Design of Image and Sound at the University of Buenos Aires, and a researcher on genocide, imagery, and society. He has written several works on memory and cinema. Email: liorzylberman@gmail.com

Resources and Further Reading

Compiled by Adam Jones and Sasha Johnston,
with input from individual contributors

"All My Inner Self Protested"
Raphael Lemkin

Books:
• Raphael Lemkin, *Axis Rule in Occupied Europe: Laws of Occupation, Analysis of Government, Proposals for Redress*, 2nd ed. (The Lawbook Exchange, 2008). With introductions by genocide scholars Samantha Power and William Schabas.
• John Cooper, *Raphael Lemkin and the Struggle for the Genocide Convention* (Palgrave Macmillan, 2008)
• Facing History and Ourselves, *Totally Unofficial: Raphael Lemkin and the Genocide Convention*. See http://www.facinghistory.org/resources/publications/lemkin
• Samuel Totten and Steven Jacobs, eds., *Pioneers in Genocide Studies* (Transaction Publishers, 2002)
• Steven L. Jacobs, ed., *Raphael Lemkin's Thoughts on the Nazi Genocide: Not Guilty?* (Edwin Mellen Press, 1992)
• Samantha Power, *"A Problem from Hell": America and the Age of Genocide* (Basic Books, 2002). Chapters 2–5 deal with Lemkin's life and thought.

Plays:
• Robert Skloot, *If the Whole Body Dies: Raphael Lemkin and the Treaty Against Genocide* (Parallel Press, 2006)
• Catherine Filloux, *Lemkin's House* (Playscripts, Inc., 2006)

Web Resources:
• Prevent Genocide International, "Key Writings of Raphael Lemkin on Genocide." http://www.preventgenocide.org/lemkin
• John Docker, "Raphael Lemkin's History of Genocide and Colonialism," US Holocaust Memorial Museum, July 2004. http://www.ushmm.org/conscience/analysis/details.php?content=2004–02–26

Lost Worlds
John M. Cox
Diego Rivera, "La Gran Tenochtitlán"
Books: Diego Rivera

• Luis Martin Lozano and Juan Coronel Rivera, *Diego Rivera: The Complete Murals* (Taschen, 2008)

• Patrick Marnham, *Dreaming with His Eyes Open: A Life of Diego Rivera* (University of California Press, 2000)

• Diego Rivera with Gladys March, *My Art, My Life: An Autobiography* (Dover Publications, 1992)

Books: Historical Background

• Frances F. Berdan, *Aztecs of Central Mexico: An Imperial Society* (Wadsworth, 2004)

• Charles C. Mann, *1491: New Revelations of the Americas before Columbus* (Knopf, 2005)

• Hugh Thomas, *Conquest: Cortes, Montezuma, and the Fall of Old Mexico* (Simon & Schuster, 1995)

Video:

• *Frescoes of Diego Rivera*, dir. Michael Camerini (VHS, Homevision 2000)

Web Resources:

• Diego Rivera Web Museum, Murals Page: http://diegorivera.com/murals/index.php

• Wikipedia page: http://en.wikipedia.org/wiki/Diego_Rivera

• Diego Rivera Mural Project, City College of San Francisco: http://www.riveramural.com

• Diego Rivera Prints: http://www.diego-rivera.org

• The Cubist Paintings of Diego Rivera: Memory, Politics, Place, National Gallery of Art, Washington, DC: http://www.nga.gov/exhibitions/2004/rivera/intro.shtm

• Palacio Nacional, Mexico City, photos and pictures by George And Audrey DeLange: http://www.delange.org/PresPalace/PresPalace.htm

The Wound at the Heart of the World
Christopher Powell
The Mission
Video:

• *The Mission*, dir. Roland Joffé (DVD, Warner Home Video 2003, ASIN B00003CXBH; Blu-Ray, Warner, ASIN B00198X0WW)

Books:

• R.B. Cunninghame Graham, *A Vanished Arcadia: Being Some Account of the Jesuits in Paraguay, 1607 to 1767* (ICON Group International, 2008)

• Richard Gott, *Land Without Evil: Utopian Journeys Across the South American Watershed* (Verso, 1993)

• C.J. McNaspy and Jose Maria Blanch, *Lost Cities of Paraguay: Art and Architecture of the Jesuit Reductions, 1607–1767* (Loyola Press, 1982)

• Ronald Wright, *Stolen Continents: 500 Years of Conquest and Resistance in the Americas* (Mariner Books, 2005)

Audio:

• *The Mission* soundtrack by Ennio Morricone (CD, Virgin Records 1986)

Web Resources:

• *The Mission* Internet Movie Database page: http://www.imdb.com/title/tt0091530

• *The Mission* Wikipedia page: http://en.wikipedia.org/wiki/The_Mission_(film)

• *The Mission* Rotten Tomatoes page: http://www.rottentomatoes.com/m/1014027-mission

• An interview with Roland Joffé (2003): http://www.dvdmg.com/interviewrolandjoffe.html

"A Bargain Indeed"
Ward Churchill
Buffy Sainte-Marie, "My Country 'Tis of Thy People You're Dying"

Books:

• *The Buffy Sainte-Marie Songbook* (Grosset & Dunlap, 1971)

• Ward Churchill, *A Little Matter of Genocide: Holocaust and Denial in the Americas 1492 to the Present* (City Lights, 2001)

Audio:

• "My Country 'Tis of Thy People You're Dying," by Buffy Sainte-Marie © Gypsy Music, 1966. From *Little Wheel Spin and Spin* (1966, CD Vanguard Records 1992, ASIN B000000EIS)

Video:

• *Buffy Sainte-Marie: A Multimedia Life*, dir. Joan Prowse (2006, DVD CineFocus Canada). See http://cinefocus.com/public/television/buffy.htm

Articles:

• Fiona Morrow, "Ever the Activist, Singer Can't Put Politics Aside," *The Globe and Mail*, 31 October 2008

Web Resources:

• Buffy Sainte-Marie website: http://www.creative-native.com, http://www.buffysainte-marie.com
• Buffy Saint-Marie MySpace page, with free listenable songs from her latest CD, *Running for the Drum*: http://www.myspace.com/buffysaintemarie
• Buffy Sainte-Marie Wikipedia page: http://en.wikipedia.org/wiki/Buffy_Sainte-Marie
• Lyrics for "My Country . . .": www.fortunecity.com/tinpan/parton/2/mycount.html
• Adam Jones, "12 Great Songs about Genocide": www.genocidetext.net/gaci_songs.htm
• A 1960s-era live performance of "My Country . . .": http://www.youtube.com/watch?v=tl08n8_b3Sw
• Ward Churchill Solidarity Network website: www.wardchurchill.net

The Westering Holocaust
Benjamin Whitmer
Cormac McCarthy, *Blood Meridian*

Books:

• Cormac McCarthy, *Blood Meridian: Or the Evening Redness in the West* (Picador, 1994)
• Cormac McCarthy, *The Border Trilogy* (Picador, 2002)
• Barcley Owens, *Cormac McCarthy's Western Novels* (University of Arizona Press, 2000)
• Shane Schimpf, ed., *A Reader's Guide to Blood Meridian* (Bon Mot Publishing, 2008)

Audio:

• *Blood Meridian* (unabridged), narrated by Richard Poe (Recorded Books, 2007)

Web Resources:

• *Blood Meridian* Wikipedia page: http://en.wikipedia.org/wiki/Blood_Meridian
• Lecture on *Blood Meridian* by Amy Hungerford of Yale University:
    Part 1: http://www.youtube.com/watch?v=FgyZ4ia25gg
    Part 2: http://www.youtube.com/watch?v=7ZFmf4T5L3o
• Film adaptation planned for 2010: http://uk.imdb.de/name/nm0748784

• The New Canon (works of fiction since 1985): http://www.thenewcanon.com/Blood_Meridian.html

My Grandfather's Testimony
Sara Cohan

Books:
• Taner Akçam, *A Shameful Act: The Armenian Genocide and the Question of Turkish Responsibility* (Metropolitan Books, 2006)
• Peter Balakian, *The Burning Tigris: The Armenian Genocide and America's Response* (HarperCollins, 2003)
• Donald Bloxham, *The Great Game of Genocide: Imperialism, Nationalism, and the Destruction of the Ottoman Armenians* (Cambridge University Press, 2005)
• Vahakn N. Dadrian, *The History of the Armenian Genocide: Ethnic Conflict from the Balkans to Anatolia to the Caucasus* (Berghahn Books, 1995)
• Donald E. Miller and Lorna Touryan Miller, *Survivors: An Oral History of the Armenian Genocide* (University of California Press, 1999)

Video:
• *The Armenian Genocide* (DVD, PBS 2006). See http://www.shoppbs.org/sm-pbs-armenian-genocide-dvd--pi-2283958.html
• *Screamers*, dir. Carla Garapedian (DVD, Sony 2008)

Web Resources:
• Armenian genocide Wikipedia page: http://en.wikipedia.org/wiki/Armenian_Genocide
• Henry Morgenthau, Ambassador Morgenthau's Story (memoirs of the US ambassador to Constantinople during the Armenian genocide): http://www.cilicia.com/morgenthau/MorgenTC.htm
• The Genocide Education Project, www.genocideeducation.org
• International Association of Genocide Scholars, www.genocidescholars.org

Werfel, *Musa Dagh*, and the Armenian Genocide
William Schabas
Franz Werfel, *The Forty Days of Musa Dagh*

Books:
• Franz Werfel, *The Forty Days of Musa Dagh* (DaCapo Press, 2002)
• William A. Schabas, *Genocide in International Law*, 2nd edition (Cambridge University Press, 2009)

Video:
• *The Forty Days of Musa Dagh* (1982) (DVD, Parseghian Records, 2002)

Web Resources:
• *The Forty Days of Musa* Dagh Wikipedia page: http://en.wikipedia.org/wiki/The_Forty_Days_of_Musa_Dagh
• *Musa Dagh*, http://www.mousaler.com/musa-dagh
• More on the events at Musa Dagh: http://www.armenian-genocide.org/musa_dagh.html
• Franz Werfel Wikipedia page: http://en.wikipedia.org/wiki/Franz_Werfel
• Franz Werfel biography: http://www.kirjasto.sci.fi/fwerfel.htm
• 1982 film adaptation: http://www.imdb.com/title/tt0138989

"The Desire to Communicate Something of My Torment"
Nina Krieger
Armin T. Wegner, photographs and letters
Book:
• Armin T. Wegner, *Die Austreibung des armenischen Volkes in die Wüste: Ein Lichtbildvortrag* (Wallstein, 2009)
Audio:
• *Armin T. Wegner: Bildnis einer Stimme / Picture of a Voice* (CD, Wallstein Verlag 2008)
Web Resources:
• Online collection of Armin T. Wegner's photographs: http://www.armenian-genocide.org/photo_wegner.html#photo_collection
• Homepage of the Armin T. Wegner Society of USA: http://www.armin-t-wegner.us/ATW/About_Us.html
• Armin T. Wegner Wikipedia page: http://en.wikipedia.org/wiki/Armin_T._Wegner
• Biography of Armin T. Wegner: http://www.armenian-genocide.org/wegner-bio.html

Warning: Here There Be Experts
Benjamin Lieberman
Bernard Lewis, *The Emergence of Modern Turkey*
Book:
• Bernard Lewis, *The Emergence of Modern Turkey*, 3rd ed. (Oxford University Press, 2001)
Web Resources:
• Bernard Lewis Wikipedia page: http://en.wikipedia.org/wiki/Bernard_Lewis

- Bernard Lewis Princeton faculty profile: http://www.princeton.edu/~nes/faculty_lewis.html
- "Bernard Lewis condemned for having denied the reality of the Armenian genocide," *Le Monde*, 23 June 1995. http://users.ids.net/~gregan/lemd_eng.html
- More on the Lewis denial controversy: http://www.armeniangenocidedebate.com/Bernard-Lewis-Armenian-Genocide
- Yervant Herian/Armenian Genocide Poster Campaign: http://www.armeniangenocideposters.org/voting/posters.asp

Conspiracy of Silence
Ani Kalayjian
Voices from the Lake
Video:
- *Voices from the Lake*, dir. J. Michael Hagopian (DVD 2003). Order through the Armenian Film Foundation, http://www.armenianfilm.org

Web Resources:
- J. Michael Hagopian Wikipedia page: http://en.wikipedia.org/wiki/J._Michael_Hagopian
- J. Michael Hagopian IMDB page: http://www.imdb.com/name/nm2062776/bio
- *Voices from the Lake* press release: http://www.anca.org/press_releases/press_releases.php?prid=1161
- *Voices from the Lake* description: http://www.armenian-genocide.org/Education.97/current_category.0/multimedia_detail.html

Discovering the Haitian Massacre
Edward Paulino
The Norweb communiqué
Document:
- Letter from Ambassador R. Henry Norweb to President Franklin Delano Roosevelt, FDR Library, Hyde Park, NY, Box 70 State, 1937, pp. 2–3.

Books:
- See footnote 1, page 54

Web Resources:
- Franklin D. Roosevelt Presidential Library and Museum: http://www.fdrlibrary.marist.edu
- "Haitian Migrants Face Rising Backlash Next Door," *The Christian Science*

Monitor, 24 January 2006. http://www.flacso.org/hemisferio/al-eeuu/boletines/01/08/mig_04.pdf
• Amnesty International, "Dominican Republic: Haitian Migrants Denied Their Rights," bulletin, 21 March 2007. http://www.amnesty.org/en/library/info/AMR27/003/2007/en

Journal Article:
• Edward Paulino, "Anti-Haitianism, Historical Memory, and the Potential for Genocidal Violence in the Dominican Republic," *Genocide Studies and Prevention*, 1: 3 (Winter 2006), pp. 265–88

Where It All Began
Paul R. Bartrop
Stefan Lorant, *I Was Hitler's Prisoner*

Books:
• Stefan Lorant, *I Was Hitler's Prisoner: A Diary* (G.P. Putnam's Sons, 1935); paperback edition, *I Was Hitler's Prisoner: Leaves from a Prison Diary* (Penguin, 1940)
• Michael Hallett, *Stefan Lorant: Godfather of Photojournalism* (The Scarecrow Press, 2005)

Video:
• *Stefan Lorant, Man in Pictures*, dir. Paul Cohen (1997, see http://www.imdb.com/title/tt0203155)

Web Resources:
• Stefan Lorant Wikipedia page: http://en.wikipedia.org/wiki/Stefan_Lorant
• Librarything page for *I Was Hitler's Prisoner* with the cover of the Penguin edition: http://www.librarything.com/work/3123777
• Stefan Lorant obituary: http://www.independent.co.uk/news/obituaries/obituary-stefan-lorant-1294687.html

Documenting Torture in the Early Nazi Camps
Joseph Robert White
Karl Schwesig, *Schlegelkeller*

Books:
• Karl Schwesig, *Schlegelkeller* (Frölich und Kaufmann, 1986, ISBN–10: 3887250222)
• *Karl Schwesig: Leben und Werk* (Frölich and Kaufmann, 1984)
• Klaus Drobisch and Günther Wieland, *System der NS-Konzentrationslager 1933–1939* (Akademie Verlag, 1993)

• Jane Caplan, "Political Detention and the Origin of the Concentration Camps in Nazi Germany, 1933–1935/6," in Neil Gregor, ed., *Nazism, War and Genocide: Essays in Honour of Jeremy Noakes* (University of Exeter Press, 2005), pp. 22–41

Web resources:

• "Declaration of Tokyo." Adopted by the World Medical Association, Tokyo, Japan, October 1975. http://www.cirp.org/library/ethics/tokyo

• Karl Schwesig Wikipedia entry: http://de.wikipedia.org/wiki/Karl_Schwesig

• Profile of Karl Schwesig on the "Learning about the Holocaust through Art" website: http://holocaust-education.net/explore.asp?langid=1&submenu=200&id=25

Sexuality and Genocide
Jack Nusan Porter
Magnus Hirschfeld

Books:

• Magnus Hirschfeld, *The Sexual History of the World War* (University Press of the Pacific, 2006)

• Magnus Hirschfeld, *The Homosexuality of Men and Women* (Prometheus Books, 2000)

• Charlotte Wolff, *Magnus Hirschfeld: A Portrait of a Pioneer in Sexology* (Quartet Books, 1987)

Video:

• *Different from the Others*, dir. Richard Oswald (DVD, Kino Video 2004, ASIN B0006GAOOA)

• *The Einstein of Sex: Life and Work of Dr. M. Hirschfeld*, dir. Rosa von Praunheim (DVD, TLA Releasing, 1999)

Web Resources:

• Magnus Hirschfeld Wikipedia page: http://en.wikipedia.org/wiki/Magnus_Hirschfeld

• A biography: http://www.stonewallsociety.com/famouspeople/magnus.htm

• *Different from the Others* Wikipedia page: http://en.wikipedia.org/wiki/Anders_als_die_Andern

• Hirschfeld's legacy: http://en.wikipedia.org/wiki/Hirschfeld_Eddy_Foundation; http://www2.hu-berlin.de/sexology/index.htm

The Multiple Meanings of Lidice

Atenea Acevedo

Monument to the Child Victims of War

Books:

• *Lidice: Sacrificial Village* (Ballantine's, 1972)

Web Resources:

• Lidice massacre Wikipedia page: http://en.wikipedia.org/wiki/Lidice

• "The Massacre at Lidice": http://www.holocaustresearchproject.org/nazi-occupation/lidice.html

• "New Czech Film about Massacre in Lidice in the Works," Aktualne.cz, 7 August 2008. http://admin.aktualne.centrum.cz/clanek.phtml?id=612938

• Information on the monument: http://www.lidice.cz/OBEC/HISTORIE/pamatnik_sochy/detiuk.html

• More on the monument: http://www.lidice-memorial.cz/default_en.aspx

A Boy Who Refused to Grow Up, and One Who Did

Michael Hayse

Günter Grass, *The Tin Drum*

Books:

• Günther Grass, "Danzig Trilogy":

    The Tin Drum (Die Blechtrommel), 1959

    Cat and Mouse (Katz und Maus), 1961

    Dog Years (Hundejahre), 1963

• John Reddick, *Danzig Trilogy Of Gunter Grass: A Study of the Tin Drum, Cat and Mouse, and Dog Years* (Harvest Books, 1975)

• The revelation (or translation) of Grass's Waffen-SS past is dealt with in Günther Grass, *Peeling the Onion* (Harcourt, 2007)

• Siegfried Mews, *Günter Grass and His Critics: From 'The Tin Drum' to 'Crabwalk'* (Camden House, 2008)

• Bill Niven, *Facing the Nazi Past: United Germany and the Legacy of the Third Reich* (Routledge, 2002)

Video:

The Tin Drum, dir. Volker Schlöndorff (1979, DVD Criterion 2004)

Web Resources:

• Grass's Nobel Prize biography: http://nobelprize.org/nobel_prizes/literature/laureates/1999/grass-bio.html

A Tale of Two Children
Diane F. Afoumado
Hans Peter Richter, *Mon Ami Frédéric*

Books:
• Hans Peter Richter, *Mon ami Frédéric* (Hachette Jeunesse, 1963). English version: *Friedrich* (Puffin, 1987)

Web Resources:
• Hans Peter Richter Wikipedia page: http://en.wikipedia.org/wiki/Hans_Peter_Richter
• *Friedrich* Wikipedia page: http://en.wikipedia.org/wiki/Friedrich_(novel)

The Attic and the Imagination
Jina Moore
Anne Frank: The Diary of a Young Girl

Books:
• *Anne Frank—The Diary of a Young Girl* (Pocket Books, 1958, ISBN–10: 0671835467)
• Netherlands Institute for War Documentation, *The Diary of Anne Frank: The Revised Critical Edition* (Doubleday, 2003)
• Rian Verhoeven, *Anne Frank: Beyond the Diary—A Photographic Remembrance* (Puffin, 1985)
• Miep Gies and Alison Leslie Gold, *Anne Frank Remembered: The Story of the Woman Who Helped to Hide the Frank Family* (Simon & Schuster, 2009)

Video:
• *The Attic: The Hiding of Anne Frank*, dir. John Erman (VHS Cabin Fever, 1995)
• *The Diary of Anne Frank*, dir. Frankie Glass (1959, DVD, Twentieth-Century Fox 2004)
• *Anne Frank Remembered*, dir. Jon Blair (DVD, Sony Pictures 2004)
• *Anne Frank—The Whole Story*, dir. Robert Dornhelm (DVD, Walt Disney Video, 2001)

Web Resources:
• Anne Frank Wikipedia page: http://en.wikipedia.org/wiki/Anne_Frank
• Anne Frank biography: http://www.gale.cengage.com/free_resources/whm/bio/frank_a.htm
• Anne Frank Center USA: http://www.annefrank.com
• Anne Frank House webpage: http://www.annefrank.org
• IMDB page for *The Attic: The Hiding of Anne Frank*: http://www.imdb.com/title/tt0094685

- Miep Gies Wikipedia page: http://en.wikipedia.org/wiki/Miep_Gies
- "Miep Gies and the Diary of Anne Frank": http://www.auschwitz.dk/miepgies.htm
- "Rescuer of Anne Frank's Diary Marks Her 100th Birthday," http://www.usatoday.com/news/world/2009-02-12-annefrank-helper_N.htm
- Mike and Doug Starn, Starn Studio, http://www.starnstudio.com

Lessing's Wisdom
Viktoria Hertling
Gotthold Ephraim Lessing, *Nathan the Wise*

Play:
- *Nathan the Wise* (Dodo Press, 2009)
- Gotthold Ephraim Lessing, *Nathan the Wise: A Dramatic Poem in Five Acts* (1779). http://www.gutenberg.org/etext/3820

Book:
- Jo-Jacqueline Eckardt, *Lessing's Nathan the Wise and the Critics: 1779–1991* (Camden House, 1993)

Video:
- *Nathan the Wise*, dir. Manfred Noa (1922, DVD Filmuseum 2006, see http://www.silentera.com/DVD/nathantheWiseDVD.html)

Web Resources:
- Gotthold Ephraim Lessing Wikipedia page: http://en.wikipedia.org/wiki/Gotthold_Ephraim_Lessing
- *Nathan the Wise* Wikipedia page: http://en.wikipedia.org/wiki/Nathan_the_Wise
- Judi Herman, "Nathan the Wise by Gotthold Ephraim Lessing": http://www.jewish-theatre.com/visitor/article_display.aspx?articleID=1568

Not the Holocaust Memorial
Pam Maclean
Or-Sarua Synagogue, Vienna

Print Resources:
See the bibliographic note on page 90

Web Resources:
- "Memorial and Museum for the Austrian Victims of the Shoah": http://www.wien.gv.at/english/culture/museums/memorial.html
- Judenplatz Holocaust Memorial Wikipedia page: http://en.wikipedia.org/wiki/Judenplatz_Holocaust_Memorial

The Processes of Destruction
Joyce Apsel
Raul Hilberg, *The Destruction of the European Jews*

Books:
• Raul Hilberg, *The Destruction of the European Jews*, 3rd ed., 3 vols. (Yale University Press, 2003)
• Raul Hilberg, *The Destruction of the European Jews*, one-volume edition (Holmes & Meier, 1985)
• Raul Hilberg, *The Politics of Memory: The Journey of a Holocaust Historian* (Ivan R. Dee, 2002)

Video:
• Hilberg is interviewed at length in Claude Lanzmann's classic nine-and-a-half-hour documentary, *Shoah* (1985, DVD New Yorker Video 2003). See also Claude Lanzmann, *Shoah: The Complete Text of the Acclaimed Holocaust Film* (Da Capo Press, 1995).

Web Resources:
• *The Destruction of the European Jews* Wikipedia page: http://en.wikipedia.org/wiki/The_Destruction_of_the_European_Jews
• Raul Hilberg Wikipedia page: http://en.wikipedia.org/wiki/Raul_Hilberg
• Christopher Browning, "The Revised Hilberg": http://motlc.wiesenthal.com/site/pp.asp?c=gvKVLcMVIuG&b=395051
• Raul Hilberg obituary: http://www.timesonline.co.uk/tol/comment/obituaries/article2217692.ece
• Norman Finkelstein, "Remembering Raul Hilberg": http://www.norman-finkelstein.com/remembering-raul-hilberg-2

The Look of Terror
Robert Skloot
The Shop on Main Street

Video:
• *The Shop on Main Street*, dirs. Ján Kadár and Elmar Klos (1966, DVD Criterion Collection 2003, ASIN B00005NFZD)

Web Resources:
• *The Shop on Main Street* IMDB page: http://www.imdb.com/title/tt0059527
• *The Shop on Main Street* Wikipedia page: http://en.wikipedia.org/wiki/The_Shop_on_Main_Street
• "The Shop on Main Street: Not the Six Million but the One," by Ján Kadár: http://www.criterion.com/current/posts/139

• Review by Steven Banovac: http://www.kinokultura.com/specials/3/obchod. shtml

• Andrew James Horton, "Just Who Owns the Shop?": http://archive.sensesof-cinema.com/contents/00/11/shop.html

The Role of the Bystander
Fred Grünfeld
Elie Wiesel, *The Town beyond the Wall*

In addition to the sources cited in the following entry, see:

Books:

• Elie Wiesel, *The Town beyond the Wall: A Novel* (Schocken, 1995, ISBN-10: 0805210458)

• Elie Wiesel, *After the Darkness: Reflections on the Holocaust* (Schocken, 2002)

Video:

• *First Person Singular: Elie Wiesel*, dir. Robert H. Gardner (DVD, PBS 2002)

Web Resources:

• Elie Wiesel Wikipedia page: http://en.wikipedia.org/wiki/Elie_Wiesel

• The Elie Wiesel Foundation for Humanity: http://www.eliewieselfoundation. org

• Elie Wiesel Nobel Peace Prize lecture, 1986: http://nobelprize.org/nobel_ prizes/peace/laureates/1986/wiesel-lecture.html

• *The World of Elie Wiesel*, PBS program: http://video.google.com/ videoplay?docid=-541754502934590928

"Revisiting Again and Again the Kingdom of Night"
Steven L. Jacobs
and
Will Only the Darkness Remain?
John K. Roth
Elie Wiesel, *Night*

In addition to the sources cited in the preceding entry, see:

Books:

• Elie Wiesel, *Night* trans. Marion Wiesel (Hill and Wang, 2006, ISBN-10: 0374500010)

• Alan Rosen, ed., *Approaches to Teaching Wiesel's Night* (Modern Language Association of America, 2007)

• *Elie Wiesel's Night*, Bloom's Modern Critical Interpretations (Chelsea House, 2001)

• John K. Roth, *Holocaust Politics* (Westminster John Knox Press, 2001)

Audio:

• *Night* (CD, Recorded Books, 2006)

Web Resources:

• *Night* Wikipedia page: http://en.wikipedia.org/wiki/Night_(book)

• *Night* teaching resources: http://www.facinghistory.org/resources/publications/night

• *Night* page on Oprah's Book Club, with additional resources: http://www.oprah.com/article/oprahsbookclub/night/book_excerpt_01/1

The Holocaust as the Holocaust

Jonathan C. Friedman

The Grey Zone

In addition to the sources cited in the following entry, see:

Video:

• *The Grey Zone*, dir. Tim Blake Nelson (DVD, Lions Gate 2003, ASIN: B000087EYX)

Books:

• Primo Levi's essay "The Gray Zone" is found in his *The Drowned and the Saved* (Vintage, 1989, ISBN-10: 067972186X). It has been widely reprinted, including in Adam Jones, ed., *Genocide, vol. 3: Perpetrators, Victims, Bystanders, Rescuers* (Sage Publications, 2009).

• Shlomo Venezia, *Inside the Gas Chambers: Eight Months in the Sonderkommando of Auschwitz* (Polity, 2009)

• Gideon Greif, *We Wept Without Tears: Testimonies of the Jewish Sonderkommando from Auschwitz* (Yale University Press, 2005)

Web Resources:

• *The Grey Zone* IMDB page: http://www.imdb.com/title/tt0252480

• *The Grey Zone* Wikipedia page: http://en.wikipedia.org/wiki/The_Grey_Zone

• Sonderkommando Wikipedia page: http://en.wikipedia.org/wiki/Sonderkommando

• Auschwitz Sonderkommando video testimonies: http://www.youtube.com/watch?v=5SoTJ9cv028

• Testimony of Sonderkommando member Filip Müller, taken from Claude Lanzmann's 1985 documentary Shoah: http://www.class.uidaho.edu/thomas/Holocaust/thomas/shoah/Muller-Singing.rtf

Keeping Memory Alive

Henry Maitles

Primo Levi

In addition to *The Drowned and the Saved*, cited in the preceding entry, see:

Books:

• Ian Thomson, *Primo Levi: A Life* (Picador, 2004)

• Ferdinando Camon, *Conversations with Primo Levi* (Marlboro Press, 1989)

• Primo Levi, *If This is a Man* (Everyman's Library, 2000). This is the omnibus edition of Levi's Auschwitz-and-after memoirs, which were also published in separate volumes as *Survival in Auschwitz* (Classic House, 2008), *The Reawakening* (Touchstone, 1995), and *Moments of Reprieve* (Penguin, 1995).

• Anthony Rudolf, *At an Uncertain Hour: Primo Levi's War against Oblivion* (Menard Press, 1990)

• Myriam Anissimov, *Primo Levi: Tragedy of an Optimist* (Aurum Press, 1998)

Video:

• *Primo Levi's Journey*, dir. Davide Ferrario (DVD, New Yorker Video 2008)

• *Primo—Primo Levi*, starring Anthony Sher (DVD, Kultur Video 2005)

Article:

• Henry Maitles, "Surviving the Holocaust: The Anger and Guilt of Primo Levi," *Journal of Genocide Research*, 4: 2 (2002), pp. 237–251

Web Resources:

• Primo Levi Wikipedia page: http://en.wikipedia.org/wiki/Primo_Levi

• The Scriptorium—Primo Levi: http://www.themodernword.com/scriptorium/levi.html

• Diego Gambetta, "Primo Levi's Last Moments": http://www.bostonreview.net/BR24.3/gambetta.html

Identity and Contested Authenticity

Dominik J. Schaller

Binjamin Wilkomirski, *Fragments*

Books:

• Binjamin Wilkomirski, *Fragments: Memories of a Wartime Childhood* (Schocken, 1997, ISBN-10: 080521089X)

• Blake Eskin, *A Life in Pieces: The Making and Unmaking of Binjamin Wilkomirski* (W.W. Norton & Co., 2002)

• Lawrence L. Langer, *Using and Abusing the Holocaust* (Indiana University Press, 2006)

Web Resources:

• Binjamin Wilkomirski Wikipedia page: http://en.wikipedia.org/wiki/Binjamin_Wilkomirski

• A review of *Fragments* in *The Nation*: http://www.writing.upenn.edu/~afilreis/Holocaust/children-camps-bk-review.html

• Renata Salecl, "Why One Would Pretend to be a Victim of the Holocaust": http://www.othervoices.org/2.1/salecl/wilkomirski.html

The Language of Klemperer

Jens Meierhenrich

Victor Klemperer, *LTI: Lingua Tertii Imperii*

Books:

• Victor Klemperer, *The Language of the Third Reich: LTI—Lingua Tertii Imperii: A Philologist's Notebook* (Continuum 2006, ISBN–10: 0826491308)

• Klemperer's diaries are compiled and abridged in English as *I Will Bear Witness 1933–1941: A Diary of the Nazi Years* (Modern Library, 1999); *I Will Bear Witness 1942–1945: A Diary of the Nazi Years* (Modern Library, 2001); and *The Lesser Evil: The Diaries of Victor Klemperer 1945–59* (Orion, 2004).

• Peter Jacobs, *Victor Klemperer: Im Kern ein deutsches Gewachs : eine Biographie* (Aufbau Taschenbuch Verlag, 2000)

Article:

• Omer Bartov, "The Last German," *The New Republic*, 28 December 1998

Video:

• *La langue ne ment pas*, dir. Stan Neumann (2003, see http://www.imdb.com/title/tt0897265)

Web Resources:

• Victor Klemperer Wikipedia page: http://en.wikipedia.org/wiki/Victor_Klemperer

• *LTI* Wikipedia page: http://en.wikipedia.org/wiki/LTI_-_Lingua_Tertii_Imperii

• Thomas Powers, "The Everyday Life of Tyranny": http://books.guardian.co.uk/print/0,3858,4063747-99793,00.html

Trauma and Transcendence

William L. Hewitt

Viktor E. Frankl, *Man's Search for Meaning*

Books:

- Victor E. Frankl, *Man's Search for Meaning* (Beacon Press, 2006, ISBN–10: 0807014273)

Audio:

- *Man's Search for Meaning* (CD, Blackstone Audiobooks, 2008)

Web Resources:

- Website of the Viktor Frankl Institute, Vienna: http://logotherapy.univie.ac.at/
- Viktor Frankl Wikipedia page: http://en.wikipedia.org/wiki/Viktor_Frankl
- *Man's Search for Meaning* Wikipedia page: http://en.wikipedia.org/wiki/Man%27s_Search_for_Meaning

On Visiting the Auschwitz Museum
Jacques Semelin
State Museum of Auschwitz-Birkenau

Books:

- Laurence Rees, *Auschwitz: A New History* (PublicAffairs, 2006)
- Rudolf Höss, *Death Dealer: The Memoirs of the SS Kommandant at Auschwitz* (Da Capo Press, 1996)

Video:

- *Auschwitz: Inside the Nazi State* (DVD, BBC Warner 2005)

Web Resources:

- Auschwitz-Birkenau Memorial and Museum: http://en.auschwitz.org.pl/m
- US Holocaust Memorial Museum Auschwitz page: http://www.ushmm.org/wlc/article.php?ModuleId=10005189
- Auschwitz concentration camp Wikipedia page: http://en.wikipedia.org/wiki/Auschwitz
- Auschwitz Museum photo montage: http://www.youtube.com/watch?v=Y4isG90mWJo
- *New York Times*, "In the Shadow of Horror, SS Guardians Frolic": http://www.nytimes.com/2007/09/19/arts/design/19photo.html

At the Wall
Alexander George
Judy Ellis Glickman, "Execution Wall"

In addition to the sources cited in the preceding entry, see:

Web Resources:

• Other views of the wall: http://www.panoramio.com/photo/6780890; http://www.travelphotoarchive.com/main.php?g2_itemId=5367
• Information on Judy Glickman at the June Fitzpatrick Gallery: http://www.junefitzpatrickgallery.com/jegresume.html

"The Wealth of All Humanity"
Donna-Lee Frieze
Train of Life

Video:
• *Train de vie*, dir. Radu Mihaileanu (DVD-PAL, ASIN B00004VYD3)
• *Train of Life* (VHS, Paramount 2000, ASIN 6305849579)

Web Resources:
• *Train de vie* IMDB page: http://www.imdb.com/title/tt0170705/
• *Train of Life* Wikipedia page: http://en.wikipedia.org/wiki/Train_of_Life
• Radu Mihaileanu Wikipedia page: http://en.wikipedia.org/wiki/Radu_Mih%C4%83ileanu

Confronting the *Porrajmos*
Fiona de Londras
Alexander Ramati, *And the Violins Stopped Playing*

Books:
• Alexander Ramati, *And the Violins Stopped Playing: A Story of the Gypsy Holocaust* (F. Watts, 1986, ISBN 0531150283)
• Sybil H. Milton, "'Gypsies' as Social Outsiders in Nazi Germany," in Robert Gellately and Nathan Stoltzfus, *Social Outsiders in Nazi Germany* (Princeton University Press, 2001)
• Benno Muller-Hill, *Murderous Science: Elimination by Scientific Selection of Jews, Gypsies, and Others in Germany, 1933–1945* (Cold Spring Harbor Laboratory Press, 1997)
• *The Nazi Genocide of the Sinti and Roma* (Documentary and Cultural Centre of German Sinti and Roma, 1995)

Video:
• *And the Violins Stopped Playing*, dir. Alexander Ramati (DVD-PAL, ASIN B000A10LTE)

Web Resources:
• *I skrzypce przestaly grac* IMDB page: http://www.imdb.com/title/tt0096815

• Prevent Genocide International resources on Roma-Sinti genocide: http://www.preventgenocide.org/edu/pastgenocides/nazi/parajmos/resources
• US Holocaust Memorial Museum, "Genocide of European Roma (Gypsies), 1939–45": http://www.ushmm.org/wlc/article.php?ModuleId=10005219
• Porrajmos Wikipedia page: http://en.wikipedia.org/wiki/Porrajmos
• Yehuda Bauer, "Interpretation of the Porrajmos": Google "Porrajmos Bauer"
• Ian Hancock, "A Brief Romani Holocaust Chronology": http://www.osi.hu/rpp/holocaust.html
• Images compiled by Ian Hancock: http://www.chgs.umn.edu/histories/victims/romaSinti/index.html
• Romani rights resources: http://www.geocities.com/~Patrin/rights.htm

There's No Place Like Home
Simone Gigliotti
The Illustrated Auschwitz

Video:
• *The Illustrated Auschwitz*, dir. Jackie Farkas (1992, Super 8 and 16mm film; apparently not released on DVD or VHS)
Web Resources:
• Jackie Farkas IMDB page: http://www.imdb.com/name/nm1241257
• An analysis of *The Illustrated Auschwitz* by Karli Lukas: http://archive.sensesofcinema.com/contents/cteq/00/10/illustrated.html

Genocide and the Shock Process
Stephen C. Feinstein
Zbigniew Libera, LEGO Concentration Camp

Books:
• Norman L. Kleeblatt, ed., *Mirroring Evil: Nazi Imagery/Recent Art* (Jewish Museum/Rutgers University Press, 2001)
Web Resources:
• Stephen C. Feinstein, "Zbigniew Libera's Lego Concentration Camp: Iconoclasm in Conceptual Art About the Shoah": http://www.othervoices.org/2.1/feinstein/auschwitz.html
• Zbigniew Libera artist's biography: http://raster.art.pl/gallery/artists/libera/libera.htm
• Zbigniew Libera Wikipedia page: http://en.wikipedia.org/wiki/Zbigniew_Libera
• Exhibition of Libera's Lego work at the University of Minnesota: http://

www.chgs.umn.edu/museum/exhibitions/absence/artists/zLibera
• Personal Cyber Botanica, "Zbigniew Libera's Sharp Art": http://www.
lomodeedee.com/2009/03/26/zbigniew-liberas-sharp-art
• A description of "Konzentrationslager": http://users.erols.com/kennrice/
lego-kz.htm

The Moral Capital of the World
Winton Higgins
Weapons of the Spirit

Video:
• *Weapons of the Spirit*, dir. Pierre Sauvage (1987, VHS 1989, ASIN 0967651204)

Books:
• Carol Rittner and Sondra Myers, *The Courage to Care* (NYU Press, 1989)
• Albert Camus, *The Plague* (Vintage, 1991)
• Karen Gray Ruelle & Deborah Durland Desaix, *Hidden on the Mountain: Stories of Children Sheltered from the Nazis in Le Chambon* (Holiday House, 2006)
• Pierre Fayol, *Le Chambon-sur-Lignon sous l'Occupation, 1940–1944: les résistances locales, l'aide interalliée, l'action de Virginia Hall (O.S.S.)* (L'Harmattan, 1990)

Web Resources:
• *Weapons of the Spirit* IMDB page: http://www.imdb.com/title/tt0100905
• Le Chambon-sur-Lignon Wikipedia page: http://en.wikipedia.org/wiki/Le_Chambon-sur-Lignon
• Le Chambon-sur-Lignon US Holocaust Memorial Museum page: http://www.ushmm.org/wlc/article.php?lang=en&ModuleId=10007518
• Chambon Foundation: http://www.chambon.org
• Pierre Sauvage, "Le Chambon's Challenge Today": http://www.chambon.org/sauvage_lcsl_challenge_en.htm
• Bronwyn Hanna, "Rescue and Resistance on the Plateau": http://www.publicchristianity.org/Lechambon1.html
• Bill Moyers interview with Pierre Sauvage: http://www.chambon.org/weapons_moyers_interview_en.htm

"You and I, We Must Change the World"
Helen Bond
Raphael Lemkin, photographed by Hans Knopf

See the resources on Raphael Lemkin cited in the first entry of this section.

Print Source:
• The image of Lemkin accompanied Herbert Yahraes's profile, "He Gave a Name to the World's Most Horrible Crime," *Collier's* Magazine, 3 March 1951

Web Resources:
• Photography by Hans Knopf:
http://gallery.pictopia.com/jacobspillow/gallery/46172/photo/4740013
http://www.gettyimages.fr/detail/50470505/Time-Life-Pictures
http://www.life.com/image/50472360/in-gallery/25671/first-ladies-signature-styles

Eichmann, Mulisch and Me
G. Jan Colijn
Harry Mulisch, *De Zaak*

In addition to the Adolf Eichmann resources cited in the "Ugliness and Distance" entry, below, see:

Books:
• G. Jan Colijn and Izaak Colijn, *Ruin's Wheel: A Father on War, A Son on Genocide* (Comteq, 2006)
• Harry Mulisch, *De Zaak 40/61: Een reportage* (1962), published in English as *Criminal Case 40/61: The Trial of Adolf Eichmann: An Eyewitness Account*, trans. Robert Naborn (University of Pennsylvania Press, 2009, ISBN–10: 081222065X)
• Bob Moore, *Victims and Survivors: The Nazi Persecution of the Jews in the Netherlands* (Edward Arnold, 1997)

Web Resources:
• Harry Mulisch website (in Dutch): http://www.mulisch.nl
• Harry Mulisch Wikipedia page: http://en.wikipedia.org/wiki/Harry_Mulisch
• Harry Mulisch biography: http://www.marshillaudio.org/resources/topic_detail.asp?ID=138
• Foundation for the Production and Translation of Dutch Literature
page for Harry Mulisch: http://www.nlpvf.nl/book/book2.php?Book=80
• Resources and references on *Criminal Case 40/61*: http://www.complete-review.com/reviews/mulischh/case4061.htm
• On Miep Gies: "Rescuer of Anne Frank's Diary Marks 100th Birthday," http://www.usatoday.com/news/world/2009-02-12-annefrank-helper_N.htm

Ugliness and Distance
Eric Gordy
Hannah Arendt, *Eichmann in Jerusalem*

Books:
• Hannah Arendt, *Eichmann in Jerusalem: A Report on the Banality of Evil* (1963, Penguin Classics edition 2006, ISBN-10: 0143039881)
• *The Portable Hannah Arendt* (Penguin Classics, 2003)
• Richard H. King and Dan Stone, eds., *Hannah Arendt and the Uses of History: Imperialism, Nation, Race, and Genocide* (Berghahn, 2008)

Video:
• *The Trial of Adolf Eichmann* (DVD, Great Projects Film Company, 2007; see http://remember.org/eichmann/odyssey.htm)

Web Resources:
• The Hannah Arendt Papers at the Library of Congress: http://lcweb2.loc.gov/ammem/arendthtml/about.html
• Adolf Eichmann Wikipedia page: http://en.wikipedia.org/wiki/Adolf_Eichmann
• US Holocaust Memorial Museum Eichmann trial page: http://www.ushmm.org/wlc/article.php?lang=en&ModuleId=10005179
• Newsreel footage of the Eichmann trial: http://www.youtube.com/watch?v=6cOyYAgK1eg
• A session of the trial on the Wannsee Conference of 1942: http://www.youtube.com/watch?v=OqbWOYO6bAg
• Philip Guston Wikipedia page: http://en.wikipedia.org/wiki/Philip_Guston
• Philip Guston biography at the Museum of Modern Art: Google "Guston MOMA"
• "Holidays in the Sun" Wikipedia page: http://en.wikipedia.org/wiki/Holidays_in_the_Sun

Morality, Indifference, and Evil
Ernesto Verdeja
Gitta Sereny, *Albert Speer: His Battle with Truth*

Books:
• Gitta Sereny, *Albert Speer: His Battle with Truth* (Vintage, 1996, ISBN-10: 0679768122)
• Gitta Sereny, *Into That Darkness: An Examination of Conscience* (Vintage, 1983)

Video:

• *Nuremberg—Nazis on Trial: Albert Speer* (BBC, 2006; see http://www.bbc. co.uk/history/worldwars/wwtwo/nuremberg_article_03.shtml; on YouTube at http://www.youtube.com/watch?v=deGwMxn_HU8)

Web Resources:

• Albert Speer Wikipedia page: http://en.wikipedia.org/wiki/Albert_Speer

• Gitta Sereny Wikipedia page: http://en.wikipedia.org/wiki/Gitta_Sereny

• A 2000 interview with Gitta Sereny by Charlie Rose: http://www.charlierose. com/view/interview/3499

• BBC, "Gitta Sereny: Biographer with Bite": http://news.bbc.co.uk/2/hi/uk_ news/86021.stm

Journey through Denial
John C. Zimmerman
Walter Sanning, *The Dissolution of Eastern European Jewry*
Books:

• Walter N. Sanning, *The Dissolution of Eastern European Jewry* (Noontide Press, 1986, ISBN-10: 0939484110)

• Michael Shermer and Alex Grobman, *Denying History: Who Says the Holocaust Never Happened and Why Do They Say It?*, 2nd ed. (University of California Press, 2009)

• John C. Zimmerman, *Holocaust Denial* (University Press of America, 2000)

Web Resources:

• "The Crazy World of Walter Sanning": http://holocaustcontroversies. blogspot.com/2007/08/crazy-world-of-walter-sanning-part-1.html

• Holocaust denial Wikipedia page: http://en.wikipedia.org/wiki/Holocaust_denial

At Seventeen
Lee Ann Fujii
Amnesty International, Cambodia photo exhibition
In addition to the sources cited in the following entry, see:

Books:

• David Chandler, *Voices from S-21: Terror and History inside Pol Pot's Secret Prison* (University of California Press, 1999)

• Douglas Niven and Chris Riley, *The Killing Fields* (photos from S-21) (Twin Palms Press, 1996)

Video:

• *S21: The Khmer Rouge Killing Machine*, dir. Rithy Panh (First Run Features, 2005)

Web Resources:
• Tuol Sleng Genocide Museum Wikipedia page: http://en.wikipedia.org/wiki/Tuol_Sleng
• "Tuol Sleng: Photographs from Pol Pot's Secret Prison": http://www.tuolsleng.com/
• Andy Carvin, "From Sideshow to Genocide: Stories of the Cambodian Holocaust": http://www.edwebproject.org/sideshow
• Amnesty International website: http://www.amnesty.org

Beyond Good and Evil
Scott Laderman
The Killing Fields
In addition to the sources cited in the preceding entry, see:
Video:
• *The Killing Fields*, dir. Roland Joffé (1984, DVD Warner Home Video 2001, ASIN B00004RF82)
Books:
• Haing S. Ngor and Roger Warner, *Survival in the Killing Fields* (Basic Books, 2003)
• Sydney Schanberg and Dith Pran, *The Killing Fields: The Facts behind the Film* (Hodder, 1984)
• William Shawcross, *Sideshow: Kissinger, Nixon and the Destruction of Cambodia*, rev. ed. (Cooper Square Press, 2002)
Articles:
• Ben Kiernan, "The American Bombardment of Kampuchea, 1969–1973," *Vietnam Generation* 1:1 (1989), pp. 4–41
• Kenton Clymer, "Jimmy Carter, Human Rights, and Cambodia," *Diplomatic History*, 27:2 (April 2003), pp. 245–278
• Taylor Owen and Ben Kiernan, "Bombs over Cambodia," *The Walrus*, October 2006, pp. 62–69. Available at http://www.yale.edu/cgp/Walrus_CambodiaBombing_OCT06.pdf
Web Resources:
• *The Killing Fields* IMDB page: http://www.imdb.com/title/tt0087553
• *The Killing Fields* Wikipedia page: http://en.wikipedia.org/wiki/The_Killing_Fields_(film)
• Killing fields Wikipedia page: http://en.wikipedia.org/wiki/Killing_Fields
• *The New York Times*, "Cambodian Physician Who Won an Oscar for

'Killing Fields' Is Slain": http://www.nytimes.com/1996/02/27/us/cambodian-physician-who-won-an-oscar-for-killing-fields-is-slain.html

The Horror
Stefanie Rixecker
Apocalypse Now

Video:

• *Apocalypse Now*, dir. Francis Ford Coppola (1979; DVD Apocalypse Now: The Complete Dossier, Paramount 2006, ASIN B000FSME1A)

• *Hearts of Darkness—A Filmmaker's Apocalypse*, dir. Eleanor Coppola (Paramount 1991). A making-of documentary nearly as wild as the movie itself.

Books:

• Francis Ford Coppola and John Milius, *Apocalypse Now Redux: A Screenplay* (Miramax Books, 2001)

• Peter Cowie, *The Apocalypse Now Book* (Da Capo Press, 2001)

• Eleanor Coppola, *Notes on the Making of Apocalypse Now* (Limelight Editions, 2004)

• Joseph Conrad, *Heart of Darkness*, Norton Critical Editions, 4th ed. (W.W. Norton & Co., 2005)

Audio:

• *Apocalypse Now Redux* (soundtrack) (CD, Nonesuch 2001)

Web Resources:

• *Apocalypse Now* Wikipedia page: http://en.wikipedia.org/wiki/Apocalypse_Now

• *Apocalypse Now* IMDB page: http://www.imdb.com/title/tt0078788

• The classic helicopter attack scene, set to Wagner's *Ride of the Valkyries*, and Robert Duvall's napalm-smells-like-victory speech: http://www.youtube.com/watch?v=vHjWDCX1Bdw

• Roger Ebert review: http://rogerebert.suntimes.com/apps/pbcs.dll/article?AID=/19991128/REVIEWS08/911280301/1023

Apocalypse Soon
Adam Jones
Midnight Oil, "Hercules"

Audio:

• "Hercules," by Jim Moginie/Peter Garrett/Rob Hirst. © 1985 Sony BMG Australia. From *Species Deceases* (1985, CD Sony Music 1990, ASIN B00000273S)

Video:

• *20,000 Watts RSL: The Midnight Oil Collection* (DVD, Sony Music 2002, ASIN B00006AUHL). Includes a live version of "Hercules" from Sydney in 1989.

Books:

• Mark Dodshon, *Beds Are Burning: Midnight Oil, The Journey* (Penguin, 2005)

• Jonathan Schell, *The Fate of the Earth and The Abolition* (Stanford University Press, 2000)

• Rex Wyler, *Greenpeace: How a Group of Ecologists, Journalists, and Visionaries Changed the World* (Rodale Books, 2004)

Web Resources:

• Midnight Oil website: http://www.midnightoil.com

• Peter Garrett website: http://www.petergarrett.com.au

• Art Nuko World Tour: http://www.pej.ca/artnuko/index.htm

• A powerful 1985 live performance of "Hercules": http://www.youtube.com/watch?v=y-_YICL9g9c—includes interview footage on the nuclear threat with Peter Garrett.

• Another live performance from 1985 at Le Spectrum, Montreal, with fluffed lyrics: http://www.youtube.com/watch?v=BE9i-NxAmNE

• *Rainbow Warrior* Wikipedia page: http://en.wikipedia.org/wiki/Rainbow_Warrior_(1955)

The Question of the Act
Lior Zylberman
The Act in Question

Video:

• *El acto en cuestión*, dir. Alejandro Agresti (1993, so far unreleased on VHS or DVD)

Web Resources:

• *El acto en cuestión* IMDB page: http://www.imdb.com/title/tt0106217

• Alejandro Agresti Wikipedia page: http://en.wikipedia.org/wiki/Alejandro_Agresti

Photography, Memory, and Denial
Marcia Esparza
Jonathan Moller, photographs from Guatemala

In addition to the sources cited in the following entry, see:

Books:

• *Our Culture Is Our Resistance: Repression, Refuge, and Healing in Guatemala*, photographs by Jonathan Moller (powerHouse Books, 2004)

• Rigoberta Menchú with Elisabeth Burgos-Débray, *I, Rigoberta Menchú: An Indian Woman in Guatemala* (Verso, 1984)

• Stephen Schlesinger and Stephen Kinzer, *Bitter Fruit: The Story of the American Coup in Guatemala*, revised and expanded edition (David Rockefeller Center Series on Latin American Studies, 2005)

Video:

• *When the Mountains Tremble* (1983, DVD New Video Group 2004)

Web Resources:

• "Our Culture is Our Resistance: Photographs by Jonathan Moller": http://www.jonathanmoller.org

Images of Impunity
Victoria Sanford
Guatemala crime scene photos

In addition to the sources cited in the preceding entry, see:

Books:

• Victoria Sanford, *Guatemala: Del genocidio al feminicidio* (F & G Editores, 2008)

• Victoria Sanford, *Buried Secrets: Truth and Human Rights in Guatemala* (Palgrave Macmillan, 2004)

• Diana Washington Valdez, *The Killing Fields: Harvest of Women* (Peace on the Border, 2006)

Video:

• *Killer's Paradise*, dir. Giselle Portenier (2006, DVD NFB/BBC, see http://www3.nfb.ca/collection/films/fiche/?id=54178)

Web Resources:

• Victoria Sanford webpage: http://www.fygeditores.com/sanford

• José Steinsleger, "Feminicidio en Guatemala": http://www.jornada.unam.mx/2005/03/09/020a1pol.php

• Gendercide Watch: http://www.gendercide.org

• Guatemala: Yale Genocide Studies Program page: http://www.yale.edu/gsp/guatemala/index.html

• Prevent Genocide International resources on Genocide in Guatemala: http://www.preventgenocide.org/edu/pastgenocides/guatemala/resources

A Reluctant Genocide Activist

Thomas Nagy

US Defense Intelligence Agency document

See footnote 1, page 220, and:

Books:

• Hans C. von Sponeck, *A Different Kind of War: The UN Sanctions Regime in Iraq* (Berghahn, 2006)

• Geoff Simons, *The Scourging of Iraq: Sanctions, Law and Natural Justice*, 2nd ed. (Macmillan, 1998)

• Anthony Arnove, ed., *Iraq under Siege: The Deadly Impact of Sanctions and War* (South End Press, 2000)

Web Resources:

• Iraq Sanctions Wikipedia page: http://en.wikipedia.org/wiki/Iraq_sanctions

• "Former UN Official Says Sanctions Against Iraq Amount to Genocide": http://www.news.cornell.edu/chronicle/99/9.30.99/Halliday_talk.html

• "Iraq: Genocide by UN Sanctions": http://www.youtube.com/watch?v=2irN1G5HiRo

Children's Photos

Daniel H. Magilow

Early photos of Saddam Hussein and Adolf Hitler

Books:

• Ron Rosenbaum, *Explaining Hitler: The Search for the Origins of His Evil* (HarperPerennial, 1999)

• Ian Kershaw, *Hitler 1889–1936: Hubris* (W.W. Norton & Co., 2000)

• Said K. Aburish, *Saddam Hussein: The Politics of Revenge* (Bloomsbury, 2001)

Web Resources:

• "Adolf Hitler—The Child and Youth": http://military-leaders.suite101.com/article.cfm/adolf_hitler_the_child_and_youth

The Face of Genocide

Donna-Lee Frieze

Photo by Ron Haviv from *Blood and Honey*

Books:

• Ron Haviv and Chuck Sudetic, *Blood and Honey: A Balkan War Journal* (TV Books, 2000, ISBN-10: 1575001357)

• Leslie Fratkin, *Sarajevo Self-Portrait: The View from Inside* (Umbrage Editions, 2000)

• Steve Horn and Dewi Lewis, *Pictures without Borders: Bosnia Revisited* (Dewi Lewis Publishing, 2005)

• Miroslav Prstojevic, *Sarajevo Survival Guide* (FAMA, 1993)

• Sean Hand, ed., *The Levinas Reader* (Blackwell, 1992)

• Roy Gutman, *A Witness to Genocide: The 1993 Pulitzer Prize-Winning Dispatches on the "Ethnic Cleansing" of Bosnia* (Lisa Drew Books, 1993)

Video:

• *Eyes of the World*, dir. Michael Perlman, profiles Haviv (2003, see http://www.nationalfilmnetwork.com/Store/ProductDetails.aspx?ProductID=184)

Web Resources:

• Ron Haviv, "Blood & Honey": http://www.photoarts.com/haviv/bloodandhoney

• Ron Haviv Wikipedia page: http://en.wikipedia.org/wiki/Ron_Haviv

• Interview with Ron Haviv by Charlie Rose: http://www.charlierose.com/view/interview/3257

The Death of 'King' Habyarimana

Christopher C. Taylor

Cartoon in *Kangura*, Rwanda

Books:

• Christopher C. Taylor, *Sacrifice as Terror: The Rwandan Genocide of 1994* (Berg, 2001)

• Marcel Kabanda, "*Kangura*: The Triumph of Propaganda Refined," in Allan Thompson, ed., *The Media and the Rwanda Genocide* (Pluto Press, 2007). Version available online at http://www.idrc.ca/rwandagenocide/ev–108184–201–1–DO_TOPIC.html

Web Resources:

• *Kangura* Wikipedia page: http://en.wikipedia.org/wiki/Kangura

A Simple Task

Shayna C. Parekh

Ghosts of Rwanda

Books:

• *Alison Des Forges, Leave None to Tell the Story: Genocide in Rwanda* (Human Rights Watch, 1999)

• African Rights, *Rwanda: Death, Despair and Defiance*, rev. ed. (African Rights, 1995)

Video:

• *Frontline: Ghosts of Rwanda*, dir. Greg Barker (2006, DVD PBS Paramount, ASIN B0007TKI06). Available on YouTube at http://www.youtube.com/watch?v=xON22c7pZ6c

Web Resources:

• PBS Frontline *Ghosts of Rwanda* page: http://www.pbs.org/wgbh/pages/frontline/shows/ghosts

• *Ghosts of Rwanda* Wikiversity page: http://en.wikiversity.org/wiki/Ghosts_of_Rwanda

• Samantha Power, "Bystanders to Genocide": http://www.theatlantic.com/doc/200109/power-genocide

"Never Again," Again
David J. Simon
Pablo Picasso, "Guernica";
Dachau and Kigali memorials

Books:

• Gijs van Hensbergen, *Guernica: The Biography of a Twentieth-Century Icon* (Bloomsbury, 2005)

• Rudolf Arnheim, *The Genesis of a Painting: Picasso's Guernica* (University of California Press, 2006)

• Paul Berben, *Dachau: The Official History, 1933–1945* (LIPP GmbH, 1986)

Video:

• *Guernica*, dir. Alain Resnais (1950). On YouTube at http://www.youtube.com/watch?v=FOEZJC74gVs

Web Resources:

• "Guernica" Wikipedia page: http://en.wikipedia.org/wiki/Guernica_(painting)

• "Picasso's Guernica in 3–D": http://www.lena-gieseke.com/guernica/movie.html

• "Guernica: Testimony of War": http://www.pbs.org/treasuresoftheworld/a_nav/guernica_nav/main_guerfrm.html

• Dachau Concentration Camp Memorial Site: http://www.kz-gedenks-taette-dachau.de/index-e.html

• Dachau Concentration Camp Wikipedia page: http://en.wikipedia.org/wiki/Dachau_concentration_camp

• Kigali Genocide Memorial Centre: http://www.kigalimemorialcentre.org/old/index.html

• Kigali Genocide Memorial Centre Wikipedia page: http://en.wikipedia.org/wiki/Kigali_Genocide_Memorial_Centre

• Ardyn Halter Art: http://www.ardynhalterart.com

• Ardyn Halter Works: http://www.redfern-gallery.com/pages/thumbnail-list/251.html

Dili on Fire

Russell Schimmer

Landsat photo of East Timor

Books:

• Thomas M. Lillesand, Ralph W. Kiefer, and Jonathan W. Chipman, *Remote Sensing and Image Interpretation* (Wiley, 2007)

• Joseph Nevins, *A Not-So-Distant Horror: Mass Violence In East Timor* (Cornell University Press, 2005)

Web Resources:

• Yale Genocide Studies Program, Maps and Satellite Images: http://www.yale.edu/gsp/maps/index.html

• Remote Sensing Wikipedia page: http://en.wikipedia.org/wiki/Remote_sensing

• Gendercide Watch East Timor case-study: http://www.gendercide.org/case_timor.html

Different Kinds of People

Wendy C. Hamblet

American History X

Video:

• *American History X*, dir. Tony Kaye (1998, DVD New Line Home Video 1999, ASIN 6305313687, Blu-Ray New Line Home Video 2009, ASIN B001O7JHSE)

Books:

• Israel W. Charny, *Fascism and Democracy in the Human Mind* (University of Nebraska Press, 2006)

• Wendy C. Hamblet, *The Sacred Monstrous* (Lexington Books, 2004)

• Nevitt Sanford and Craig Comstock, *Sanctions for Evil: Sources of Social Destructiveness* (Jossey-Bass, 1971)

• Ervin Staub, *The Psychology of Good and Evil* (Cambridge University Press, 2003)

Web Resources:

• *American History X* webpage: http://www.newline.com/properties/american-historyx.html

• *American History X* IMDB page: http://www.imdb.com/title/tt0120586/

• *American History X* Wikipedia page: http://en.wikipedia.org/wiki/American_History_X

• Neo-Nazism Wikipedia page: http://en.wikipedia.org/wiki/Neo-Nazism

• Review by Janet Maslin: http://movies.nytimes.com/movie/review?res=9c07e4de103cf93ba15753c1a96e958260

• A key moment from the film: http://www.youtube.com/watch?v=8hEtN0-vF90

"The Enemy We Seek To Destroy"
R. Charli Carpenter
"I, Borg," episode of *Star Trek: The Next Generation*

Video:

• "I, Borg," Episode 123 of *Star Trek: The Next Generation*, originally aired 11 May 1992. Available on DVD on disk two of the four-disk *Star Trek: Fan Collective—Borg* (Star Trek 2006, ASIN B000CCBCIA).

Books:

• Richard Hanley, *The Metaphysics of Star Trek* (Perseus Books, 1997)

• Jutta Weldes, ed., *To Seek Out New Worlds: Science Fiction and World Politics* (Palgrave MacMillan, 2003)

Web Resources:

• "I, Borg" Wikipedia page: http://en.wikipedia.org/wiki/I,_Borg

• "I, Borg" at StarTrek.com: http://www.startrek.com/startrek/view/library/episodes/TNG/detail/68552.html

• Detailed plot summary: http://memory-alpha.org/en/wiki/I_Borg_(episode)

Brotherhood
Alex Hinton
Octavio Paz, "Hermandad"

Books:

• Octavio Paz and Eliot Weinberger, *Octavio Paz: Collected Poems* (New Directions Publishing Corp., 1988)

• Octavio Paz, *Obras Completas* (Fondo de Cultura Economica USA, 2003)

Web Resources:

• Octavio Paz Wikipedia Page: http://en.wikipedia.org/wiki/Octavio_Paz

• Octavio Paz Nobel Prize biography: http://nobelprize.org/nobel_prizes/literature/laureates/1990/paz-bio.html
• Excerpt from an Octavio Paz TV interview: http://www.youtube.com/watch?v=Yg5D4s5YBmA
• A child recites "Hermandad":
http://www.youtube.com/watch?v=crBCiXQjwZk

"A Single Child"
Eric Reeves
Paul Jeffrey photo; Ursula K. Le Guin, "The Ones Who Walk Away from Omelas"

Books:
• Ursula K. Le Guin, *The Ones Who Walk Away from Omelas* (Creative Education, 1992)
• Eric Reeves, *A Long Day's Dying: Critical Moments in the Darfur Genocide* (The Key Publishing House Inc., 2007)

Video:
• *Frontline: On Our Watch* (DVD, PBS 2008)

Web Resources:
• "The Ones Who Walk Away from Omelas" Wikipedia page: http://en.wikipedia.org/wiki/The_Ones_Who_Walk_Away_from_Omelas
• Ursula K. Le Guin website: http://www.ursulakleguin.com
• Eric Reeves website: http://www.sudanreeves.org
• Photos by Paul Jeffrey: http://www.gbgm-umc.org/honduras/photos
• Genocide Intervention Network/STAND: http://www.standnow.org

Index